PACIFIC NATIONS AND TERRITORIES

The Islands of Micronesia, Melanesia, and Polynesia

Second Edition, Revised

By Reilly Ridgell

Bess Press, Inc.
P.O. Box 22388
Honolulu, Hawaii 96822

Dedicated to Neipi, Clynton, Davin, and Joel

Every effort has been made to trace the ownership of all copyrighted material in this text book and to obtain permission for its use. This book is for educational purposes.

Library of Congress Cataloging in Publication Data

Catalog Card No: 88-70787

Ridgell, Reilly

Pacific Nations and Territories, The Islands of Micronesia, Melanesia, and Polynesia; Second Edition

Honolulu, Hawaii: Bess Press, Inc.

ISBN: 0-935848-50-9

CONTENTS

FOREWORD TO ISLAND EDUCATORS

While teaching world geography to ninth graders at Father Duenas Memorial High School on Guam, I became very frustrated at the lack of materials on the Pacific islands. The world geography textbook we were using was decent enough, but covered Micronesia, Melanesia, and Polynesia with a paltry paragraph apiece. Those paragraphs were included in the chapter on New Zealand in a unit on Australia and Oceania. I decided that if my students were to learn anything about the islands around them, I would have to develop my own materials.

What happened next was a natural progression. With encouragement bordering on insistence from Brother Gregory Seubert, principal of Father Duenas, I first developed a quick two-week unit on the islands of the Trust Territory of Micronesia. The next year it became a full nine-week unit on all of Micronesia, Melanesia, and Polynesia. Each student was assigned to write to an island and information began to trickle in. The next year I changed schools and began teaching in the high school division of Guam Community College. I was assigned to develop and teach a full semester course on Pacific Studies. After two semesters of teaching without any text for my students, I proposed to write one. The proposal received enthusiastic support from Dr. John Salas, Provost of Guam Community College, and formal approval from the College Board of Trustees. Many months of hard work followed, and the result is this book.

The purpose of this textbook is to give students a background in Pacific geography, culture, and history, plus a general overview of the different Pacific island groups. It is not intended to be used for a detailed, in-depth course on any one group. Students on Guam, for example, take other courses that deal specifically with Guam. They will use this book to learn about other Pacific islands and how they compare to Guam. It is my hope that teachers in Kiribati, or the Solomons, or Tonga, or any of the islands included in this text will find it useful for the same purpose: not to teach detail about their own islands, but to teach about the rest of the Pacific. To that end this book should help fill a void in Pacific instructional materials. I will gladly accept any comments or suggestions.

Reilly Ridgell
Guam 1982

ABOUT THE FIRST EDITION

The first edition of *Pacific Nations and Territories* was published by Guam Community College (copyright 1982). The first printing was released in January 1983, followed by a second in November 1983, a third in April 1984, and a fourth in December 1984.

The first edition was written and produced entirely on Guam. The text was reviewed by Luther Myrvold, Sandra Liberty, Frank Castro, Dr. Dirk Ballendorf, and Dr. Robert Craig. Editing was by Carol Simpson, artwork by Jan Stevens, typesetting by Expert Secretarial Services, title heads by *The Guam Tribune*, and graphic layout by Wordsmiths, Inc. All copies of the first edition were printed by American Printing, Guam. I would like to acknowledge the assistance of the following individuals and organizations who aided in the development and successful continuation of this project: Dr. John Salas, former Provost of Guam Community College; the Board of Trustees of Guam Community College; the Guam Community College President's Office; many individual members of the faculty, staff, and administration of Guam Community College; the Guam Community College Library; the Guam Community College Bookstore; the Guam Community College Procurement and Supply Division; the Guam Community College Business Office; the Micronesian Area Research Center of the University of Guam; and the Naval Oceanographic Command Center, Guam. There were also many friends and associates on Guam and throughout the Pacific academic community who offered suggestions and support.

PREFACE TO THE SECOND EDITION

Since its original release in January, 1983, the first edition of *Pacific Nations and Territories* has gone through four printings, sold 4500 copies, and has been purchased for use by at least some high schools or colleges in Guam, the Northern Marianas, Belau, Yap, Truk, Pohnpei, Kosrae, the Marshall Islands, Nauru, American Samoa, Papua New Guinea, Hawaii, and even one private high school in South Carolina. In addition, copies were purchased by high school, college, or public libraries in Australia, New Zealand, and throughout the United States. *Pacific Nations and Territories* was designed to fill a void in Pacific instructional materials, and it remains the only textbook of its type covering the islands of Micronesia, Melanesia, and Polynesia.

Five years have passed since the first edition was written, and many important changes have happened in the Pacific since then. Because of those changes, and since the first edition had been successful and had become established in many island schools and school systems, the time was right for a second edition. This second edition contains expanded and updated information for all the island groups. The addition of a hard cover will improve the book's durability and usefulness as a textbook. It is my hope that the book will continue to be helpful to the islands that have already acquired it, and that this improved edition will fill the needs of even more schools in more island groups.

I would like to acknowledge the following people who helped with the revision for the second edition: Richard Randall, University of Guam Marine Laboratory; Craig Brittain, Nauru Secondary School Library; M. Liliu, Department of Secondary and Further Education, Vanuatu; Dr. Ron Crocombe, University of the South Pacific, Fiji; Joseph Theroux and Teresa Stanley, Department of Education, American Samoa; O. Faraimo, Office of Tokelau Affairs, Apia, Western Samoa; G.D. Harraway, Office of the Governor of Pitcairn, Auckland, New Zealand; Ana Maria Arredondo, Professor of History, Easter Island; and T. Varet, Le Chef du Service de la Culture, Tahiti, French Polynesia. For the island groups whose education departments did not respond to my request for help in the revision, I relied on the various resources available to me on Guam. The material in this edition is current up through December, 1987. I would like to acknowledge two Pacific periodicals for their usefulness in keeping up to date with Pacific events and recommend them for anyone wishing to follow current political, social, and economic developments in the Pacific islands:

Pacific Island Monthly, Pacific Publications (Aust.) Pty. Ltd., GPO 3408, Sydney, 2001, Australia; (US subscriptions — PIM Hawaii, Box 22250, Honolulu, Hawaii, 96822)

Pacific Magazine, Box 25488, Honolulu, Hawaii, 96825

I would also like to thank Mr. Peter Nelson, President of Guam Community College, his assistant Mr. Chris Perez Howard, and the chairman of the Guam Community College Board of Trustees, Dr. Antonio Yamashita, for their help with this project. In addition I wish to thank Benjamin Bess and Ann Rayson of Bess Press for making this second edition possible, and my wife and family for their understanding and support.

All the drawings and maps in this book, except where indicated, are by Jan Stevens.

Reilly Ridgell
Guam 1988

INTRODUCTION FOR ISLAND STUDENTS

You live on a Pacific island. Every day this fact has impact on your lives. The kind of life you have right now, as well as the kind of life you may be able to have in the future, is directly related to your home being an island. Islands are different from mainland continents. They are limited in space, resources, and transportation.

In this book you will learn about other islands, your neighbors, and how their situations and problems compare to those of your island and to each other. You will look at the similarities and differences between the various island groups. You will also learn some of the history and geography of the Pacific area as a whole.

The time will come when you will have to make choices — choices about your own future, and choices about the future of your island. This book will help you make those choices from the point of understanding what it means to be living on an island in the Pacific.

ABOUT THE AUTHOR

Reilly Ridgell has been living and teaching in the Pacific since 1971. Born in Santa Monica, California, in 1947, he received a Bachelor of Arts in Political Science from the University of California at Los Angeles in 1969; and a Master of Arts in the same field from the University of California at Santa Barbara in 1970.

In 1971 Ridgell joined the Peace Corps and became an English teacher on several outer islands in the Truk District of the Trust Territory of the Pacific Islands. This was followed in 1973 by a two-year teaching contract in Truk. The author then came to Guam in 1975, teaching first at Father Duenas Memorial High School and currently at Guam Community College. Ridgell has written many Micronesia-related articles for *The Pacific Daily News Islander*, *Pacific Magazine*, and *The People's Almanac 2*. He is fluent in three dialects of Trukese: Western, Mortlockese, and Lagoon. His wife, Blora, is from the island of Ta in the Lower Mortlock Islands of Truk. They have three boys, Clynton, Davin, and Joel.

PHOTOGRAPHIC ACKNOWLEDGEMENTS

The following people and organizations were instrumental in helping to locate and acquire photographs for this textbook:

Mike Malone; Sue Terlaje; Glimpses of Guam; Gordon Tydingco; Micronesia Regional Tourism Council; Naval Oceanographic Command Center, Guam; James Miculka; War in the Pacific National Historical Park, Guam; Sam McPhetres; Trust Territory of the Pacific Islands Archives; Al Williams; Marjorie Driver; Micronesian Area Research Center, University of Guam; Real Academea de la Historia, Madrid, Spain; Joe Murphy; John Simpson; Kathy Flynn; Mark Skinner; Joe Novotny; *Pacific Daily News*, Guam; John Berry; Pacific Publications Pty. Ltd., Australia; Dr. Jerry Loveland; Leu Fonoti; Institute for Polynesian Studies, Brigham Young University, Hawaii; Tropical Color Center, Guam; Phyllis Koontz; Carlos Viti; Mark Berg; Bob Richards; Jimmy Cornell; Craig Brittain; Terrence Debao; Carol Diaz; Guam Visitors Bureau; William Penn; Solomon Islands Tourist Authority; Vanuatu Visitors Bureau; Cook Islands Tourist Authority; Tahiti Tourist Development Board; New Caledonia Government Office of Tourism; Papua New Guinea Government Office of Information; Hawaii Visitors Bureau; South Pacific Commission; District Committee Publisher, Nauru

PART ONE: PACIFIC BACKGROUND
Unit One: Basic Pacific Geology and Geography

Chapter 1: Pacific Geology

1. Some Definitions

The Pacific Ocean. Pacific means peaceful. Ferdinand Magellan named it when he became the first European to sail across the ocean in 1521. Since it was so calm, he called it the Pacific Ocean. Magellan never saw one of the Pacific's typhoons. A few years before Magellan, a Spanish explorer named Balboa was the first European to see the ocean when he walked across the isthmus of Panama. Since he was facing south, he named the ocean the South Seas. Actually, most of the ocean was to the west of him. Today we call it the Pacific Ocean. South Seas is used more as a nickname for the southern Pacific.

If you look at a globe of the earth, you will notice that the Pacific Ocean is the single largest feature on earth. All other oceans and all continents are smaller than the Pacific.

Oceans are large bodies of salt water. They cover about 70% of the earth's surface. There are four oceans: the Pacific, the Atlantic, the Indian, and the Arctic. The ocean is very uniform in depth — about two and one-half to three miles (4-4.8 km). The bottom's uniform depth is broken by underwater mountain ranges, individual sea mounts, trenches, and shallow areas near islands and continents. The rocks forming the ocean's beds are different kinds than continental rocks. They are heavier and more dense than the rocks forming the continents.

Continents are large land masses. There are six continents: Eurasia, North America, South America, Africa, Antarctica, and Australia. Europe and Asia are part of the same land mass, but since they are so different culturally, they have been considered two different continents throughout history. Since continents are exposed to the erosion of wind and water, they are not as level as the ocean bottoms. Also, the rocks making up the continents are less dense and lighter than the rocks in the ocean beds.

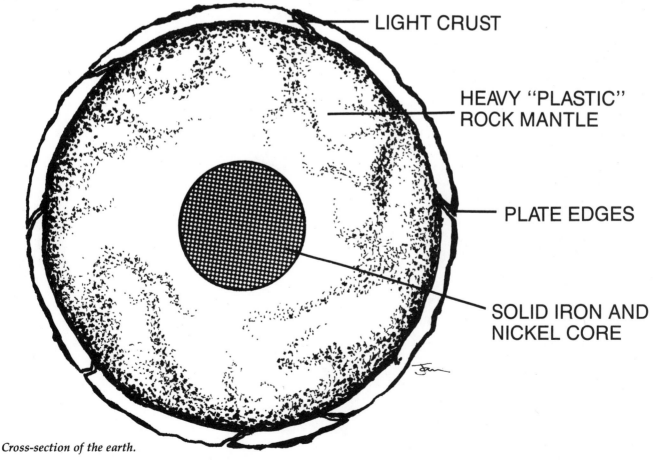

LIGHT CRUST

HEAVY "PLASTIC" ROCK MANTLE

PLATE EDGES

SOLID IRON AND NICKEL CORE

Cross-section of the earth.

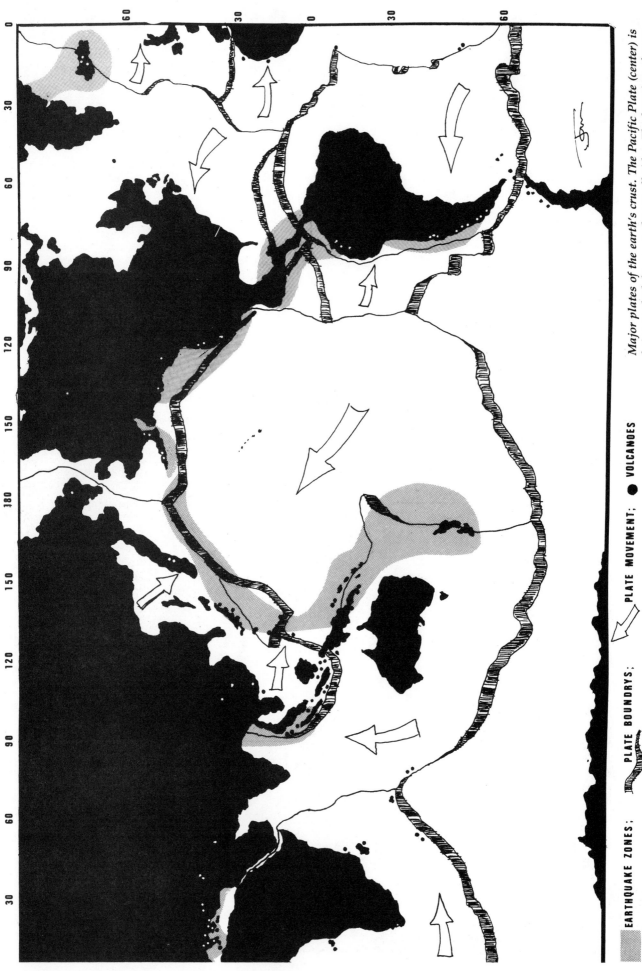

EARTHQUAKE ZONES;   PLATE BOUNDRYS;   PLATE MOVEMENT;   ● VOLCANOES

Major plates of the earth's crust. The Pacific Plate (center) is being pushed down on almost all sides. The location of most earthquake zones and volcanoes is near the plate boundaries.

Islands are smaller land masses than continents and are completely surrounded by water. Greenland is the world's largest island. Australia looks like an island, but is several times larger than Greenland. Australia is thus considered the smallest continent. A continental shelf is part of a continent extending under the ocean from the shore. It creates a relatively shallow area up to 200 miles (320 km) from the continent before dropping down to the ocean deep. Ocean ridges are underwater mountain ranges, and sea mounts are single underwater mountains.

2. Plate Tectonics (continental drift), Earthquakes, and Volcanoes

Scientists have evidence that the earth is about four and one-half billion years old. This is such a long time that it is hard to understand how long it really is. Man has only been civilized for about 7000 years at the most. If you count to a hundred in one minute, and a thousand in ten minutes, it will take you one week to count to a million. That's if you don't stop

(a) The earth's land masses as they appeared about 200 million years ago.

(b) The earth as it is today.

(c) The earth in about eight-and-a-half million years. Part of California has broken off from North America and formed an island. Part of East Africa has separated from the rest of Africa.

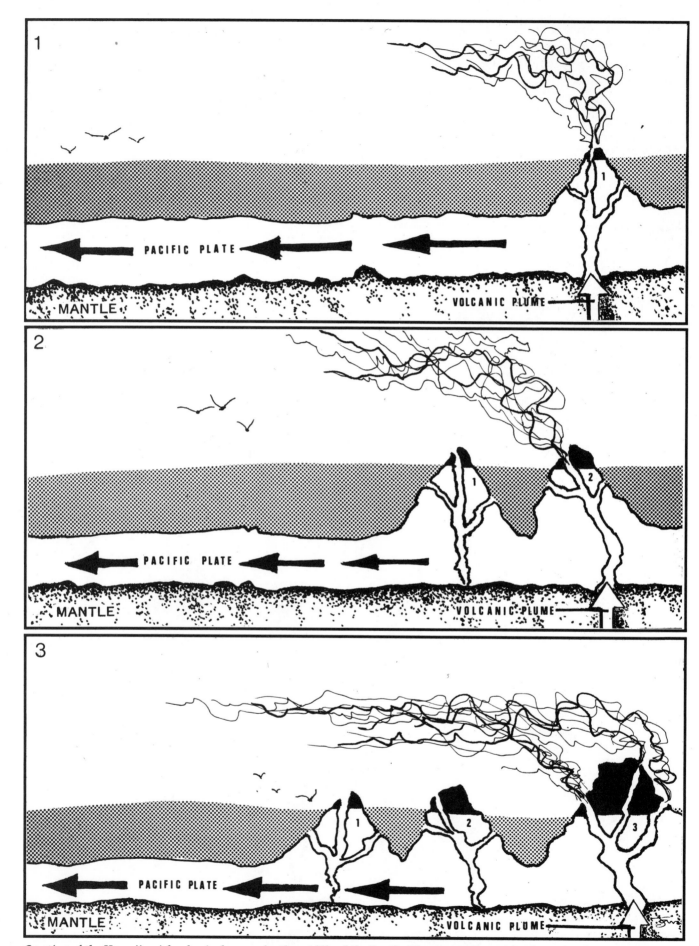

Creation of the Hawaiian islands. A plume under the middle of the Pacific Plate created new islands as the plate moved.

Pagan volcano still smoking one year after driving the 52 residents off this Northern Marianas island in May of 1981. (Photo by Dave Link, courtesy Glimpses Magazine)

to sleep or eat. If you keep going you will reach one billion after 19 years.

It is necessary to understand how long four and one-half billion years is so you can understand how the continents, which seem so hard and set, can actually have moved halfway around the globe. This movement is the theory of continental drift or plate tectonics.

Look at South America and Africa on the globe. See how they look like puzzle pieces that could fit together? At one time they did fit together. Then, slowly, they began drifting apart at the rate of only a few inches a year at most. But since they've been moving for millions of years, they are now far apart.

Plate tectonics is the slow movement of continents and oceans. This theory was not accepted by most scientists until the late 1960s. Today there is much evidence that supports the theory, and the theory itself explains much about the earth.

If we could cut the earth in half like an apple, we would see three parts. The crust covers the outside. It is made of solid rocks, but is very thin. The crust is only 50 miles (80 km) thick at most. Below the crust is the mantle. The mantle is made of heavy rock that moves and behaves somewhat like a plastic and is about 2000 miles (3200 km) thick. Inside the mantle is the earth's core. It is made up of solid nickel and

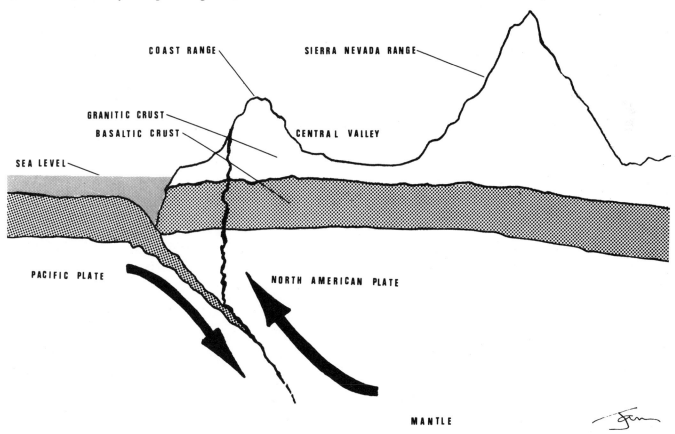

Cross-section of a plate boundary. The lighter North American continental plate is riding up over the heavier Pacific Ocean plate. The ocean plate is pushed down, creating a deep trench off the coast. The continental plate is pushed up, creating mountain ranges.

iron. The temperature in the core is hot enough for those metals to be liquid, but the pressure from the weight of the mantle has compressed them into solids.

The crust is not a single solid shell covering the mantle. It is broken into several pieces called plates. These plates "float" on top of the mantle. Certain currents or forces inside the mantle push on the plates and make them move. This process is not yet completely understood. When two plates are pushed apart, liquid rock called magma is formed in the mantle and rises through volcanic vents to fill the gap. Once on the surface, magma is called lava. It cools to form new rock for the crust. If two plates are pushed together, something has to give. If a continent plate and ocean plate are pushed together, the denser ocean plate will be forced back into the mantle, creating a deep ocean trench. The lighter continent plate will be pushed up to form a mountain range. If two continent plates crash together, they will both be pushed up to form a giant mountain range. If two ocean plates come together, they will form a very deep trench.

Down the middle of the Atlantic is the Mid-Atlantic Ridge. This underwater mountain range contains many volcanoes bringing new material to the crust from the mantle. All the plates that border the Mid-Atlantic Ridge are moving away from each other. This means the Americas are moving away from Africa and Eurasia. Two hundred million years ago they were all together as one continent.

Wherever plates come together there are cracks or faults in the earth's crust. As the plates push against each other, pressure builds up. When the pressure is great enough, the plates slip. This is an earthquake. Earthquakes from slipping plates can cause much damage by shaking the ground, often destroying buildings and roads. Near the oceans, earthquakes can cause tsunamis, formerly known as tidal waves. These waves are barely noticeable in the open ocean, but upon reaching shallow water near a coast, they can get huge and wash far inland.

Volcanoes are the openings through the earth's crust where molten rock (magma) comes up from the mantle. The mountain formed by this rock (now called lava), as it cools, hardens, and builds up around the opening, is also called a volcano. Volcanoes can cause much damage when they erupt. Sometimes they explode, or sometimes they send flows of lava that destroy any buildings in the way. They always cause earthquakes when they erupt. Active volcanoes are those which continue to pour out lava or gasses. Dormant volcanoes are those which have not done anything for a long time, but

still have the potential to erupt. Extinct volcanoes are those no longer considered to have openings through to the mantle and will never erupt again. Most of the world's volcanoes and earthquakes are located along the boundaries where the plates come together.

The processes discussed in this chapter are responsible for the formation of the two types of high islands: continental and volcanic. Continental islands are those large islands that used to be part of much larger land masses or continents. Due to the shifting of plates and rising sea levels from the melting of the last Ice Age, these pieces of continents have become islands. Continental islands are the largest type of island. They have much diversity of landform, plants, and animals, and can support the most people. New Guinea and New Caledonia are examples of continental islands.

Volcanic islands are formed by undersea volcanoes pouring out lava rock into a pile on the ocean floor. If the volcano stays active, the volcano opening at the top of the pile will continue to pour out lava and make the pile larger and larger. If the volcano continues to pour out lava, the pile will eventually break the surface of the ocean and become an island. The island will get larger and the volcano higher as long as the lava keeps flowing.

Volcanic islands are considered a large type of island, even though they are much smaller than continental islands. Often much of the land of a volcanic island is very steep. People must live along the coast and in the narrow valleys. There is less variety of plants and animals. Tahiti and Pohnpei are examples of volcanic islands. Low islands or atolls are formed by coral, and will be discussed in the next chapter.

One exception to earthquakes and volcanoes being located near plate boundaries is Hawaii. The Hawaiian islands were formed by volcanoes building up rock on the ocean floor until breaking the ocean's surface and becoming islands. But these volcanoes are right in the middle of the Pacific plate — nowhere near plate boundaries. Scientists believe these islands were formed by a plume — an upwelling or hot spot in the mantle that turns on and off. The plume is able to burn a hole through the crust and build up a volcanic island. When the plate moves, the plume merely makes a new hole and a new island. Many years from now, there will be a new Hawaiian island.

CHAPTER REVIEW

Vocabulary: Pacific, ocean, continent, island, continental shelf, ocean ridge, sea mount, continental drift, plate tectonics, crust, mantle, magma, core, plates, Mid-Atlantic Ridge, earthquake, volcano, lava, tsunami, plate boundaries, faults, plume, continental island, volcanic island.

Questions:

1. What is the theory of plate tectonics and how does it work? (Be sure to explain crust, mantle, and plates.)

2. Where do earthquakes and volcanoes usually occur and why?

3. In what ways are continents and oceans different from each other?

4. How do volcanoes make islands?

5. How were the Hawaiian Islands formed?

For Further Reading:

Siever, Raymond and Press, Frank. *EARTH* (Third Edition). Freeman and Co., 1982.

Chapter 2: Coral

1. The Coral Polyp

The movement of plates and the eruption of volcanoes play an important role in making islands. The other important ingredient in island formation is the coral polyp, which together with certain types of algae, mollusks, and other life forms, creates coral reefs.

The coral polyp is an animal. Most individual coral polyps are very small, but coral polyps can form huge colonies. The polyps secrete lime to make hard, bony cups outside their bodies. When they die, the bodies dissolve but the cups or skeletons remain. New coral builds on top of these skeletons. Thus a coral colony keeps getting bigger and bigger, as new coral builds on the skeletons of old. This is how reefs are formed.

There are only four parts to a coral animal: the outside skin, several stinging tentacles, an all-purpose cavity, and the skeletal cup that the animal lives in. The coral eats plankton, tiny floating plants and animals. The tentacles sting the plankton which then fall through the mouth into the cavity. The cavity digests the food and spits out the waste through the same opening or mouth.

The cavity also produces the coral's sex cells. Sexual reproduction varies from species to species. Some are hermaphrodites, producing both sperm and eggs though not at the same time. Some have exclusively male polyps, or exclusively female, or both. In some cases, the sperm is made in the cavity then put into the water, eventually entering the cavity

of a polyp producing eggs. The fertilized eggs, now called larvae, are then spit out from the cavity. In other cases, both sperm and eggs are simply spit out into the water where fertilization takes place.

In all cases, the larvae swim through the ocean looking for a place to attach themselves. Many die or are eaten, but a few attach themselves to a rock. They then start a different type of reproduction. The single larva, now attached to a rock, becomes a polyp and starts budding or dividing. It will grow new polyps from its own body, or divide into two complete polyps. When a polyp dies, it leaves its skeleton as a base for the new polyps. Only the outer layer of a coral colony is alive; underneath are the skeletons of the previous generations.

Thus coral has two kinds of reproduction. Sexual reproduction produces larvae to start new colonies. Asexual reproduction makes the colonies larger by budding or dividing.

Reef building coral can only live under certain conditions. The larvae looking for a new home cannot land just anywhere. The water must be salt, with all the minerals of ocean water so the coral can get the calcium it needs to make its skeleton. The water must be warm, at least 70 degrees F (21 degrees C), and must be shallow, 180 feet (54 m) or less, and clear. It must be shallow and clear so there will be enough light for a certain type of algae to grow. Algae are plants and need light. A special type of algae lives with the coral. They live in symbiosis, which means they help each other. The algae help coral take calcium out of the water and help cement the coral skeletons together. The coral gives the algae animal waste, which is plant fertilizer. Reef-building coral can only grow in warm, shallow, clear saltwater.

2. How Atolls Are Formed

If a volcano makes an island in warm, clear, ocean water, coral can grow on its shallow surfaces. The coral will grow away from the island. It can't grow above the surface, down into deeper water, or into the volcano. But as parts of the reef die and are broken down by the waves, an apron of debris is deposited underwater around the volcano. The coral can continue to grow on this apron shelf as it builds up ever farther from the volcano shore, forming a fringing reef.

For reasons still being debated by scientists, the volcano may begin to sink. This may be due to a subsiding sea floor, the cooling of the volcano, or a ris-

Aerial view of a coral atoll: Majuro in the Marshall Islands — long, skinny, and flat islands surrounding a large lagoon. (Photo courtesy Glimpses Magazine)

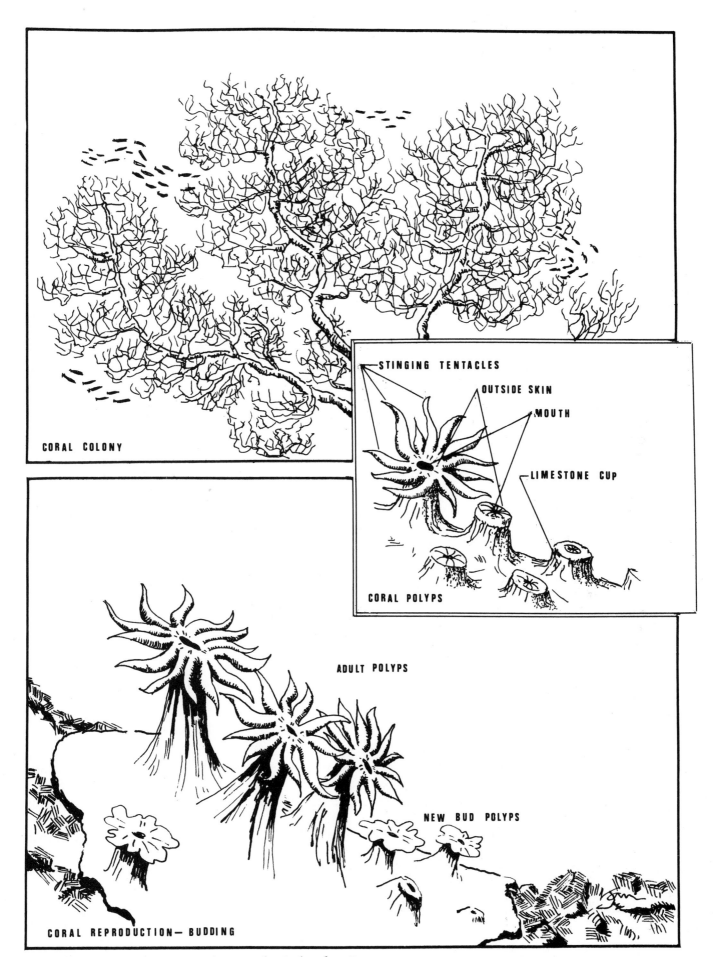

CORAL COLONY

STINGING TENTACLES

OUTSIDE SKIN

MOUTH

LIMESTONE CUP

CORAL POLYPS

ADULT POLYPS

NEW BUD POLYPS

CORAL REPRODUCTION— BUDDING

Coral. (Top: a coral colony. Center: the parts of a single polyp. Bottom: coral reproducing by budding.)

The birth of an atoll. Coral grows on the sides of a tropical volcano, forming a fringing reef. As the volcano sinks, the coral grows up as well as out, forming a barrier reef with a lagoon. Finally, the volcano disappears leaving only the barrier reef and lagoon.

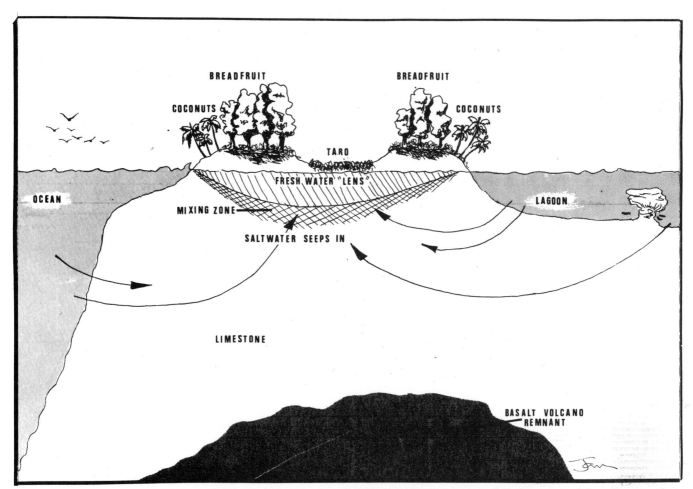

Cross-section of a reef island. A limited amount of fresh rain water is held in the limestone and floats on top of the salt water that saturates the porous rock from the ocean. Coconuts grow near the beach, breadfruit a little farther inland, and taro in a low, swampy area in the middle.

ing of the sea level due to melting ice from the last Ice Age, or a combination of all of these. As the volcano sinks, the live coral at the edge of the fringing reef must now start growing up as well as out. This way the coral will stay in the shallow water it needs to survive. The reef will now be separated from the sinking volcanic island. This is a barrier reef. The shallow water between the island and the reef is called a lagoon. The bottom of the lagoon is usually sand from broken coral and parts of the mountain which have washed down. Underneath that will be the old coral of the original fringing reef.

Eventually the volcano will sink completely. The coral will continue to build on top of the sunken mountain. There will now be a reef shaped roughly like a circle. There will be no mountain, no volcanic island, but only a lagoon in the middle. This is an atoll.

3. The Reef Environment

The coral reef, whether fringing, barrier, or atoll, is one of the richest environments in the world. The reef is the home for many types of plants and animals. Fish of many kinds inhabit the reef. They are usually smaller and more colorful than open ocean fish. Many types of sharks can also be found. The octopus is a reef animal, living in holes and cracks in the reef. It is not dangerous to man. Moray eels also live in holes in the coral. They can be dangerous to people poking their hands into the coral. Crabs, lobsters, clams, starfish, slugs, and anemones all live in the reef. None of these animals inhabit the open ocean. There are also many kinds of algae and other plants living in the environment of a coral reef. Without coral, they would probably not exist.

The coral reef — one of the richest environments in the world. How many creatures can you recognize?

4. Reef Islands

Since the coral reefs are just below the surface of the water, it is easy for them to become filters that trap and collect sand and other debris. Much of the sand is made from pieces of coral broken down by the waves. As waves break and crash across the reef, this sand is often deposited on the lagoon side of the reef. This sand can build up until it breaks sea level. Sometimes it remains only a sandbar. But it can become a reef island — limestone covered with sand. If it is high enough, it can hold rainwater. If it holds water, plants can grow permanently. The plants' roots help the island hold more water. When the plants die, they make the sandy soil richer. This makes it even easier for more and more plants to grow. Soil, or dirt, is made from broken down rocks, dead plants, and dead animals. The limestone is the compacted dead coral of the reef itself.

There are four ways plants can get to an island. Some, like coconuts and pandanus, have seeds that can float for hundreds of miles. The waves eventually toss them up onto an island. Some seeds can be blown by the wind, especially in typhoons. Sometimes birds eat seeds that are not digested. They can land on an island and leave the seeds in their droppings. Finally, man brings new plants to islands.

As rain falls on an atoll, it is soaked up by the land. In the porous limestone rocks, the lighter fresh water floats on top of the salt water that has already seeped into the rock from the ocean. The fresh water level stays just a little above the sea level in a convex lens, and rises and falls with high and low tide. Thus wells can be dug on reef islands to get fresh rainwater, and canals can be dug which will fill up with fresh water for taro patches.

There are no rivers on atoll reef islands. The islands are flat, rarely more than 15 feet (4.5 m) above sea level. Reef islands are very similar to each other. There is almost no variety of land forms. Size and shape of the islands may vary. Likewise, atolls themselves vary in size, shape, and number of islands on the reef. Reef islands are very vulnerable to typhoons and heavy seas, which can sometimes wipe out whole islands. It is easy to wash away the thin topsoil. Coral islands also keep changing. They usually erode on the windward side and build up to leeward.

Geologically coral reef islands are not very old — maybe a few thousand years. Compared to the rich coral reefs, the thin soiled reef islands have very little variety of plants and animals. Most plants and animals migrated across the Pacific from Asia. The farther an island is from Asia, the fewer species of plants and animals it has. This is true for the reefs also.

Coral islands have no mineral resources except, on a few islands, phosphate. Phosphate is used to make fertilizer.

Reef islands can support several plants important to man. Pandanus and coconuts can grow almost anywhere. Breadfruit and taro need fresh ground water, which most reef islands have. Also bananas, papayas, sweet potatoes, and a few other food plants can grow. Most of these plants were spread by man.

There are very few animals on reef islands. Land crabs, insects, and lizards were likely there before man. Many of these animals may have come on drifting plants. There are also some land birds on the islands. Sea birds fish out on the ocean during the day then nest at night on the island. Their droppings fertilize the soil and make it richer. Chickens, pigs, dogs, and rats were all probably brought by man. The rats may have hidden in canoes.

In addition to the two types of high islands, continental and volcanic, there are two types of low islands.

Atolls have the flat reef islands just discussed. They are the smallest, have the least variety of plants and animals, and support the smallest populations of all types of islands. Atoll dwellers usually do the most sailing. They have to go to high islands to trade for things that won't grow on the atoll islands.

The last type of island is the raised coral island. These are atolls that have been raised up into the air. The walls of the reef now form cliffs above the water. The lagoon in the middle drains out, leaving dry land. These islands are still fairly flat on top. Some may even be considered high islands, as they can get up to several hundred feet above sea level.

The Marshall Islands are all atolls. Niue is a raised coral island.

CHAPTER REVIEW

Vocabulary: coral polyp, plankton, hermaphrodite, larvae, budding, sexual reproduction, asexual reproduction, algae, calcium, symbiosis, fringing reef, barrier reef, lagoon, atoll, reef island, phosphate, pandanus, raised coral island

Questions:

1. What conditions does coral need to survive and why?

2. What methods does coral use to make new colonies and build reefs?

3. How are atolls formed?

4. How are reef islands formed?

5. Compare the environment of the reef to the environment of the reef island.

6. Explain what happens to rainwater on a coral island.

For Further Reading:

Randall, Richard H. and Myers, Robert F. *THE CORALS*, Guide to the Resources of Guam, Vol. 2. Guam: University of Guam Marine Laboratory, University of Guam Press, 1983.

Chapter 3: Tropical Pacific Weather and Climate

1. The Tropics

Because of the tilt of the earth, the sun appears to move throughout the year. It never rises or sets in exactly the same spot everyday. Each day it rises or sets a little farther north or south than it did the day before. It will only go so far north before it appears to start moving south again. It takes one year for it to complete one cycle. This "movement" explains why we have seasons. When the sun is north of the equator, the northern hemisphere (half) of the earth gets direct sunlight. The southern hemisphere gets sunlight at an angle. The more direct the rays of the sun, the hotter it is. Thus the north will have summer and the south will have winter. When the sun crosses back across the equator, the south will have summer and the north will have winter. Of course the sun doesn't really move. As the earth revolves around the sun, the tilt of the earth makes the sun appear to move.

The area of the earth that the sun passes directly overhead, from the farthest north to the farthest south, is known as the tropics. This zone is from 23½ degrees north to 23½ degrees south of the equator.

At the extreme north and south of the earth are the polar zones. These are zones where the sun sometimes disappears for days or weeks or, at the exact poles, for six months. In summer the sun never sets for six months.

Between the polar zones and the tropics are the temperate zones.

Most Pacific islands that we will study are located in the tropics.

Because the tropic zone gets more direct sunlight than other parts of the earth, it is usually warm or hot, even in winter. Because the Pacific is a large ocean, Pacific tropics are hot and humid. Humidity is moisture in the air. Direct sunlight causes the ocean water to evaporate and warm air can hold more moisture than cold air. Thus there is always much moisture in the air of the Pacific tropics.

2. The Rainy and Dry Seasons

As the sun passes back and forth across the tropics, it heats up the water. The part of the tropics where the ocean is warmest is known as the inter-tropical convergence zone, or ITCZ. This is where the air masses of the northern and southern hemispheres come together. This zone chases the sun. Sometimes it is directly under the sun, but sometimes it is behind and following the sun. This happens when the sun heads back across the equator. The water where the sun left is warmer than the water where the sun is headed. Then the water the sun left cools, and the water under it heats up, and the zone catches up with the sun. Usually, the zone is centered just north of the equator, but it will stretch to the north or south following the sun and warm water.

Evaporation is the process of a liquid becoming a gas. Warm water evaporates easier than cool water, and warm air holds more moisture than cooler air. Where the ocean is hottest, near the ITCZ, warm, moist, air rises. When it gets up high enough, it cools. This condenses the moisture, turning it back into liquid. It then rains back down. This happens during the rainy season.

When the ocean is cooler, the air has less humidity (moisture). Since the air near the equator and ITCZ is rising, this creates a low pressure area and air over the cooler water, under higher pressure, flows towards the warmer water. This makes the trade winds which come during the dry season. Trade winds are steady winds that blow towards the equator usually during winter months. Because of the spin of the earth to the east, trade winds do not head directly for the equator, but come at an angle from the east.

The nearer the equator and ITCZ, the more unpredictable and unsteady the winds. This area is often known as the doldrums, or area without wind.

There are thus two basic seasons in the tropics: a hot, wet, rainy season and a slightly cooler, dry, trade wind season. The tropics really don't have seasons known as summer, spring, winter, and fall.

The winds make it feel drier and cooler because they help evaporate perspiration. Hot and humid is more uncomfortable than hot and dry.

The human body cools itself by perspiring. Perspiration cools the body by evaporation. Perspiration takes the heat from the body as it evaporates. But if the air is already very humid, it is hard for the perspiration to evaporate. The humid air already has too

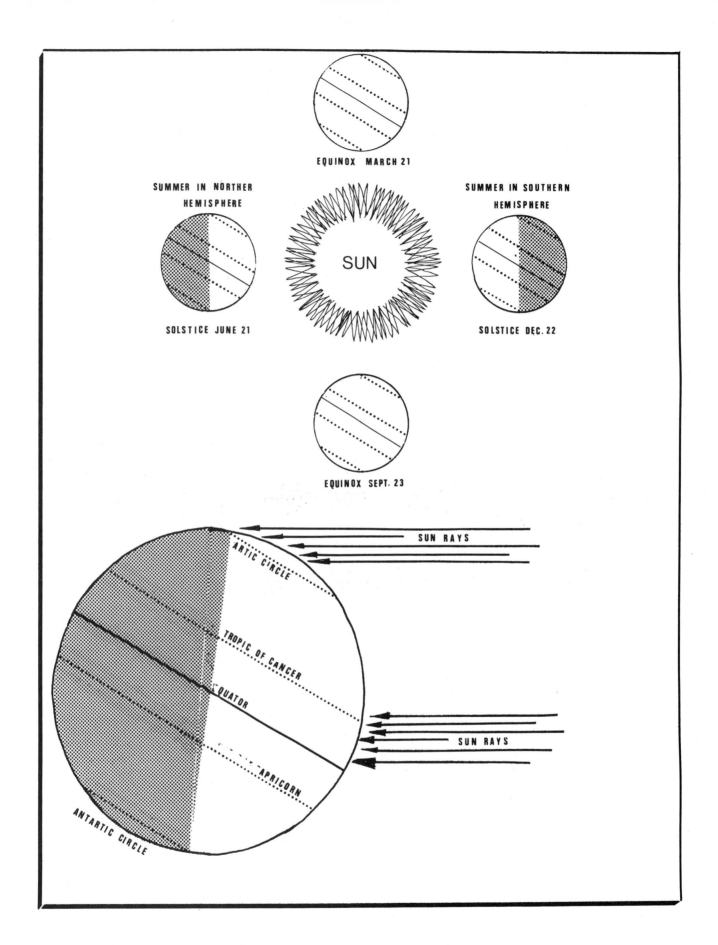

The tilt of the earth determines the seasons. In June, the northern hemisphere is receiving direct sunlight and has warmer weather. In December, the earth has moved to the opposite side of the sun, and due to the tilt of the earth, the southern hemisphere now has the direct rays and warmer weather.

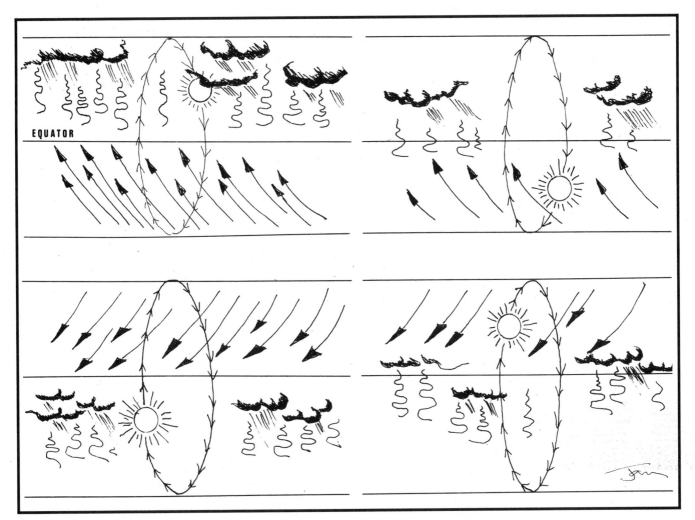

Top left: August; the sun has been north of the equator since March, the ocean water is very warm, so the northern Pacific tropics has rainy/typhoon season, the southern tropics has dry/trade wind season.

Bottom left: February; full rainy season in southern tropics, trade winds become established in northern tropics.

Top right: November; the sun has just crossed the equator, but north of the equator still has warmer water, rain continues in the northern tropics but trade winds are starting, trade winds continue but taper off in the southern tropics.

Bottom right: May; trade winds continue in north, but rains will arrive soon; south is cooling off, trades will pick up soon.

much moisture. So the perspiration stays on our body, our body doesn't feel cool, and it perspires even more. Our clothes beome wet and sticky.

This is why Pacific islanders used to wear very little clothing. In order for perspiration to evaporate in a hot and humid climate, you must expose as much skin as possible to the air. The best clothing in this type of climate is no clothing at all.

3. Typhoons

Typhoons are very large and powerful Pacific storms. The same kind of storm is called a hurricane in the Atlantic. Typhoons have winds from 75 to 200 miles per hour (120 to 320 km/hr). They also usually bring much rain, high seas, and high surf. Some-

times they are very destructive to islands, especially the flat atolls.

A typhoon is most often anywhere from 350 to 600 miles (560 to 960 km) across. There is a very low pressure area in the center, and the wind and clouds spiral around it. This is the eye, usually a very calm place in the middle of the storm that most typhoons develop. This eye can be anywhere from five to 35 miles (8 to 56 km) across. The strongest winds are right next to the eye. The better formed the eye, the stronger the winds.

Scientists are still not sure exactly what starts a typhoon. Not all storms develop into typhoons, but any can if the conditions are right. As a storm gets stronger it is classified from an area of disturbed weather, to a tropical depression, to a tropical storm, to a typhoon, to a supertyphoon. These classifications are based on wind speed.

There are several conditions necessary for a

SUPER TYPHOON TIP
DATE: 11/2117Z OCT 79
CENTER FIX: 16.2N 138.5E
MAX WIND: 160 G 190 KTS
MAX TOPS: 50,000 FT +
EYE DIAM: 13 NM
MIN SLP: 870 MB
AREA OF CIRCULATION: 1200 NM

←YAP

←KOROR

←———— 300NM ————→

Satellite photo of Supertyphoon Tip, October, 1979. Tip was unusually large. Note the eye and the counterclockwise spiral of the clouds. (Photo courtesy Naval Oceanographic Command Center, Guam)

Damage caused by Typhoon Karen, Guam, 1962. This wooden house was completely destroyed. Coconut trees, able to bend with the wind, fared a little better. (Photo courtesy MARC)

typhoon to form. It must be very humid. The water surface temperature must be at least 80 degrees F (27 degrees C). Typhoons form only over warm water, usually near the end of summer when the water is warmest. This is during the rainy season. There must be an upper level high pressure system. And there must also be warm, moist, rising air that is warmer than the surrounding air up to about 30,000 feet (9000 m).

When this warm air rises and condenses rapidly, it gives off much heat. Remember evaporation uses heat to change liquid to gas. Condensation is the reverse process. It changes gas back into a liquid, giving off much heat. Heat is energy, and is the main energy of a typhoon. The heat given off by rapid condensation is energy that begins moving the air — thus the strong wind.

Storms cannot become typhoons too close to the equator. This is because of the Coriolis effect. The Coriolis effect governs the spin and energy of whirlpools. Typhoons are big whirlpools of air. North of the equator, typhoons spin counterclockwise. South of the equator, they spin clockwise. Near the equator, the Coriolis force is very weak and whirlpools barely spin at all. Storms cannot reach typhoon strength closer than five degrees latitude of the equator. Because of this, typhoons tend to move away from the equator. Due to the general atmospheric flow, typhoons tend to move to the west. As a general rule then, typhoons move away from the equator and to the west. There can be temporary exceptions, and sometimes typhoons do double back or loop in the wrong direction. But eventually they will head away from the equator and west. (Note: south of the equator in the Pacific the storms tend to be smaller in diameter and altitude. They are thus less influenced by the atmospheric flow and are as likely to head east as west.)

The typhoon will move at a speed of 9-14 miles per hour (14-22 km/hr). It will last from one to two weeks. As soon as it gets over a large land mass or cold water, it will begin to break up. Remember it needs heat from warm water to make strong winds.

Nobody knows how to stop or slow down the winds of a typhoon. Scientists think that if you can seed the clouds next to the eye and make them rain out, the eye will get larger and the winds weaker. This has not been tried.

The northwest Pacific has more than twice the number of typhoons than any other part of the world.

CHAPTER REVIEW

Vocabulary: tropics, hemisphere, polar, temperate, humidity, evaporation, ITCZ, condense, rainy season, trade winds, dry season, doldrums, typhoon, hurricane, eye, equator, Coriolis effect

Questions:

1. What causes the seasons and climate zones of the earth and why?

2. What kind of clothing is best in humid tropics and why?

3. What causes the rainy season? What causes the dry season?

4. What conditions are necessary for a typhoon to form?

5. Which direction to typhoons usually head and why?

For Further Reading:

Fritzen, Dorothy. *THE SPINNING WINDS*. Agana, Guam: Agency Service, 1972.

Nieuwolt, S. *TROPICAL CLIMATOLOGY*. London: John Wiley and Sons, Ltd., 1977.

Unit Two: Peopling of the Pacific
Chapter 4: Migration

1. The Scientific Questions

The Pacific islands were settled long ago by the ancestors of today's Polynesians, Melanesians, and Micronesians. Since the cultures of these people lacked writing, they left no written historical records of this settlement. They do have legends and oral history, but the accuracy of these is always in question. When, why, how, and from where these islands were settled has been a matter of controversy among modern scientists. Many theories have been proposed to explain these questions.

Since there are no written records, scientists have to use other methods to find answers. Racial studies were once often used. Comparisons would be made based on the physical and racial characteristics of islanders. It was assumed that an island of brown-skinned people could not have originally come from an island of black-skinned people. These racial or genetic studies have not proved very accurate. The problems with these will be explained later.

Another way is to study and compare the cultures of islands. This can be done by looking at tools and customs in use, but also by digging to find tools used long ago. Similar tools and customs may mean a connection. The existence of certain types of pottery shards is helpful in tracing migrations. Only certain groups made pottery, and the art had mostly died out by contact times. These studies tend to be better than racial studies.

Language studies have proved very useful in recent years. Using computers and newly developed methods, the vocabulary and structure of two languages can be compared and any overlap can be found. Languages overlap when they use similar sounding words for similar meanings. These studies have proved the most accurate so far.

Ancestors of today's Pacific islanders crossed hundreds of miles of open ocean to find and settle new islands. Their craft were often as small as these 27-foot-long Carolinian outriggers. The canoes pictured here sailed over 600 miles from Satawal in Yap to Saipan. (Photo by Carlos Viti)

2. The Pattern of Migration

Today most scientists agree that Pacific islanders migrated from Southeast Asia. There is one opposing theory that they came from South America. The sweet potato is an American plant, but it is also found on Pacific islands. It is not native to Asia. Also, the prevailing winds and currents make it much easier to sail east to west than west to east. Language studies, however, despite some place name overlap between Pacific and South American languages, mostly connect the languages of the Pacific islands with the languages of Southeast Asia. There definitely was some contact between Polynesia and South America, but most scientists feel that Pacific islanders sailed to South America and brought back the sweet potato.

The most likely sequence for Pacific migration and settlement is: 40,000 years ago dark-skinned hunter/gatherers known as Australoids settled in New Guinea and later the Bismarck and Solomon Islands. They may have been able to walk on land that existed where only ocean is today, but they still had to cross some open water. They were undisturbed for thousands of years. Then, 5000 years ago, when the Egyptians were building their pyramids, lighter brown-skinned and slightly more advanced Austronesians moved in. They could not completely wipe out or conquer the Australoids, but they settled in. There began to be some mixing and intermarriage between the two groups. After a thousand more years (about 4000 years ago) some groups of Australoids began moving on down into Vanuatu and New Caledonia. About the same time, different groups of Austronesians began moving directly from the Philippines and Indonesia into Belau, Yap, and the Marianas. After another 500 years (3,500 years ago) Austronesians began leaving the Melanesian islands and moving into both central Polynesia and eastern Micronesia. Over the next 26 centuries (to 900 years ago) all of Polynesia was settled.

3. The Reasons for and Methods of Migration

Why these people moved and how they found new land have been equally hard questions to answer. The simple Australoids may have been seeking more game as they moved into the large islands of Melanesia. The Austronesians were probably pushed out of Southeast Asia by advancing Malay tribes. The more primitive hill tribes of Southeast Asia may be descendents of the Austronesians.

But why, once established on an island, did people continue to leave and search for new land? Most Pacific islands are small and can support only a limited population. When Pacific islanders' ancestors had migrated from Southeast Asia, the sick and weak had been left behind. Thus there were very few diseases in the Pacific. That means the causes of death were old age, accident, suicide, murder, or war. A small island could quickly become overpopulated. There would not be enough food for all the people. There might be a war between villages. The losing village would either be completely wiped out, or forced to pay regular tributes of food to the winner, making life even harder. The losing chief thus might decide to leave. He would take his strongest, healthiest people, load up his canoes, and look for a new home.

And how could they find a new island? Western scholars for years refused to believe that Pacific islanders had the skills and knowledge necessary to deliberately find new islands. Many believed new islands were discovered by accident. Perhaps a canoe of fishermen was blown by a storm to a new island. But women don't usually go fishing. How could the men reproduce on the new island? And even if women were along, the canoes would not be stocked with the food plants necessary to survive on a new island which might not even have coconuts. They would have to have enough navigational skill to find their way home, pick up some women and plants for settlement, then find their way to the new island again.

As we shall see in the next chapter, Pacific islanders knew much about navigation. Most likely the islanders conducted a purposeful, educated search for land. It was not accidental. Nor was it random — just sailing around until they found an island. They noticed things like birds heading into empty ocean and not returning for long periods. They also saw vegetation float in from afar. They knew land was out there. By the time Magellan came, all Pacific islands were either settled or known about by islanders. There was also much contact among the different islands within island groups.

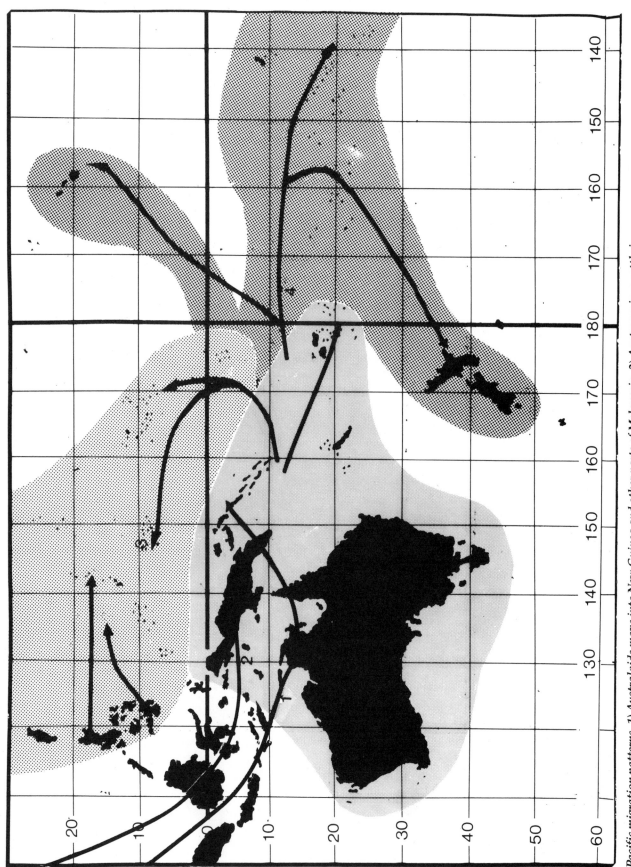

Pacific migration patterns. 1) Australoids move into New Guinea and other parts of Melanesia. 2) Austronesians settle in same area much later. 3) Austronesians leave Melanesia and back-migrate into Micronesia, while some move directly from the Philippines or Indonesia into Western Micronesia. 4) Austronesians move out of Melanesia and spread across Polynesia.

4. Sampling Error

It is possible that the ancestors of an island of brown-skinned people migrated from an island of black-skinned people. This is because of sampling error. In any population, some will be lighter skinned than others. Suppose an island has 80% darker-skinned people and 20% whose skin, while dark, is noticeably lighter. For any of the reasons discussed before, canoes leave the island to find new land. But for some reason, the people on the canoes are not 80% dark and 20% light. It just so happens that the ones who choose to leave are 70% light skinned and only 30% dark, almost the reverse of the island as a whole. Thus they do not represent the same proportion of skin colors of the population as the original population — they are a non-representative sample. And since many of them are light, after they leave, the home island has an even higher ratio of dark to light, maybe 90% to 10%. When the canoes find land, the population of the new island will be much lighter. As years go by, the people of the two islands will look very different. When a non-representative sample reproduces in isolation from the original population, it will look different. Sampling error confused many scientists who refused to believe brown Micronesians could have come from black Melanesia. Language studies have proven that this is probably what happened.

CHAPTER REVIEW

Vocabulary: racial studies, genetic studies, language studies, overlap, Australoids, Austronesians, random search, sampling error, non-representative sample

Questions:

1. What caused early islanders to leave Southeast Asia? What caused them to keep looking for new islands?

2. Why is it unlikely that all islands were found either by accident or random search?

3. What is sampling error? What does it explain?

For Further Reading:

Bellwood, P.S. "The Peopling of the Pacific," *SCIENTIFIC AMERICAN*. November, 1980. pp. 174-175.

Chapter 5: Navigation and Canoe Technology

1. Outrigger Canoes

Pacific islanders used outrigger sailing canoes. These craft were very sturdy and easily capable of open ocean voyages. The hulls were usually made of breadfruit wood. The sail was woven pandanus leaves. Rope and lines for the vessel were made from coconut fibers. Polynesian canoes could be quite large, with double hulls capable of carrying 50 or more people. Dogs, pigs, and chickens could be taken for stock on a new island. It was also a good idea to take coconuts, breadfruit, taro, bananas, potatoes, and other crops for planting on a new island. The canoes could hold all this easily.

Micronesian canoes tended to be smaller, 25' to 30' long. To tack, or change direction when sailing upwind, the whole sail could be lifted and moved to the other end. The bow would become the stern and vice versa.

Early European explorers were always impressed with the seaworthiness of Pacific canoes. Even caught in a typhoon, they would at least stay afloat. Many cases have been recorded of islanders surviving a typhoon by lashing themselves to their canoe and riding out the storm.

2. Navigation Problems

In navigation there are two problems. One is how to tell which direction you are going. The other is how to tell your exact position. In the open ocean, out of sight of land, these are very real problems.

Man from Kapingamorangi, a Polynesian atoll in Micronesia, uses an adze to carve out a paddling canoe on Pohnpei. (Photo courtesy MRTC)

In the European method of navigation, a compass can be used to tell direction. The needle will point north. But this does not tell you where you are. The needle will point north regardless of your position. (Of course it will point to magnetic north, which is not the same as true north.)

To find position, you must know your latitude and longitude. Latitude lines, or parallels, run east-west around the earth. They measure how far north or south of the equator you are. Longitude lines, or meridians, run north-south, meeting at the poles. They measure how far east or west you are of the prime meridian, which runs through Britain. If you know your degrees of latitude and longitude, you can locate yourself on a map.

These values can be found using a sextant, an accurate watch, the proper tables, and good charts and maps. Latitude is easier to find. The North Star never moves; it is located right above the North Pole. The farther north you are, the higher the North Star. South of the equator, the North Star disappears. But if you are north of the equator, simply use the sextant to measure the angle of the North Star to the horizon. That gives you exact latitude.

Longitude is much more difficult. You must use the sextant to take a sight of the sun exactly at 12:00 noon. Then you need the proper tables and charts. Early European navigators were very poor at fixing longitude.

Today there are many electronic navigation aids. Loran stations are large radio transmitters located on certain islands. They send out steady signals to help ships and planes pinpoint their locations. Various types of navigation radar are being used, and satellites are proving useful to navigation.

3. Islander Navigation Methods

Pacific islanders had neither compass, nor sextant, nor watches, nor tables, nor maps. They had no Loran stations, satellites, or radar. If below the equator, they did not even have the North Star. (They did, however, have the Southern Cross, a constellation giving a fairly accurate reading for south.)

One way to navigate is to use dead reckoning. This means you start from one island and head straight in the direction of the island you want to reach. If you keep straight, you should hit the island. But ocean currents can take you off course without your knowing it. You will miss the island. Storms and squalls may also throw you off your path.

Pacific island navigators had many methods for telling direction and position. For direction, the sun

Outrigger sailing canoe tied up in the Puluwat Lagoon, Truk State. (Photo by Carlos Viti)

and stars are very useful. By their rising and setting, they give a general heading for east and west. They also serve as a directional guide to locate islands. From the time he is a small boy, a prospective navigator memorizes hundreds of star courses. He memorizes which stars to follow to get to each island from any island he might be on.

If it is cloudy, the navigator can use waves to tell direction. Waves are made by wind. During the trade wind season, which is also the sailing season, the steady trade winds make steady swells or waves. These swells go in a steady direction. The navigator feels the waves under the boat. He can tell which are the steady swells coming from the northeast (or southeast below the equator). He feels the rocking of the canoe as the waves pass under. Depending on how the boat rocks, he can judge the angle of the canoe to the swells. He thus knows in which direction he is heading.

Keeping track of position is more difficult. The navigator simply keeps track mentally of speed and direction to judge how far the canoe has travelled. This is also dead reckoning, and means he has to be on the lookout for currents. There are three main currents in the Pacific area we are studying. The North Equatorial Current flows east to west. The Equatorial Counter Current flows west to east just north of the equator. Below it is the South Equatorial Current which flows east to west. The navigator already knows where these and other regular currents are, and can judge their strength by the shape of the waves. Waves are made by wind, and a current will change the way a wave looks. All this information will be in the navigator's head.

The navigator also knows the location of all undersea reefs. He can recognize a reef by the shape along its edge. Once he finds a reef and recognizes which one it is, he knows his exact location. Some reefs are many miles from land, but they are valuable sea marks. Once you know your exact position, you can adjust your course.

Land nesting sea birds also help navigators. These birds fish anywhere from 20-30 miles (32-48 km) from land. If a navigator spots such a bird, he knows land is close. At sunset, the birds will head in a straight line for their island. Since flat atolls can be seen from about ten miles (16 km) away at most, the birds give the navigator a bigger target and more insurance.

Certain island groups had additional methods. Kiribati navigators could see islands reflected in the clouds above the islands. Marshallese navigators used the northeast swells. The steady waves would be bent by the long reefs of the Marshallese atolls.

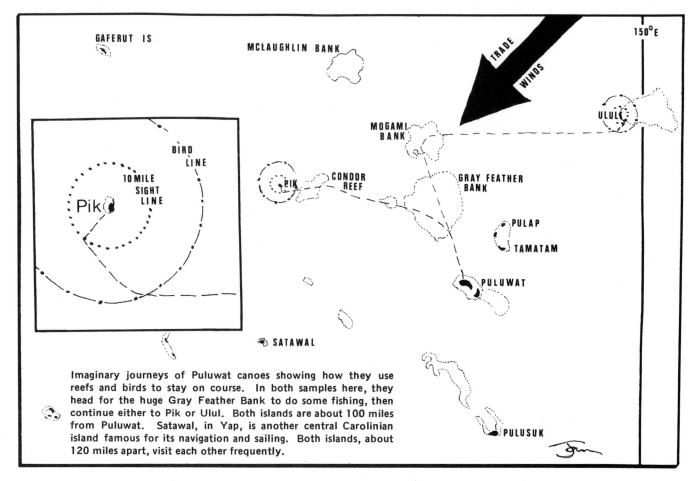

Imaginary journeys of Puluwat canoes showing how they use reefs and birds to stay on course. In both samples here, they head for the huge Gray Feather Bank to do some fishing, then continue either to Pik or Ulul. Both islands are about 100 miles from Puluwat. Satawal, in Yap, is another central Carolinian island famous for its navigation and sailing. Both islands, about 120 miles apart, visit each other frequently.

The famous Marshallese stick charts were really only used as training aids for young navigators.

Today, most of this knowledge has been lost. Only in a few islands in the central Carolines of Micronesia are there still navigators who dare to cross hundreds of miles of open ocean. Even on those islands, the skill may be dying. The brighter children go off to school, away from their fathers and uncles who can teach them navigation. It takes years of study and practice to become a navigator. Some of these islands have, however, experienced a revival of canoe building and navigation learning in the late 1970s and early 1980s. Whether the current revival on islands like Puluwat will keep such skills alive for more than a generation or two remains to be seen.

CHAPTER REVIEW

Vocabulary: outrigger canoes, tack, direction, position, compass, latitude, longitude, parallels, meridians, prime meridian, sextant, North Star, Loran stations, dead reckoning, northeast or southeast swell, undersea reefs

Questions:

1. Explain the problems of determining direction and position.

2. What are some of the methods Pacific islanders used to navigate?

For Further Reading:

Dodd, Edward. *POLYNESIAN SEAFARING*. New York: Dodd, Mead, and Co., 1972.

Gladwin, Thomas. *EAST IS A BIG BIRD*. Cambridge, Massachussetts: Harvard University Press, 1970.

Lewis, David. *WE, THE NAVIGATORS*. Honolulu: University of Hawaii Press, 1972.

Chapter 6: Pre-Contact Lifestyle

1. Subsistence Living

Before Europeans came to the Pacific, islanders had a subsistence lifestyle. Subsistence is when you do everything for yourself. You catch, raise, or grow all your own food. You make your own tools from materials on the island. You also build your own shelters and make your own clothes from local materials.

Any trading was usually done as simple barter. Micronesian atoll islanders would trade woven mats to high islanders for food that doesn't grow on atolls. Papua New Guinea coastal tribes would trade with highlanders. Also in Melanesia, pigs were used to buy brides. Polynesians did very little trading. Only a few islands had any kind of money system, mostly for ceremonial purposes.

From local materials islanders could make many things. But the main thing islanders lacked was metal. This put a limit on the durability of tools.

For food, islanders had coconut, breadfruit, taro, pandanus, banana, and a few others. The high islands had sweet potatoes and yams in addition to the above. For protein, they had their chickens, pigs, and dogs. Pig raising was especially important in parts of Melanesia. Another protein source was the big land crabs, but most protein came from the sea.

Fish hooks were made from wood or shell. Lines were coconut rope. Hermit crabs served as bait. With hooks and lines, islanders could either troll on the sailing canoes for open ocean fish like tuna, or they could stop the canoe over a deep reef and drop the lines over for bottom fish like red snapper.

To get reef fish they used wooden spears without rubber slings. Or they could make a large net from coconut leaves and have several people drive the fish into it. They also made small throw nets for catching fish in shallow water. The reef also yielded octopus, clams, and lobster.

Fish traps were also used on many islands. Sticks would be lashed together to make a cage-like trap. The trap would be placed on the reef in the trap maker's favorite spot. The fish would swim into the trap, become confused, and not be able to swim out. Poisons, made from local plants, were also used, making stunned fish float to the surface.

Since there was no metal, tools were made of wood, stone, and shell. The main tool used in the Pacific was the adze. Clam shell was usually used as its cutting edge before metal came into the Pacific.

A fish hook carved from wood.

The adze — main tool of the Pacific.

Ikuliman in his canoe house on Puluwat, Truk, making rope from coconut husk fiber. (Photo by Carlos Viti)

This shell adze was used for hollowing and shaping canoes and for almost any carving chore.

Weaving coconut and pandanus leaves could produce baskets, thatch, sails, and mats.

On a few atolls, clothing was made from weaving banana or hibiscus fibers on wooden looms. On other islands, the bark of certain trees was pounded into tapa cloth. There were also other plants like pandanus used to make clothing.

Buildings were constructed of wood and thatch, all lashed together by coconut rope. Sometimes they would have raised floors. The roof would be high with a steep peak. This type of construction was very airy and cool. Huge, impressive canoe houses and men's houses could be constructed this way.

Melanesians had knowledge of the bow and arrow. But for Micronesians and Polynesians, the weapon of choice was the war club. Made of hard wood and carved with intricate, sharp-edged knotches, the war club could easily crush a man's skull. Shark's teeth were often imbedded in clubs, spears, and smaller weapons. Sting ray tails were often used as spears. Using slings to hurl stones was also widespread.

Medicine men were skilled at the use of plants and herbs to cure infection and poison. For many ailments, excellent massage techniques proved useful. Magic chants were also often used in the healing process. These chants caused many missionaries to object to local medicine.

Personal decorations were quite important to most islanders. Melanesians developed elaborate and colorful costumes. Tattooing was widespread in most of Polynesia and Micronesia. Islanders often adorned themselves with flowers and the yellowish turmeric powder.

2. Social Organization

Religion on Pacific islands was polytheistic — meaning belief in many gods, spirits, and ghosts. Ancestor worship was extremely important in Melanesia especially. Magical powers for telling future or distant events; causing illness, insanity, or death; or causing one to fall in love were widely used and believed.

If two islands worshipped different gods and went to war with each other, the winning island was assumed to have the stronger god. The losing island would sometimes adopt and worship the winning god. This is one explanation of why many islanders accepted Christianity so quickly. The European god must be powerful, because the Europeans were so powerful and had so many good things.

Social organization and specific customs varied from island to island. Some islands had very strict caste or class systems. Depending on birth, some people would be upper, middle, or lower class. Some islands had royalty systems, with kings and other nobles with titles by birth. Slavery was practiced on some islands, the slaves being either prizes of war or born to other slaves. Cannibalism, the eating of human flesh, was practiced on some islands. This was usually done more for post-war tribal ritual than for a real food source. Cannibals would eat defeated enemies as a sign of disgust and disrespect. In some cases, the victors ate their enemies to acquire their strength, courage, or wisdom. Recently, a few people have challenged the existence of cannibalism. They believe stories of cannibalism were made up by Europeans who only assumed Pacific islanders were savage enough to eat human flesh. The evidence does support its existence, however. Headhunting was definitely practiced on some islands. Infanticide, the killing of unwanted babies, was often used as a method for controlling population on some islands. Human sacrifice was also a feature of some island religions.

The basis for most Pacific island cultures was and still is the extended family. Brothers, sisters, aunts, uncles, grandparents, and cousins all lived and worked together. They helped each other by building houses and getting food. They shared the watch-

The little grass shack. Comfortable, cool, dry, repairable or replaceable with local materials. This one is on Kapingamorangi, Pohnpei. (Photo by Carlos Viti)

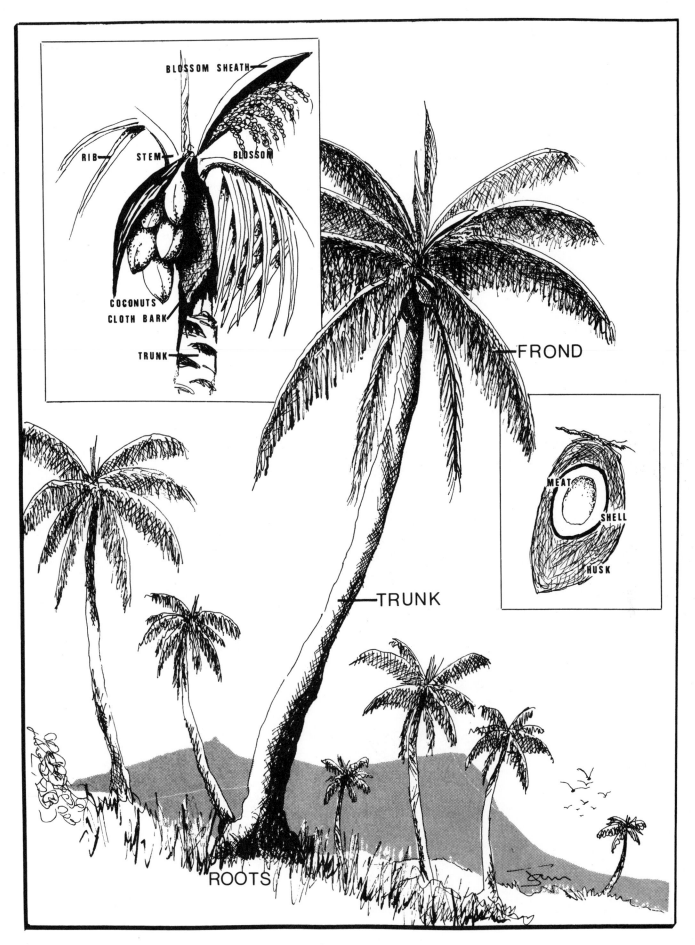

The coconut tree.

ing of children. This was a very good system for a subsistence economy. Family members shared both their resources and labor. A nuclear family, a man with his wife and their children, would be inefficient. They would not have the time or the resources to do all the necessary chores for survival. Also in an extended family system, each person had a secure place with plenty of support in the family.

For islanders it is important not to show true feelings. They never say anything offensive. Living on a small island, people see each other everyday. They must be nice to each other to keep the peace. This is hard for many Europeans and Americans to get used to. Westerners expect straight and honest answers, but islanders will say what they think the listener wants to hear. This is the polite thing to do for islanders.

Islanders lived in a very narrow balance with nature. Many of their customs and traditions developed from a need to preserve that balance.

3. The Coconut Tree

The coconut tree is by far the most useful plant in the Pacific. All its parts can be used. The following is a chart of the parts of the tree and their uses:

USES OF THE COCONUT TREE

Roots: medicine, fertilizer

Trunk: furniture, construction, simple bridges

Bark: (cloth-like material near leaves) strainer, rag, clothing, sandals

Blossom sheath: firewood, funnel, toy

Blossom: tapped for tuba, which can be either sweet, alcoholic, vinegar, or syrup

Nut stems: decoration, firewood, fertilizer

Baby Nut: eaten, used as toy

Immature Nut:
husk — fiber rope, to buff or wipe, sponge, mosquito smoker, toilet paper, cut spoon to scrape soft meat, fertilizer
shell — eaten (if young enough)
meat — eaten (is very soft), make soup
water — drink (main stage of nut that is used for drinking)

Making thatch from pandanus leaves on Kapingamorangi. (Photo by Carlos Viti)

Mature Nut:

husk — same as above plus carving decoration, cork for bottle stopper

shell — cup, scraper, various spoons and utensils, decoration, bra, firewood

meat — make copra (cash crop), make cooking sauce, eaten, a candy, soap, coconut oil

water — can be drunk

Sprouting Nut:

husk — same as above

shell — same as above

meat — eaten but is thinner and drier

spongy center (no more water) — eaten as a candy

Leaf:

mid-rib (stem) — paddle, stirring utensil, rollers under a canoe

ribs (veins) — toothpicks, brooms

individual leaf — decoration, folded into a spoon, magic, body squeegee

whole frond — weaving — thatch, baskets, hats, mats, fans

Heart: eaten (removing the heart kills the tree)

CHAPTER REVIEW

Vocabulary: subsistence, barter, troll, fish traps, adze, polytheistic, caste, royalty, cannibalism, infanticide, extended family, nuclear family

Questions:

1. Why is an extended family well suited for a subsistence economy?

2. What are some of the tools, weapons, utensils, and clothing islanders used?

3. Why do islanders tend to tell a person what they think he wants to hear?

For Further Reading:

Alkire, William H. *AN INTRODUCTION TO THE PEOPLES AND CULTURES OF MICRONESIA.* Addison-Wesley Publishing Company, 1972.

Oliver, Douglas L. *THE PACIFIC ISLANDS.* Garden City, New York: Natural History Library Edition, Anchor Books, Doubleday and Company, Inc., 1961 (original 1951).

Unit Three: Post-Contact History and Development

Chapter 7: Explorers

1. Exploration Begins

Contact means contact between Pacific islanders and white civilization — Europe and then later America. For thousands of years, Europeans and Pacific islanders did not know of each other. But changes began happening in Europe. For about 1000 years after the fall of the Roman Empire (c. 450 AD) Europe was a backward place. Europeans were not interested in trade or improving their lifestyle. During the Crusades, when Christian Europeans tried to capture the Holy Land from the Moslem Arabs and Turks in a series of wars (1096 AD-1230 AD), the Europeans saw that the Moslems lived better. Due in part to the Crusades, Europeans began trading for spices, silk, and other goods that came from India, China, and Southeast Asia. At first, Italy controlled the trade routes that came overland from the east. Other European countries wanted their own trade routes to by-pass the Italians. Portugal began exploring and found a way to go around Africa to get to India. Columbus tried to get to India for Spain by sailing west, but ran into the New World. So Magellan, also sailing for Spain, tried to find a way around South America to get to India. He thus found the Pacific.

Europe began exploring mainly to find new trade routes to the orient. But there were some other reasons. European countries also wanted to find new land for more power. The more land area controlled, the better a country's military advantage over competing countries. New lands also could be rich in raw materials, and have populations that could become markets for European goods. There was also the missionary purpose: converting the pagans to Christianity. Finally, there were scientific reasons — sailing to expand the knowledge of the earth.

In the early days of exploration, the condition of European ships and sailors was very poor. European ships of the 15th century were designed for short journeys along the coast, not for long open sea voyages. Also, the early explorers were usually given older, rotten ships. Ship owners did not want to risk expensive new ships on a voyage from which the ship might not return.

Most sailors were from the lower classes of European society. They were poor, uneducated, illiterate, and superstitious. Often they were tricked, bribed, or even kidnapped into sailing. At sea they were mean, surly, and hard to control. Often the only thing preventing mutiny was the fact that only the captain and one or two officers knew anything about navigation. The sailors were afraid to kill the officers because they could never get home. Also, the punishment for mutiny was always death.

The small ships would only be provisioned for six months. The Europeans didn't realize that voyages would take two and three years. So the ships would always run low on supplies. The main food was salt pork, salt beef, and hard tack biscuits. Fruits and vegetables were not taken since they could not be preserved. The Europeans didn't realize it, but this meant a lack of vitamin C in the diet. On a long voyage, lack of vitamin C causes scurvy. Gums swell and bleed, teeth fall out, and eventually the sailor dies. Ships began taking at least twice as many men as they needed, hoping at least half would survive to finish the voyage.

Early European navigators were not very accurate. They could usually get a good reading for latitude, but they hardly ever could tell correct longitude. This meant islands could be found, but not found again for many years.

2. Some Important Explorers

Magellan was the first European to visit a Pacific island. After rounding South America, he sailed for months across the Pacific. He saw only a few deserted islands and ran out of food. His men ate all the rats, then began eating leather. Magellan was lost and in a hopeless condition when he sighted the Mariana Islands. He pulled into Umatac Bay on Guam. The islanders swarmed over the ship, taking everything that was not nailed down. They were especially interested in metal. After a small boat was stolen, Magellan took an armed party ashore. He burned several houses and killed several islanders with crossbows and arquebuses (primitive rifles). Thus, the first meeting between Pacific islanders and whites ended in bloodshed. Unfortunately, many more meetings would end the same. Time and again, explorers would punish petty thievery and other crimes the islanders didn't understand by burning and killing. Island after island suffered a similar fate.

A ship of the type used by early Spanish explorers. It was only 86 feet long.

Europeans and islanders were unable to understand each other. On many Pacific islands, the custom was to accept any visitors and provide them with food, but at the same time all of the visitor's possessions then became the property of the islanders. So after offering coconuts, bananas, and other items, the islanders felt justified in helping themselves, and were completely bewildered at the explorers' violent responses.

The Europeans of the 16th and 17th centuries were usually incapable of seeing things from the islanders' viewpoint. Even amongst Europeans there was little tolerance. Catholics and Protestants mistrusted and hated each other. Pacific islanders were viewed as heathen, non-Christian savages. Killing savages was considered more sport than murder.

In the late 18th century this attitude began to change. The man who most reflected the change was Captain James Cook. Cook was the best, the most respected, and the most famous of Pacific explorers. He sailed for Britain (the United Kingdom).

Cook was the most accurate navigator and map maker of his time. Some of his charts can still be used today. He was also extremely thorough, checking out any island he sighted. After discovering that daily rations of sauerkraut prevented scurvy, he never lost a sailor from scurvy. Sailors liked to go with Cook because they had a good chance of coming back alive.

The islanders liked Cook even more. His cardinal rule was: "Don't kill islanders." To keep things from getting stolen, he would keep them locked up. He would trade metal to the islanders for food, so they would try to steal less. If anything important was stolen, he would ask the chief to return it. If worst came to worst, he would take the chief hostage on board ship until the stolen items were returned. But sometimes he would get violent and burn houses and canoes.

For Cook's sailors, and indeed for the sailors of all explorers, the islands offered many pleasures. In addition to warm weather and fresh food, most Pacific island women were more than willing to make love to the lonely white men. Island men were more curious than jealous; in fact they readily used their women's sexual favors as a trade item. Sexual customs of the islands were different from those in Europe. After many months at sea with no women, sailors were very eager to stop on the islands. During one stop on Tahiti, Cook's men learned that for three or four nails, they could have any girl they wanted. Cook soon had to put an armed guard on the ship's supply of nails. To Pacific islanders it often seemed that these strange white men must come from a land where there was little food and no women. As soon as they came to an island, all they wanted was food and sex — both in large quantities.

Cook only made one serious mistake in dealing with islanders, but it cost him his life. On his third voyage, Cook was the first European to visit the Hawaiian Islands. The Hawaiians thought he was a god, since he came during a festival celebrating the return of the god Lono. After staying a few weeks, and eating up much of the island's food supply, Cook's ships left. They soon ran into a storm and one ship was damaged. Cook decided to return to Hawaii to make repairs. This time, their food reserves low, the islanders were not happy to see him. A small boat was stolen, and when Cook went ashore to take the chief hostage, an angry crowd killed him.

One very interesting story of Pacific exploration is the mutiny on the *Bounty*. The *Bounty* was a British ship sent to Tahiti to get breadfruit. The breadfruit was to be taken to the West Indies to be planted as cheap food for slaves. The captain was William Bligh, a former officer of Cook. The *Bounty* stayed at Tahiti for several months. Many of the sailors fell in love with island girls. After the *Bounty* left, Bligh was strict in his treatment of the sailors, who by now were used to the easy life ashore.

About 15 of the crew of 44 mutinied and took over the ship. Bligh and 18 men were put adrift in a small boat. In a remarkable feat of navigation, Bligh managed to sail the small boat 3500 miles (5600 km) to the nearest civilization. Meanwhile, after a failed attempt to settle on Tubuai, the *Bounty* returned to Tahiti. There the men who were not mutineers but couldn't fit in the boat with Bligh got off to wait for a British ship. A few of the mutineers decided to stay on Tahiti too. The rest of the mutineers left with the *Bounty* to find a hiding place. No matter what the cause, in those days mutiny was always punished by hanging.

After Bligh told his story in Britain, a ship was sent to Tahiti to look for the mutineers. They captured all the *Bounty* sailors on Tahiti, even the innocent ones, and put them in chains. Some died in a shipwreck, some were hanged in Britain, and some were acquitted or pardoned.

Meanwhile the *Bounty*, with nine mutineers, six Tahitian men, and 12 Tahitian women, found a hiding place. It was Pitcairn Island. Pitcairn was uninhabited, had many cliffs with no easy place to land a boat, and was not charted correctly on the maps. This made it a perfect hiding place. Fletcher Christian, the leader of the mutiny, burned the *Bounty*. They would stay there forever. Soon there was trouble. There were not enough women for all the men, and the British sailors treated the Tahitian men like slaves. After a bloody battle, all the Tahitian men were killed as well as five mutineers, including Christian. By the time the island was discovered again, only one mutineer was alive. He was acting husband to ten women and acting father to about 30 children. Today the descendants of the mutineers still live on Pitcairn.

3. Major Exploring Countries

There were five European countries that did most of the exploration. Portugal did very little and eventually lost its trading posts to the Dutch.

Spain set up a trading route between Mexico and the Philippines. These ships, the Manila Galleons, went back and forth across the Pacific for 250 years. Spain sent silver from Mexico in exchange for silk, ivory, jade, china, jewelry, and spices. They did little exploration after setting up this route — sailing right past Hawaii without ever realizing it was there.

The Dutch made some discoveries, but were content to stay close to their possession of the Dutch East Indies, which they had seized from Portugal. The Dutch East Indies were once known as the Spice Islands. Today they are the independent country of Indonesia.

The British, mostly due to Cook, did much of the Pacific exploration. (See chart.)

The French began relatively late, but explored a lot to compete with the British.

Some islands were discovered many times and given many names, but not the names used by the islanders who lived there. Some islands were discovered, then lost for many years due to poor navigation.

Most major islands were known by the Europeans by the 1800s. Smaller islands were discovered by whalers and traders. By 1842, western civilization had charted all Pacific islands. Of course all these islands had already been discovered by Pacific islanders.

EUROPEAN EXPLORERS OF THE PACIFIC			
DATE	NAME	COUNTRY	ISLANDS VISITED
1513	Balboa	Spain	"South Seas" (first European to see Pacific)
1521	Magellan	Spain	Guam
1525	daRocha	Portugal	Western Carolines
1527	daMeneses	Portugal	New Guinea
1565	Legaspi	Spain	Started trade route from Mexico to Philippines, set up Manila
1567	Mendana	Spain	Solomons
1578	Drake	Britain	Belau (British pirates search for Manila Galleons)
1595	Mendana	Spain	Marquesas, Santa Cruz, Guam
1605	Queiros	Spain	Vanuatu
1606	Torres	Spain	Proved New Guinea an island
1616	LeMaire	Netherlands	Tuamotu, Tonga, Bismarck
1642	Tasman	Netherlands	Tasmania, New Zealand (first in Pacific from west)
1722	Roggeveen	Netherlands	Easter, Tuamotu, Samoa
1767	Wallis	Britain	Tahiti
1767	Carteret	Britain	Pitcairn, Santa Cruz (lost since 1595), Solomons (lost since 1567)
1768	Bougainville	France	Tuamotu, Tahiti, Samoa, Solomons
1768-71	Cook	Britain	Tahiti, Bora Bora, New Zealand, Australia
1772-75	Cook	Britain	New Zealand, Tahiti, Cook Islands, Tonga, near Antarctica, Easter, Marquesas, Vanuatu, New Caledonia, Norfolk
1776-78	Cook	Britain	Hawaii
1788	La Perouse	France	Easter, Hawaii, Samoa, Tonga
by 1842 — all islands visited and charted			

CHAPTER REVIEW

Vocabulary: contact, Crusades, mutiny, scurvy, Magellan, arquebus, Cook, Manila Galleons

Questions:

1. Give several reasons why Europe began exploring.

2. What were some of the problems facing European explorers?

3. What usually happened when Europeans and islanders met and why?

4. Why is Cook considered the best of the Explorers?

For Further Reading:

Day, A. Grove. *EXPLORERS OF THE PACIFIC.* New York: Duell, Sloan, and Pearce, 1966.

Hezel, Francis and Berg, M.L. (eds.) *WINDS OF CHANGE.* Trust Territory of the Pacific Islands, 1979.

Howe, K.R. *WHERE THE WAVES FALL.* Honolulu: University of Hawaii Press, 1984.

Warner, Oliver. *CAPTAIN COOK AND THE SOUTH PACIFIC.* American Heritage Publishing Co., Inc., 1963.

Chapter 8: Outsiders

After most of the main islands had been explored, many Europeans, Americans, and even Asians began coming to the Pacific. They came for many reasons. They came from all walks of life. The lure of the tropics — warm climate, easy life, easy women — brought them all.

German traders relaxing on Truk near the turn of the century. (Photo from Max Mori collection, Truk Archives)

1. Beachcombers

Beachcombers came first, and continued to show up into the 20th century. The first beachcombers were sailors who deserted from early explorers' ships. Some had been shipwrecked. Sometimes, ship captains would just dump troublemakers on a nearby island. A few were mutineers attempting to hide or prisoners escaped from penal colonies.

Others came deliberately to be beachcombers. Hearing romantic tales of the South Seas, they would somehow manage to get to the islands. Many were running away from problems in civilization.

Basically, a beachcomber would try to live with the islanders. Islanders usually fed any outsider since it was a shameful thing to let anyone go hungry on their island. Some islands were not good for beachcombers, however, as they might be promptly killed and eaten. On the friendlier islands, a beachcomber might marry an island girl, learn the language, settle in, and become a useful member of the community. On the other hand, he might also end up being a troublemaking leech. Most beachcombers, being uneducated lower-class sailors, were lazy, shiftless, troublemakers. They often interfered with local politics, caused fights, became involved in wars, caused killings, and spread disease.

Fiji provides a good example of both good and bad beachcombers. In the early 1800s a Swede by the name of Charlie Savage established himself on Fiji. He advised chiefs on how to kill their enemies, shot islanders just for fun, raped at will, and built up a whole gang of cut-throat beachcombers. He and his men were eventually killed and eaten by the Fijians in 1813.

In 1822 David Whippey, a young American, settled in the islands. He was quite different from Savage. He married a Fijian and became useful as a go-between and translator between the Fijians and Europeans. He became very influential and was respected by both islanders and whites.

2. Whalers

Whaling ships also came to the Pacific, mostly from New England in the United States and from Britain. Whale oil used to be in big demand as a fuel for lamps. The whaling ships would stay in the Pacific until their holds were full of whale oil. Sometimes that took three years. They would have to stop at islands for fresh food and water. They would also want entertainment. Entertainment to a whaler meant two things: alcohol and women. In the 1840s there were 675 American whaling ships, mostly operating in the Pacific. During the 1840s and 1850s an average of better than 500 ships a year called at Hawaii ports, becoming the basis of Hawaiian economy. Whalers had mostly negative effects on the islands. They encouraged the development of bars, gambling, and prostitution. They frequently fought,

First missionaries in the Truk Lagoon, German Protestants Mr. and Mrs. Maeder, Tol. (Photo from Protestant Mission Collection, Truk Archives)

Lagoon Trukese in traditional hibiscus-robe dress bringing gifts to the Protestant missionaries on Dublon. (Protestant Mission Collection, Truk Archives)

often killing many islanders on smaller islands. Honolulu, Hawaii, and Papeete, Tahiti, developed as whaling towns. They were loud, rough, and rowdy. Islanders were drawn to the towns by the jobs which catered to the needs of the whalers. Many island boys joined the ships to become whalers, replacing sailors lost at sea.

Island cultures were put under much strain by the whalers. Islands like Kosrae were almost wiped out by them, especially by the diseases they spread. Smallpox, measles, flu, and venereal disease were spread rapidly. These diseases were unknown in the islands before the explorers. Thousands of islanders died from measles. Measles was a simple childhood disease for whites, but Pacific islanders had no resistance, so measles killed them. All whites helped spread these diseases, but whalers spread them even faster, especially venereal disease.

Guam managed to develop a healthy money economy supplying whaling ships without suffering many of the evils mentioned above. This was due to the strict control and protection of the Spanish colonial government.

3. Traders

Traders came to the Pacific to make money. They would either settle on one island, or travel from island to island in ships. It was hard to make a profit in the Pacific. There were not as many resources as in America, Asia, or Africa. Traders bought mostly copra (dried coconut meat) and a few goods that would sell in China. They sold clothes and tools to the islanders. Some traders settled in, married, and became useful members of the island community. Others were dishonest and cheated the islanders. They sold guns, caused wars, and tried to get rid of chiefs who wouldn't cooperate with their trading ventures. Bad traders could cause a lot of trouble.

The main effect of all traders, good or bad, was to bring a money economy to the Pacific. When things like metal knives and cloth become necessities for the islanders, they need money to get them. They have to work to get money. This takes time away from subsistence chores. And a man who makes money doesn't like to share it with his relatives, although many work hard just to support many kin. The extended family system is based on sharing and helping each other. This is fine when there is no money. The extended family gives support and help in a subsistence economy. But in a money economy, the extended family is more of a parasite. Family members without income leech off those who do have income. This causes the ones with money to want to break away from their families. Thus money helps break down the extended family system of sharing. Since the cultures of most Pacific islands are based on the extended family, money means the breakdown of traditional culture. This happens slowly, but the change is inevitable. Today families are still important in the Pacific, but not as important as they used to be. With enough money, a nuclear family — man, wife, and children — can be independent of other relatives. Thus the whole basis of Pacific cultures is undermined.

Usually, the chiefs were the ones who made the most money. They often forced their people to do the work, but they would get the money. This did not help the culture either, as people became angry at their own chiefs. And the chiefs were becoming richer and more aloof from their people. Hawaii's Kamehameha I was guilty of this — as we shall see in the next chapter.

4. Blackbirders

Blackbirders were labor traders. They would sail to an island and buy islanders from the chief or hire willing individuals. In some cases, islanders were kidnapped and treated like slaves. They were taken to work in mines and on plantations in Fiji, Australia, and even Peru. Recent research has shown that the labor trade was not as cruel as once believed.

Though there were abuses, and several cases of outright slave raids on some islands, many of the islanders hired on voluntarily to work after their original term expired, and quite a few were taken back home to their islands when their contracts expired. The returning workers were often loaded with goods purchased with their earnings and enjoyed much respect and status in their villages.

Converted Trukese in missionary-influenced dress. (Protestant Mission Collection, Truk Archives)

5. Missionaries

Finally came the missionaries. Their goal was to convert the heathen islanders and make them good Christians. Spanish Jesuits had already succeeded in converting the Chamorros of the Marianas to Catholicism, though not without some resistance and bloodshed. Many priests and catechists were killed, and Spanish troops would then burn the offending villages.

The London Missionary Society sent Protestants to Tahiti in 1797. It took several years to become established and accepted, but after that conversion of the islanders was achieved more quickly. The missionaries first had to learn local politics, customs, and, most importantly, language. Their work was not easy, and they were often in physical danger. The old Polynesian religions died hard, as they were deeply rooted in the people's culture. But the missionaries succeeded, and soon spread the faith to other islands.

The other major Protestant missionary group was from Boston — the American Board of Commissioners for Foreign Missions. They came to Hawaii in 1819, bringing very strict Puritan ethics to Polynesia. Eventually they were successful, and Christianity spread through the islands.

The Hawaiian Missionary Society was founded, and sent missionaries into Micronesia. Conversion was easier there, as local religions were less developed. Melanesia was much more difficult. The London Missionary Society tried there, but many of their missionaries were killed. Not until the late 19th and early 20th centuries did Christianity receive many converts in Melanesia.

French Marist missionaries worked spreading Catholicism in the Marquesas, New Caledonia, and Wallis/Futuna.

Much controversy surrounds the effects of the missionaries in the Pacific. Some people feel they did mostly good, some feel they did mostly harm. Catholic and Protestant missionaries often competed with each other, causing much confusion and many problems for islanders.

On the negative side, most missionaries had little respect for the islanders' traditional beliefs and customs. They looked on the islanders as uncivilized, barbarian savages. Many missionaries did not bother to try to understand the islanders' point of view. The missionaries felt that the islanders must become Christian, and they must get rid of any attitudes, rituals, customs, or ways of thinking that were against the missionaries' European/American ideas of what was a "Good Christian."

Missionaries and traders both had problems understanding islander work ethics. Instead of working at one job all day long every day, islanders were used to doing many different jobs. One day might be spent fishing, another day re-thatching a house, and another day working on a canoe. This often frustrated the missionaries and traders, who would conclude that the islanders' poor work habits, when doing steady jobs for pay, were due to laziness.

Missionaries also didn't like the scanty dress of most islanders. They did their best to get the women to cover their breasts, and the men to wear pants and shirts. The traders liked this because it meant the people would buy clothes. But wearing clothes is uncomfortable in the humid tropics. In Melanesia especially the wearing of clothes caused a spread of flu, pneumonia, and tuberculosis. Clothes would get wet in the rain, the people would not take off the wet clothes, the clothes would not dry quickly in the humidity, and the people would get sick. Many died.

Of course the missionaries didn't appreciate the Pacific islanders' sexual attitudes. They worked hard to stop promiscuity, both premarital and extramarital. In a way this was beneficial because it helped slow down the spread of venereal disease. But this was an attempt to encourage European sexual standards. Those standards were very different from island standards, and led to much confusion and guilt.

Some missionaries tried to get the islanders to give up traditional dancing. Many dances were about sex. Dances also usually involved the traditional gods and spirits of the old religions that the missionaries were trying to wipe out. This was a major reason for opposing traditional herbal medicine. Magic was often used in the preparation of various potions. Unfortunately, many of the local medicines were very useful for treating infected wounds, poisons, and muscle problems. They should have been preserved.

There were also many positive accomplishments of the missionaries. From the islanders' point of view, the missionaries were the only white men who did not come to their islands looking for food, profit, or women. In fact, the missionaries always tried to protect the islanders from exploitation. They worked against troublemaking beachcombers, cheating traders, and all whalers and blackbirders. They tried to stop tribal wars, cannibalism, and head hunting. They brought white man's medicine to fight white man's diseases. They tried to improve agriculture in the islands. They taught the islanders to write their own languages, built many schools, and helped educate many islanders.

One note of irony, however. Although they fought exploitation by other whites, some missionaries actually became traders or plantation owners themselves. Some also became powerful advisors to chiefs, thus interfering in local politics.

Except in parts of Melanesia, Pacific missionaries of the nineteenth century were successful. Often this was due to certain chiefs who saw political and material advantages to conversion, and once they converted their whole population would follow suit. Today the Pacific islands are entirely Christian. The only exceptions of note are some local religions still surviving in parts of Melanesia. One current result of this overwhelming Christian influence in the Pacific is the strong anti-communist feelings of most Pacific islanders. Most of what the islanders know about communism was taught to them by missionaries, who of course hate and fear the atheism of communist governments. This religious anti-communism has been one reason for the lack of Russian and Chinese influence in the Pacific islands. Also, the colonial powers who controlled the islands were anti-communist, and did their best to set up democratic political practices. Island leaders today, even of now-independent island groups, are very cautious when dealing with communist countries. Even with the current expansion of Russian interest in the Pacific, it is highly unlikely that communism will ever get a foothold in the Pacific islands.

6. Effects of Contact

The island cultures stumbled upon by the Europeans were not perfect. No cultures are. All cultures have aspects that are very useful and functional but they also have aspects that are undesirable. Pacific island cultures are often pictured as idyllic, perfectly balanaced, well-ordered societies that were brutally defiled and destroyed by Europeans. To a certain extent this was true. But island cultures had their darker aspects: frequent warfare, slavery, cannibalism, infanticide, despotic rulers, human sacrifice, and even exploitation of some islands by others.

The events that occurred when the more advanced Europeans came into contact with the primitive island cultures were not unique to the Pacific. Similar things happened in Africa, parts of Asia, and the Americas. Whenever a high technology culture begins to influence a primitive subsistence culture, certain things are inevitable. The culture of the less developed group changes. Sometimes the change is drastic and sudden, sometimes more gradual. Unless all the population is wiped out, at least a part of the traditional culture will survive. It adapts, it changes. But elements of the original culture always remain. The key becomes the degree of change — how much of the traditional culture is carried on, and which aspects of the culture are retained. The answers to these questions determine how well the new synthetic, combination culture will function. It must also be noted that the islanders were not completely forced into all the changes. They were often willing participants in the process, manipulating the beachcombers, traders, and missionaries for their own purposes as much as being manipulated by them.

For Pacific islanders, there were positive results from their contact with Western civilization. On a practical level was the introduction of metal. Metal made their tools last longer, and made many of their subsistence chores much easier. Tribal war, slavery, cannibalism, infanticide, and human sacrifice were

Trading station on Pohnpei, 1899. (Uranus Expedition photo courtesy Real Academia de la Historia, Madrid, Spain and MARC, University of Guam-MC 24.91)

reduced and, for the most part, eliminated. Formal education and literacy also resulted from contact. This led to a growing awareness and understanding of the outside world.

Development itself and the general "opening up" of the islands to the outside world could be considered a positive result of contact. This idea is often challenged by people who believe in the "zoo theory." This theory states that the islanders should have been left alone, to live out their lives within their cultures without outside interference. The "zoo theory" deplores the changes that have altered traditional lifestyles, and believes these changes should be completely prevented. According to this theory, the original cultures were very functional and should have been left alone.

The problem with the "zoo theory" is that it denies the islanders the right to make choices about their own lives. It decides for them how they should live, treating them like children or animals in a zoo. The "opening up" of the islands can be considered positive. Even though many bad things resulted, even though there was much needless pain and suffering, even though many good parts of island culture and lifestyle were lost or altered, the "opening up" is still beneficial. Islanders now have more options and more opportunity than when they were locked into their traditional cultures. And the original cultures were not static, they were constantly evolving like all cultures do.

But there were many negative effects of contact. On a practical level, many diseases for which the islanders had no immunity were introduced. Thousands died. Many islanders were killed in direct conflict with whites, and blackbirders took many into virtual slavery.

Most drastic of all was the resultant breakdown of traditional controls. As explained earlier in this chapter, the introduction of a money economy helped break down the extended family, thus eroding cultural controls. Island cultures depended mainly on external controls to prevent crime, enforce respect for authority, and control anti-social behavior. These controls were exerted by the families, who kept constant watch that none of their members were committing any wrongdoing. People were thus prevented from wrongdoing by fear of being caught and exposed, thus shaming their family and themselves. Any internalized belief that a certain act was just wrong was much weaker than the external fear of being caught. A man might not feel guilty cheating on his wife if she never found out. The extended family also helped control things since it was very difficult to do anything wrong without family members becoming aware of it. These external controls effectively kept order on a small island.

Western cultures depend more on internal controls. People are socialized into believing certain acts are wrong, period. Of course these internal controls are backed up by external ones, but there is much more reliance on internal controls than there is in island cultures.

This breakdown of external controls causes the most problems for island societies. If the old controls break down before new ones are developed, social decay results. Crime increases, as does alcohol usage, prostitution, the growth of slum-like towns, and confusion. The islanders are caught in between. The old ways are dying and ineffective. The new ways are confusing and ineffective. Depression and frustration may result. Today this type of decay can best be seen on the more developed Pacific islands. Guam, Hawaii, Tahiti, and American Samoa are good examples. The least developed and more traditional islands cling to the traditional cultural controls. Inevitably, they all change.

CHAPTER REVIEW

Vocabulary: beachcomber, whaler, trader, copra, blackbirder, missionary, herbal medicine, London Missionary Society, American Board of Commissioners for Foreign Missions, Hawaiian Missionary Society

Questions:

1. How did beachcombers survive?

2. How does money break down traditional cultural controls?

3. What are the positive and negative effects of missionaries?

4. What are the positive and negative effects of contact?

For Further Reading

Dodge, Ernest S. *ISLANDS AND EMPIRES*. Minneapolis: University of Minnesota Press, 1976.

Hezel, Francis and Berg, M.L. (eds.). *WINDS OF CHANGE*. Trust Territory of the Pacific Islands, 1979.

Howe, K. R. *WHERE THE WAVES FALL*. Honolulu: University of Hawaii Press, 1984.

Oliver, Douglas L. *THE PACIFIC ISLANDS*. Garden City, New York: Natural History Library Edition, Anchor Books, Doubleday and Company, Inc., 1961 (original 1951).

Chapter 9: Colonialism in the Pacific

1. The Reason for European Colonialism

In the 19th century, competition among European countries became very strong. Britain, France, and Germany were the most powerful, economically and militarily. They didn't trust each other. They each wanted to be more powerful than the other. But inside Europe, there was a balance. To get more power, these countries had to look outside Europe. Thus European countries began looking for colonies. They took over other places in Africa and Asia in order to get more resources and power. Colonies also boosted national pride and prestige. There was also the "white man's burden," the idea that modern Christian Europe was obligated to help the backward areas and people of the world. Africa, India, China, and the rest of Asia were all divided up by Europe. The European countries were more advanced militarily and simply took over these places. Finally, they began to look at the Pacific.

There was very little reason to take over Pacific islands. There were very few resources in the Pacific. The populations of islands were small and would not provide large markets for European goods. Islands were isolated and spread out, making communication, transportation, and defense difficult and expensive. A few were strategically important, but most were of little value to Europe. In fact, many European colonies in the Pacific cost much more than they ever returned. But in the end, Europeans and Americans began taking them over. Why? Usually just to keep other countries from getting them.

German gunboat **Jaguar** *fires salute at Pohnpei. (Uranus Expedition photo courtesy Real Academia de la Historia, Madrid and MARC — MC 24.108)*

2. Pacific Resources

There were a few products of value in the Pacific. Traders looked for items that would sell in China. Chinese tea and silk were in great demand in Europe. It is better to trade for the Chinese goods than to pay cash. One product the Chinese wanted was sea otter fur. In a few years sea otters were practically wiped out. Then it was discovered that sandalwood grew on a few Pacific islands. Chinese use sandalwood for incense. Traders persuaded island chiefs to send crews into the forest to cut sandalwood. The people's farms went unattended and many of the crew became sick in the forest and died. But the chiefs like Hawaii's Kamehameha I got rich. That is except in the cases where the sandalwood traders decided to kill the chief and his family so the next trader would not be well received by the people.

Similar things happened with the sea slug trade. The sea slug was a Chinese delicacy. Pearls, pearl shells, and turtle shells were also profitable. Black-birding was another money maker. Most of these ventures had a disrupting effect on islanders and their cultures. The money economy became more established. The people had to work hard for the traders and chiefs. The chiefs became hungry for money to buy good things for themselves.

After colonial governments became established, more businesses became possible. Traders usually liked the colonial governments because they gave protection from uncooperative chiefs. Colonial administrations also brought the stability and law and order necessary for the development of plantation crops. Large scale copra, sugar cane, and fruit plantations proved profitable on some larger islands like Hawaii, Fiji, and in parts of Melanesia. Phosphate, nickel, and gold were discovered and mined on a few islands. Colonial governments, backed by the military might of their mother country, made sure these operations ran smoothly. The islanders themselves, however, benefited little from this development. Only a few chiefs and the whites made much money. The traditional, supportive cultures continued to decay rapidly. This was economic exploitation.

3. How European Countries and the United States Acquired Islands

It was not very difficult for Western powers to take over islands. For smaller islands, they simply sailed in with gunboats and claimed them. There was little the islanders could do to stop them. On the larger islands like Tahiti, Samoa, Fiji, and Hawaii, things were more complicated. Port town communities had grown up, consisting mainly of European and American traders, missionaries, and planters, all owning much land. If there was political instability in the local islander government, perhaps caused by rivalries between many different chiefs, the local white residents would call on their home countries for help. Western powers would then get involved, back up one of the chiefs, and eventually obtain control of the islands from that chief. Britain, France, and Germany were the main powers involved.

The United States also became involved in the Pacific. The United States went to war with Spain in 1898. Spain didn't want the war, and the United States won easily. From this, the United States got possession of the Philippines and Guam. Spain quickly sold the Northern Marianas, the Carolines, and the Marshalls to Germany.

Samoa is a good example of the way the Western powers competed for control of islands. Germany, Britain, and the United States all wanted Samoa. It had one of the best harbors in the Pacific at Pago Pago. The harbor would make a good coaling station for steamships. All three countries sent warships to claim the islands. Each was backing a different chief for the title of high chief of all Samoa. The Samoans themselves were fighting with each other on shore, and there was much confusion and uncertainty. The different ships were close to firing on each other and starting a bigger war. Then in 1889, a typhoon came. The U.S. and German ships were sunk and only the British ship escaped. But Britain decided to give up its claim to Samoa in exchange for some German claims in Melanesia. Then the United States and Germany sat down and divided up Samoa in 1899. The United States took the eastern portion with the good harbor. Germany received the much larger western half. Today they are still separated, as American Samoa and independent Western Samoa.

The United States also ended up with Hawaii. A Hawaiian chief, the great Kamehameha, had built an army and conquered the Hawaiian Islands by 1795. He made Hawaii an independent kingdom with his family on the throne. Over the years, U.S. sugar planters built up a successful business in Hawaii, selling sugar to the U.S. mainland. Then, to protect Louisiana sugar growers, the U.S. Congress passed a tariff on foreign sugar. Hawaii, being a foreign country, would have to pay the tariff, and Hawaiian sugar would be more expensive than Louisiana sugar. Unless Hawaii could become part of the United States, the sugar planters and sugar indus-

try in Hawaii would be ruined. As a result the planters formed a small army and took over the government, arresting the queen. After a few years, the United States annexed the islands at the request of the new government. The islands became a U.S. territory, then, later, a state.

Britain and France took most of the Pacific. Britain was reluctant to take too many islands. Fiji asked several times before Britain agreed to take it as a protectorate. Because of Britain's hesitation, France was able to acquire New Caledonia, Wallis & Futuna, and French Polynesia. Britain took the Cooks, the Gilbert and Ellice Islands, Tokelau, and Niue in Polynesia and Micronesia. In Melanesia, Britain had New Guinea and the Solomons. In a unique arrangement, Britain and France agreed to share the New Hebrides (Vanuatu). Tonga was the only group never to become a colony, although Britain established a protectorate over it to keep other countries from forcible annexation. (see chart)

4. World War I in the Pacific

This situation remained until World War I in 1914. The First World War came about because the balance between the European powers finally broke down.

On one side were Germany, Austria, Bulgaria, Turkey, and some smaller countries. On the other side when the war started were Britain, France, Belgium, Russia, Italy, and some smaller ones. In the Pacific, Germany was no match for Britain or France. Germany knew it could not protect its Pacific colonies. New Zealand, fighting on Britain's side, occupied Western Samoa. Australia took over the German controlled areas of Nauru and German New

Yap — The German governor of New Guinea reads the document of cession of the Caroline Islands from Spain to Germany. (Uranus Expedition photo courtesy Real Academia de la Historia, Madrid and MARC — MC 24.9)

Guinea. Before anything else could happen, Japan declared war on Germany. The Japanese moved in and took over Germany's islands in Micronesia. The two never really fought each other. Germany was actually happy to have Japan acquire the islands instead of Britain or France.

After World War I, Germany was out of the Pacific. Japan was in. Britain gave many islands to New Zealand and Australia. This remained the situation until World War II.

COLONIAL ACQUISITION IN THE PACIFIC

SPAIN:
1565 Colonizes Marianas, claims Carolines

BRITAIN:
1788 British settlers on uninhabited Norfolk
1808 Britain takes responsibility for Pitcairn when mutineers' community discovered
1874 Fiji ceeded to Britain
1884 British protectorate established over Southeast New Guinea
1888 British protectorate established over southern Cook Islands
1889 British protectorate established over Tokelau
1892 British protectorate established over Gilberts
       British protectorate established over Ellice (Tuvalu)
1893- British protectorate established over Solomons
1900

FRANCE:
1842- French protectorate established over Windward Societies, Marquesas, Tuamotus, and some of the
1847 Australs
1853 Possesses New Caledonia
1887 French protectorate established over Wallis & Futuna
1888 Leeward Societies and rest of Australs added to protectorate of French Polynesia

GERMANY:
1884 German protectorate established over Northeast New Guinea and Bismarck Islands
1886 German protectorate established over Marshall Islands
1888 Nauru added to Marshall Islands protectorate

CHILE:
1888 annexes Easter Island

SPANISH AMERICAN WAR 1898 (Spain loses all colonies and possessions in Pacific)

UNITED STATES:
1898 Takes Guam from Spain; annexes Hawaii (previously independent)
1899 Takes Eastern (American) Samoa by cession

GERMANY:
1898 Buys Northern Marianas and Carolines from Spain
1899 Takes Western Samoa by cession

BRITAIN:
1900 British protectorate established over Niue; friendship/protectorate treaty signed with Tonga

NEW ZEALAND:
1901 Annexes Cook Islands, including northern group and Niue, from Britain

AUSTRALIA:
1906 Takes over British New Guinea (Papua)

BRITAIN AND FRANCE:
1906 Establish condominium government over New Hebrides (Vanuatu)

WORLD WAR ONE 1914-1919 (Germany loses all Pacific possessions)

AUSTRALIA:
1914 Occupies German New Guinea; occupies Nauru

NEW ZEALAND:
1914 Occupies Western Samoa
1925 Assumes administration of Tokelau from Britain

JAPAN:
1914 Occupies Northern Marianas, Carolines, Marshalls

BRITAIN:
1916 Establishes Gilbert and Ellice Island Colony (includes Banaba and, for a while, Tokelau)

WORLD WAR TWO 1941-45 (Japan loses all Pacific possessions)

UNITED STATES:
1945 Occupies Northern Marianas, Marshalls, and Carolines

UNITED NATIONS:
1947 Establishes Trust Territories:
      Trust Territory of the Pacific Islands (United States)
      Nauru Trust Territory (Australia)
      Trust Territory of New Guinea (Australia)
      Trust Territory of Western Samoa (New Zealand)

MOVING TOWARD INDEPENDENCE:

Full Independence —
      1962 — Western Samoa
      1968 — Nauru
      1970 — Fiji; Tonga
      1975 — Papua New Guinea
      1978 — Solomon Islands; Tuvalu (Ellice)
      1979 — Kiribati (Gilberts)
      1980 — Vanuatu (New Hebrides)

Forms of Self-Rule —
      Always — Tonga
      1965 — Cook Islands (Free Association with New Zealand)
      1974 — Niue (Free Association with New Zealand)
      1979 — Federated States of Micronesia, Belau, Marshall Islands (Free Association with United States)

Other Status —
      American Samoa — U.S. Territory — 1978 complete local self-government
      Guam — U.S. Territory — 1970 complete local self-government
      Northern Marianas — U.S. Commonwealth — 1978 local self-government
      Hawaii — U.S. State — 1959 local self-government
      French Polynesia — Overseas Territory of France — 1977 & 1984 increasing internal autonomy
      New Caledonia — Overseas Territory of France
      Wallis & Futuna — Overseas Territory of France
      Easter Island — Dependency of Chile
      Norfolk Island — Territory of Australia
      Pitcairn — British Dependency
      Tokelau — New Zealand Dependency

CHAPTER REVIEW

Vocabulary: colonies, strategic, sandalwood, exploitation, tariff, protectorate, annex, balance of power

Questions:

1. Why did Europe want colonies?

2. How did Europeans and the United States take over islands?

3. Why was Europe slow to become interested in the Pacific?

For Further Reading:

Dodge, Ernest S. *ISLANDS AND EMPIRES*. Minneapolis: University of Minnesota Press, 1976.

Hezel, Francis and Berg, M.L. (eds.). *WINDS OF CHANGE*. Trust Territory of the Pacific Islands, 1979.

Oliver, Douglas L. *THE PACIFIC ISLANDS*. Garden City, New York: Natural History Library Edition, Anchor Books, Doubleday & Company, Inc., 1961 (original 1951).

Chapter 10: World War Two and Post-War Changes

1. War Comes to the Pacific

Japan and Thailand were the only Asian countries that were not taken over and made colonies of European countries during the 19th century. Japan actually began capturing colonies of its own. For many years, Japan had isolated itself from the world. The Japanese did not like the interference they had experienced from Europen missionaries. After the United States forced Japan to open up in 1852, the Japnese developed very quickly. They became an industrial power just like European countries. In 1905 they had advanced enough to beat Russia in a war for control of Northern China. Japan's problem was that the home islands lacked the natural resources necessary for industry. It needed to take over other lands to get raw materials for its factories. Also, it was overpopulated and needed more space for its people. In the 1920s, Japan attacked the remaining free part of China. Many countries did not like this, but Japan did it anyway.

After World War I, the League of Nations had been formed to help prevent war. Since Japan had taken over Germany's islands, the League made it official by mandating them to Japan. The League also did this for some of the islands controlled by Australia and New Zealand. The only condition was that Japan not use the islands for military bases. When the League accused Japan of deliberately attacking China for no reason, Japan became angry and quit the League. The Japanese then began to fortify the Micronesian islands which they controlled.

World War II started in Europe, and Germany quickly conquered France. France controlled Indochina, now called Laos, Vietnam, and Kampuchea. Since Germany controlled France, Japan asked its friend Germany to make the French let Japan put troops into Indochina. The United States became angry and stopped selling oil to Japan.

This was a severe problem for Japan, which had no oil of its own. In six months Japan would be out of oil completely. Japan dreamed of being a world power and the leader of Asia. The Japanese were proud and believed Asia should belong to them because they were Asians. They had two choices. They could back down to the United States' demand and pull their troops out of Indochina. But this would be very shameful in their culture. Or, they

could attack south and take over Indonesia from the free Dutch. Indonesia had plenty of oil.

They decided to take Indonesia. To do this, they needed to protect their supply lines between Japan and Indonesia. The only country that could stop them was the United States. The U.S. forces based in the Philippines and Hawaii would be in a position to cut supply lines between Indonesia and Japan. Japan had to neutralize the U.S. military before taking Indonesia. This was the reason for the attack on Pearl Harbor, Hawaii, on December 7, 1941.

U.S. Marines, under fire from Japanese, hug the invasion beach on Guam, 1944. (National Archives photo courtesy MARC)

2. The Course of the War

During the first four months of the war in the Pacific, the Japanese were very successful. They took Malaya, Singapore, and Burma from the British. They occupied Thailand. They captured Indonesia from the Dutch. They took the Philippines, Guam, and Wake Island from the United States. They also destroyed many ships and planes at Pearl Harbor. But the big aircraft carriers had not been at Pearl. Aircraft carriers proved to be the most important weapons in the Pacific war.

Japan's drive toward Australia was stopped at the battle of the Coral Sea in May, 1942. Although the United States lost more ships, Japan was prevented from going any further. Coral Sea was the first sea battle fought entirely by carrier planes aginst ships. The ships never saw one another.

The turning point of the war was the battle of Midway in June, 1942. In that battle, four Japnese carriers fought against three American carriers. The planes from the American carriers found the

Japanese carriers first. All four Japanese carriers were sunk. One American carrier went down. For the rest of the war, Japan was on the defensive. It could never match the U.S. industrial might. The United States was not only able to replace its losses, but actually became stronger. The Japanese could not replace their losses, and became weaker and weaker.

Japan had fortified many islands. The United States developed the strategy of island hopping. Instead of attacking every Japanese-held island, only important ones would be taken. The rest would be cut off from supplies and the soldiers left to starve. Each island the United States did take gave it airfields closer to Japan. Eventually Japan was being bombed daily. In desperation, the Japanese used Kamikaze attacks. Pilots would commit suicide by flying their planes into American ships. The United States lost many smaller ships to Kamikazes, but few carriers were damaged.

Meanwhile, U.S. scientists had developed the atomic bomb. The United States was preparing to invade Japan, but didn't want to because of all the people who would be killed on both sides. Japan said it would surrender on the condition that it be allowed to keep its emperor, Hirohito. The United States refused, saying the Japanese must surrender unconditionally. Japan refused. The United States dropped an atomic bomb, first on Hiroshima, then on Nagasaki. The Japanese surrendered unconditionally. Then the United States let them keep their emperor anyway.

The dropping of the atomic bombs is still very controversial. Some feel it actually saved lives, since fewer died than would have died in an invasion. Others feel using nuclear weapons for any reason is immoral. There might have been other ways to convince Japan to surrender. The debate continues.

Today nuclear issues have become very important in the Pacific. The United States, Britain and France have used Pacific islands to test nuclear bombs. Now Japan, ironically, wants to use deep Pacific waters to dump waste from its atomic power plants. Pacific island nations are strongly opposed to this.

Empty landing craft at invasion beach on Guam. Though of shallow draft, these craft could get stuck on the fringing reef short of the beach at low tide, making for a deadly sprint through heavy Japanese fire before reaching cover on the beach. (National archives photo courtesy MARC)

3. Effects of the War

After World War II Japan was out of the Pacific. The United States took over Japan's Micronesian islands.

Islanders were strongly affected by the war. They were impressed by the power and material wealth of the United States. More and more, islanders began thinking about modernization, development, and moving into the 20th century.

At the end of the war, only Tonga was governing itself, and even then Britain controlled its foreign affairs. All other islands in Melanesia, Micronesia, and Polynesia were governed by either the United States, Britain, France, Australia, New Zealand, or in the case of Easter Island, Chile. Slowly, the islands have moved toward various forms of independence. Independence is difficult for Pacific islands because of many things. Their small size and lack of resources make economic development difficult. They usually rely on money from their colonial rulers. They usually lacked good European-style educationl opportunities which meant lack of well-trained leaders. Since most were taken care of for so long by the colonial powers, it took many years to build the confidence to believe independence was possible.

In 1962 Western Samoa became independent. Slowly, other islands begn to see independence as a realistic goal. Since 1962, most Pacific islands have attained some form of self-government. In Part II we will look at all the islands and see how they are doing today.

CHAPTER REVIEW

Questions

Vocabulary: League of Nations, mandate, Indochina, carriers, Coral Sea, Midway, island hopping, kamikaze, atomic bomb, independence

Questions

1. Why did Japan want to conquer other places like China?

2. Why did Japan attack Pearl Harbor?

3. What happened at Coral Sea and Midway?

4. Why is independence so hard for Pacific islands?

For Further Reading:

Toland, John. *THE RISING SUN*. New York: Random House, 1970.

PART TWO: THE ISLANDS

In this part we will look at all the islands of Melanesia, Micronesia, and Polynesia. To do this, we will use the following pattern of study for each island group:

1. General geography: location, size, type of island(s), number of islands, land forms, unique physical characteristics, climate, vegetation;

2. People & Culture: history, ethnic groups, population, culture and lifestyle, languages, attitude toward change, effect of 20th century on culture, interesting customs;

3. Economy & Resources: level of subsistence, level of development, balance of trade, major resources, potential for economic development and economic self-sufficiency;

4. Political status: present and possible future status, type of government, foreign relations;

5. Major problems;

Many of the problems we will discuss will repeat themselves over and over again. Most islands have the same or similar problems. Economic problems are widespread. So are problems related to cultural changes brought about by contact and development discussed in previous chapters. The most important of these include "brain drain," urban drift, development of relatively wealthy classes, and the breakdown of traditional cultural controls. Brain drain is the loss of skilled, educated, and ambitious islanders who leave their islands to get better jobs in developed countries. Urban drift is the movement of outer islanders to the more developed port towns and administrative centers of their island groups. They seek jobs, and cause overpopulation and overcrowding in the towns while draining the outer islands of people. Ironically, most administrative centers and port towns are unsightly, unhealthy, ramshackle, tin and scrapwood shanty slums. By comparison, the thatch villages of yesteryear seem cleaner and more comfortable. The standard of living may actually be worse in the modern but slummy port towns than on the undeveloped outer islands. Also those who do have good jobs become wealthy and can afford many more of the amenities of civilization than other islanders, thus creating feelings of poverty and class differences.

Finally, development tends to lead to the breakdown of traditional cultural controls before new ones develop. As explained before, the money economy tends to break down the extended family which is the basis for most island cultures. It is very frustrating for islands to try to preserve traditional customs

Drying copra on Guam in the 1930s. Today copra is still the main cash crop of the Pacific, but cannot support developed economies or modern lifestyles. It is no longer produced on Guam. (Photo courtesy MARC)

that they value, yet still develop their economy and modernize their standard of living.

To understand the islands' situation fully, it is necessary to understand some concepts about economics. Balance of trade is very important. This is the balance between imports and exports. Imports are goods bought from off island and exports are goods that the island sells to the outside. The idea is to sell more than you buy, or export more than you import. Most islands don't do this. Most islands import much more than they export. The difference has to be made up in cash. Where will the cash come from? The islands have to ask for help, usually from Britain, France, the United States, Australia, New Zealand, and international organizations like the United Nations. This keeps them dependent on the developed countries. This is not unique to the Pacific. Many of the world's countries have unfavorable trade balances. They, too, depend on other countries.

There are two ways to make a better balance. Either import (buy) less or export (sell) more. Most islands import a lot of food and a lot of fuel for power. Food imports can be reduced by more subsistence and local market farming and fishing, like in the old days. The more you grow or catch yourself, the less you have to buy. (Besides, the traditional food diet is much healthier than the now popular diet of store-bought food.) Fuel imports can be reduced by developing new sources of power. Wind, solar, and ocean thermal energy conversion (OTEC) are very promising power sources for Pacific islands. Islands with many fast rivers can develop hydroelectric power, and islands with volcanoes can develop ther-

ISLANDS OF THE PACIFIC

Island Group	Political Status	Area Square Miles	(Sq. Km)	Population
MICRONESIA:				
Guam	Unincorporated Territory of the U.S.	212	(549)	120,000
Northern Marianas	Commonwealth of the U.S.	181	(471)	20,000
Belau	Free Association with the U.S.	177	(460)	18,000
Marshalls	Free Association with the U.S.	66	(171)	35,000
Federated States of Micronesia	Free Association with the U.S.	300	(780)	95,000
Nauru	Independent	9	(22)	8,000
Kiribati	Independent	310	(806)	63,000
MELANESIA:				
Papua New Guinea	Independent	178,000	(462,840)	3,200,000
Solomons	Independent	11,500	(29,785)	250,000
Vanuatu	Independent	4,600	(11,800)	130,000
New Caledonia	Overseas Territory of France	7,370	(19,103)	150,000
Fiji	Independent	7,000	(18,272)	700,000
POLYNESIA:				
American Samoa	Unincorporated Territory of the U.S.	76	(197)	37,000
Western Samoa	Independent	1,133	(2,934)	165,000
Tuvalu	Independent	10	(26)	9,000
Tokelau	Dependency of New Zealand	4	(10)	1,700
Niue	Free Association with New Zealand	100	(260)	3,000
Cook Islands	Free Association with New Zealand	92	(240)	16,000
Tonga	Independent	258	(671)	104,000
Pitcairn	Dependency of Britain	2	(4.5)	45
Norfolk	Territory of Australia	13	(35)	2,200
Wallis & Futuna	Overseas Territory of France	48	(124)	12,000
French Polynesia	Overseas Territory of France	1,500	(4,000)	167,000
Easter	Dependency of Chile	65	(170)	2,400
Hawaii	State of the U.S.	6,500	(16,638)	1,000,000

Note: There is no universal census for the Pacific Islands. Population figures vary from source to source. Approximate numbers have been used here.

mal power. Anything that cuts dependency on imported fuel would help.

Since the Pacific has few resources, increasing exports is not that easy. Copra is the main cash crop of the islands, but does not bring in nearly enough money. Most islands are looking at either tourism and/or fishing for economic development.

For tourism, islands must have hotels, good air service, and be close to large tourist markets. Tourism is risky because if the economy is bad, people stop traveling. Sometimes tourism also helps breed gambling and prostitution. But it does bring in money to the islands to help offest a bad balance of trade.

Fishing is looking better for the islands' future. The problem with fishing is the cost of buying and operating expensive fishing ships and building expensive canneries. Most island countries don't have the capital to get started. But now new international laws are giving island nations new ways to make money from fishing.

In the old days, countries claimed the water up to three miles (4.8 km) off their coast. Cannon range was about three miles, and any foreign ship coming closer than that could be sunk. Three miles became the accepted limit for territorial waters. As time went by, cannon got much longer range. Some World War I cannon could shoot up to 75 miles (120 km). Many countries began claiming 12 miles (19.2 km) as their boundary. By the 1960s, most countries accepted the idea of a 12-mile limit.

To have a successful tourist industry, an island must be close to tourist markets, have good air service, and have good hotels. Pictured here is Tumon Bay, Guam's "Hotel Row." (Photo courtesy Guam Visitors Bureau)

Then the small South American country of Ecuador began making what seemed like outrageous claims. Ecuador was poor with few resources. But off Ecuador's coast were rich fishing grounds. Many American ships came to fish there outside the 12-mile limit. Ecuador agreed that 12 miles was the limit of its political boundary. But it began claiming an economic zone as far as 200 miles (320 km) offshore. In this zone, Ecuador claimed, foreign ships could come and go freely as long as they didn't fish. Ecuador began seizing U.S. tuna boats and charging them large fines. Soon Peru and other countries began doing the same.

Today the 200-mile economic zone is becoming recognized in international law. For Pacific islands, this means they control a lot of ocean. Island nations are now able to make money by selling licenses to countries with fishing fleets. These countries, usually Japan, South Korea, and Taiwan, may then fish inside the 200-mile zone claimed by the islands. Many island nations in the Pacific are already making money this way, and the potential for more money is great.

The Soviet Union signed a one year fishing pact with Kiribati, and in early 1987 signed a fishing treaty with Vanuatu. The agreement allows for port visits by Russian ships. There is speculation that Fiji and Papua New Guinea may also sign similar agreements with the Soviets. However, the Pacific nations do seem hesitant to deal with the Soviets, especially when it comes to allowing any type of shore facilities, and a renewal of the Kiribati pact fell through. Ironically the Soviet interest in the Pacific may have prompted a change in U.S. policy. The United States had refused to sign the 1982 Law of the Sea treaty, and maintained that tuna was a migratory fish and thus exempt from the 200-mile zone concept. This led to trouble with the Solomon Islands and even with the U.S. supported Federated States of Micronesia over charges of illegal fishing by U.S. tuna boats. However, in late 1986 the United States signed a pact with the South Pacific Forum Fisheries Agency, agreeing to pay U.S.$12 million for 35 U.S. tuna boats to fish within the 200-mile zones of the 16 Forum member states, each of which will receive a share of the money. The island governments' appreciation of this was dampened somewhat when, in February of 1987, the United States refused to sign a treaty agreeing that the Pacific should remain nuclear free.

As for current island lifestyles, most fit at either

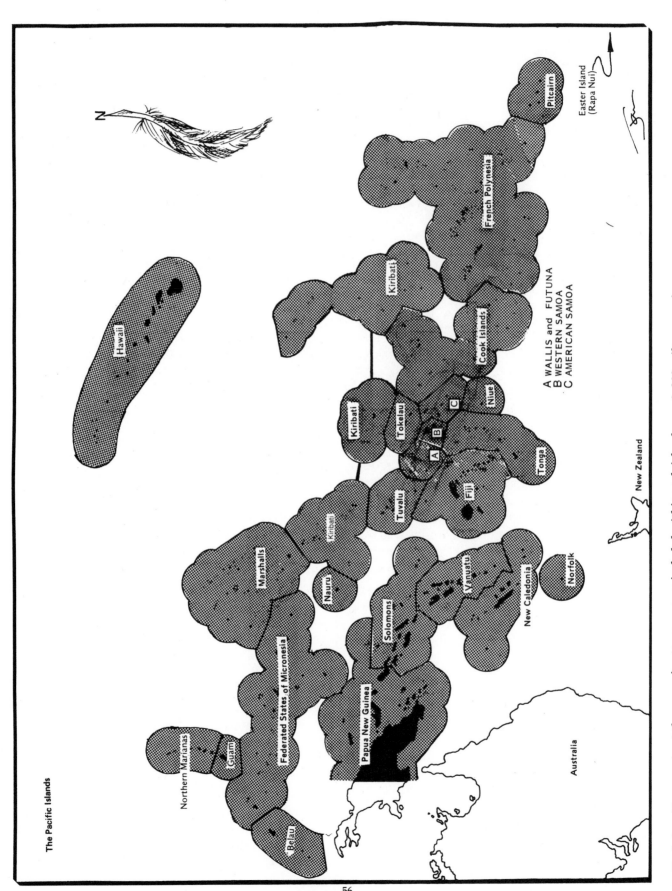

The Pacific Islands

Hawaii

Northern Marianas

Guam

Federated States of Micronesia

Belau

Marshalls

Nauru

Kiribati

Papua New Guinea

Solomons

Vanuatu

New Caledonia

Norfolk

Tuvalu

Fiji

Tonga

Kiribati

Tokelau

Niue

A

B

C

Kiribati

Cook Islands

French Polynesia

Pitcairn

Easter Island
(Rapa Nui)

A WALLIS and FUTUNA
B WESTERN SAMOA
C AMERICAN SAMOA

Australia

New Zealand

Shaded portions represent the approximate ocean area included within each island group's 200-mile economic zone.

end of two extremes. One is the more or less modernized life of the urbanized port towns and island capitals. Here people live more from cash earnings from available jobs, buying food from stores and in many cases enjoying the benefits of electricity and plumbing. These towns vary in development from completely modern cities like Noumea, Port Moresby, and Suva to much less hectic settlements like Nuku'alofa and Honiara. Outside of these towns, except on a few developed islands like Hawaii and Guam, most people live a village subsistence lifestyle. This is especially true for the outer island atolls. In this type of lifestyle there is generally no permanent electricity or plumbing, and most food is from local fishing and farming. Cash opportunities, except for a few government supported jobs like teaching in local schools, are usually limited to the sale of copra and handicrafts.

One final note of introduction — the 1980s have been devasting to the Pacific islands in terms of storm damage. Major typhoons have struck Tonga and Hawaii in 1982, Fiji in 1984, French Polynesia in 1983, the Solomons and the Northern Marianas in 1986, and American Samoa, the Cook Islands, Vanuatu, and Truk of the Federated States of Micronesia in 1987. All caused much damage to homes and crops, many caused loss of life as well. Such storms make it even harder for economic development in the islands.

REVIEW

Vocabulary: ethnic groups, balance of trade, political status, import, export, OTEC, tourism, territorial waters, economic zone, brain drain, urban drift

Questions:

1. Why is a favorable balance of trade so important?

2. What are some of the problems with tourism?

3. Why are the new 200-mile economic zones so important for islands?

UNIT FOUR: MICRONESIA

Micronesia means small islands. The islands of Micronesia are true to their name. The largest is the island of Guam, only a little more than 200 square miles (520 km²) in area. Located mostly in the Northwest Pacific, Micronesia is scattered throughout the ocean area west of the International Date Line, east of the Philippines, south of Japan, and north of New Guinea and the Solomons. There are four groups of islands in Micronesia: the Marianas, the Carolines, the Marshalls, and the Gilberts. The single island of Nauru is also part of Micronesia.

Micronesians are faced with many problems. There are about 20 languages spoken throughout the islands. Land area is small, resources are limited, and the islands are spread out over vast distances. For the most part, the people have become dependent on outside money, especially from the United States. Developing local economies that can support the lifestyle the people have become used to seems an almost impossible job. The future remains cloudy.

MICRONESIAN LANGUAGES

English	Where are you going?	I don't know.
Nauruan	Wo nim et?	Eki.
Gilbertese	Ko na era?	I aki ataia.
Marshallese	Kwaj etal nan ia?	Ijaji.
Kosraean	Kom a som nu ia?	Nga nukin.
Mokilese	Ia koanila?	Ngah jejoa.
Pingelapese	Ia kehn ala?	Ngei sehse.
Pohnpeian	Ke pahn kola ia?	Ih sehse.
Lagoon Trukese	Kepwe ne fena ia?	Use sinei.
Hall dialect	Kopwe le fela ia?	Ise silei.
Mortlockese	Opwe le fela ia?	Ise kilei.
Western Trukese	Opwe le fela ia?	Ihe kulei.
Satawalese	Opwe ne na ia?	Ise kunei.
Carolinian	Upwe le la ia?	Ise kulei.
Woleaian	Opwe lag ia?	Ite kula.
Ulithian	Opwe lag ia?	Itugla.
Sonsorolese	Hobera ia?	Ite hura.
Yapese	Ngam man ngaŋ?	Dak nang.
Belauan	Kemor ker?	Ngdiak kudengei
Chamorro	Para manu hao?	Ti hu tungo.
Nukuoro	Ga hana na goe gi hee?	Au de iloo e au.

Note: spelling variations may occur.

Chapter 11: Guam

1. Geography

Guam, the southernmost of the Mariana Islands, is located about 1300 miles (2080 km) east of the Philippines and 1500 miles (2400 km) south of Japan. Guam is a single volcanic island about 32 miles (51.2 km) long and four to eight miles (6.4 to 12.8 km) wide. At slightly more than 200 square miles (520 km²), Guam is the largest island in Micronesia.

The southern half of the island is very hilly, with mountains up to 1300 feet (390 m). There are numerous rivers and waterfalls. The northern half resembles a raised coral island. It is a relatively flat limestone plateau. There are no rivers, as the rain sinks immediately into the limestone. The climate is warm and humid, with about 100 inches (250 cm) of rain per year. Guam lies on a natural typhoon track. The island is hit head on by major typhoons several times per century. Many other storms pass close enough to do damage. Most of the island is surrounded by fringing reef with only a couple of lagoon areas. There is a good natural harbor at Apra.

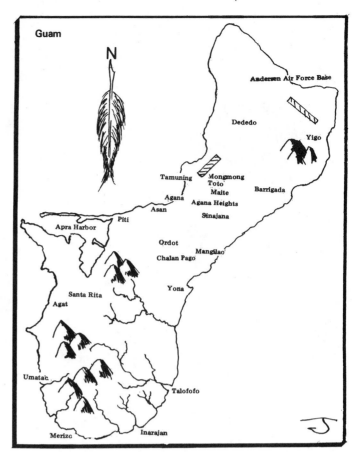

2. People and Culture

Guam was the first Pacific island visited by Europeans (Magellan 1521), and thus was the first Pacific island to have contact with Western civilization. In the 1600s the Spanish established a colony on Guam and used the island as a stopover for Manila Galleons. A Jesuit priest, San Vitores, established a Catholic mission in 1668 and began converting the Chamorros. Soon there was conflict. New diseases spread through the population, and the Chamorros blamed the practice of baptism. The high-caste Chamorros were particularly upset with baptism because the Spanish were baptizing low-caste Chamorros as well. San Vitores baptized a child against the father's orders and was killed. The Spanish began a program of wars against the Chamorros. They forced Chamorros from the Northern Mariana Islands to move to Guam.

After several years of war and disease, the Chamorro population was reduced to about 5000. There may have been as many as 40,000 before the Spanish came. These 5000 survivors began to inter-marry with the Mexican soldiers who were stationed on Guam, and with the Filipinos the Spanish had brought in. By the 20th century, there were no pure-blood Chamorros.

The United States acquired Guam from Spain in 1898 after the Spanish-American War. Spain sold the Northern Mariana Islands to to Germany. Japan captured Guam in 1941, but the United States took it back in 1944. In 1950, Guam became a U.S. Territory, its people becoming U.S. citizens.

Guam has many ethnic groups. The total population in 1987 was estimated to be about 120,000. According to the 1980 census, some 45% consider themselves Chamorros, a mixture of original Chamorro, Mexican (Spanish mixed with Native American), and Filipino. About 21% are Filipinos, 25% stateside Americans, 5% Asian (Japanese, Chinese, Korean, Vietnamese), 3% other Pacific islanders, and 1% other groups. Some Chamorros are alarmed that they are now less than half of the island's population. However the figure for stateside Americans includes the 20,000 military and their dependents who are stationed on Guam. These people only stay for two years and usually don't bother to vote in local elections, and many of the Filipinos, Asians, and other Micronesians are not U.S. citizens. Consequently the Chamorros still represent about 75%-80% of the voting population. Generally the races get along well, although some problems do

Downtown Agana, capital of Guam. Across the bay lies Tamuning, also very developed. (Photo courtesy Guam Visitors Bureau)

exist. There are many mixed marriages, and these help bring the various groups together. The people tend to have a tolerant attitude toward others.

English is the official language. Chamorro, a mixture of Spanish and original Chamorro, is widely used. Tagalog and Japanese are also prevalent.

The local culture of Guam is dominated by Spanish Catholic Church customs. Village fiestas, big weddings, wakes, and other parties are the focal point of social life. The last 25 years have brought many changes, however. Guam is one of the most modern and developed islands in the Pacific. It has rapidly become a "little America." Cars are numerous, and the downtown areas of Agana and Tamuning have modern department stores, fast food restaurants, several theaters, luxury hotels, and many other aspects of American cities. Almost everybody has a salaried job. No one survives on a subsistence level anymore. And the money economy has taken its toll. The inevitabale breakdown of the extended family has led to a loss of cultural controls. The result has been an alarming crime rate comparable to many large U.S. cities. Burglary, robbery, rape, and even murder, unheard of in the 1950s and before, are now almost commonplace. Older Guamanians are saddened. Younger ones prefer the excitement of modern Guam to the old days they have only heard about. They also like the increase in freedom from having to follow their family's wishes.

In general, Guamanians are proud to be modern and advanced compared to many other islands. They have worked hard to become developed and part of the 20th century. They do worry and talk a lot about the loss of culture and tradition. As of yet they have been unable to come up with a consensus as to what to preserve and how to preserve it.

3. Economy and Resources

Although the lifestyle has become modern and developed with American-style homes and businesses, Guam's economy depends greatly on outside money, mostly from the United States. Imports outnumber exports by a wide margin of about eight to one. The island depends heavily on imported food, fuel, and manufactured goods. Some of this is offset by tourism, the island's largest private industry. Over 400,000 tourists visit Guam each year, mostly from Japan. They bring in badly needed cash. Guam's economy also gets help from the U.S. military presence. The military personnel and their dependents stationed on Guam spend much money locally. In addition, the military also hires many civilians and provides other jobs through local construction contracts. By far the biggest employer is the local government, employing about 10,000 out of a total work force of 40,000+. The Guam government supports itself by a gross receipts tax on businesses and the U.S. income tax which is given to the Guam government. In addition, the federal government gives the island many grants and loans for different

Village of Inarajan on Guam's southeast coast. The pace here is much more relaxed than Agana/Tamuning. (Photo courtesy Guam Visitors Bureau)

projects.

Guam has few exports. Local agriculture and fishing are underdeveloped, and only supply a portion of the local market. Agricultural development is difficult due to many diseases, pests, frequent storms, and the high cost of living which forces farmers to set prices too high.

Since Guam depends so much on money from the U.S. government, any threatened spending cuts are viewed with alarm. Any cutoff of federal money has a heavily negative effect on Guam's economy. Guam is dependent on the United States. The local economy could never support the present lifestyle.

In the mid-1980s, Guam began both a tourism and construction boom. Several new hotels and hotel additions have been built, and the total number of rooms is about 4000. Many new stores and apartments have also been built, and road improvements are continuing. As a result, unemployment has dipped to new lows, and though still dependent on the United States, the economy is building some diversity.

4. Political Status

Guam is an unincorporated Territory of the United States. The people are U.S. citizens, free to go to the States to live and work. Once in the States, a Guamanian is an equal citizen, and may vote in all elections. On Guam, the people may only vote in local elections. They cannot vote for U.S. President. Guam also sends a non-voting representative to the U.S. House of Representatives. He can serve and vote on committees, but can't vote on the House floor. Guam does not have a constitution. Its government was established by the Organic Act of 1950, an act of the U.S. Congress. The governor and local legislature are elected by popular vote.

Lately Guam has been going through a lengthy process of trying to decide its future status. Everything from statehood in the United States to full independence was considered. There is also a controversy over who should be allowed to vote for future status, with a movement to limit voting to "indigenous" Guamanians, meaning the Chamorros. Most Guamanians value their U.S. citizenship and are very patriotic towards America. Guam will probably retain close ties with the United States. The dependency of the economy on the U.S. government makes most people leery of independence. In a 1982 election, the voters of Guam chose Commonwealth of the United States as the status they would like Guam to obtain. A proposed Commonwealth Act has been drafted, and a plebiscite was held in 1987. Controversial aspects of the Draft Act include sections about rights of the indigenous islanders as different from other citizens; applicability of the U.S. Constitution, laws, and court decisions; and the exact nature of the division of power between the U.S. and Guam governments.

5. Major Problems

Besides future status, Guam's major problems are its dependent economy and the current cultural breakdown that has led to crime and loss of purpose.

Also, the Guam Government has run up a huge deficit of about $100 million, yet no acceptable way has been found to either increase revenue or reduce spending. Problems with the government owned telephone, power, and water services threaten to stifle the current economic boom. And to complicate matters even more, several government officials and

Fiesta — the focal point of Guam's culture. (Photo courtesy Guam Visitors Bureau)

CHAPTER REVIEW

Vocabulary: Spanish-Chamorro War, Chamorro, fiesta, unincorporated territory

Questions:

1. What happened in the Spanish-Chamorro Wars?

2. What is the ethnic background of a modern Chamorro?

3. What is Guam's lifestyle like?

4. Explain Guam's current status.

5. Discuss Guam's major problems.

For Further Reading:

Carter, John (ed.). *PACIFIC ISLANDS YEAR BOOK*, 15th edition. Sydney: Pacific Publications, 1984.

Sanchez, Dr. Pedro and Cerano, Paul. *A COMPLETE HISTORY OF GUAM*. Tokyo, Japan: Charles E. Tuttle Co. Inc., 1964. (note: an updated edition is due for release soon).

Stanley, David, and Dalton, Bill. *SOUTH PACIFIC HANDBOOK*. Chico, California: Moon Publications, 1982.

local businessmen have either pled guilty or are awaiting trial on corruption charges. Apparently certain officials, perhaps for a long time, had been demanding payments from contractors to assure the awarding of government contracts. One of those tried in 1987 was the former Governor, Ricardo Bordallo. Another still unsettled problem revolves around claims for payment of land taken by the U.S. military after World War II. The United States has offered $40 million as a final settlement to be shared by all claimants, but many landowners are not satisfied. The federal government possesses almost one third of the total land area of Guam.

Guam needs to cut down on imports. One way is to grow more food locally. Another is to get away from burning imported fossil fuel for power. There were plans for an OTEC plant as well as a system of windmills, solar generators, and a garbage-to-power plant. However declining oil prices have made the schemes too expensive, and the importation of fuel oil continues.

For the problems related to the rapid development and changing culture of Guam, there seem to be no clear answers. The extended families grow weaker, crime increases, and many people call for "preserving the culture."

Peaceful island lifestyles pay a price for becoming modern.

Chapter 12: Trust Territory of the Pacific Islands

1. The Birth of the Trust Territory

The three island groups of the Marianas, the Marshalls, and the Carolines have had the most complicated history of involvment with colonial powers of any Pacific islands. Controlled by Spain until 1898, they then came under German control (except Guam, which became a U.S. possession). After World War I, they became a League of Nations Mandated Territory of Japan (see Chapter 10).

After World War II the United States was in control of the islands, having captured them from Japan. Shortly after the war the United Nations was formed. It was to replace the League of Nations, which had failed to prevent World War II and had ceased to exist. One of the new UN's functions was to decide what to do with all the old League of Nations Mandated Territories. Many of those territories had been captured in the war.

The United Nations has two main parts: a General Assembly and a Security Council. The General Assembly consists of all member nations, each member having one vote. The Security Council has 15 members. Five are permanent, the remaining 10 are elected from the General Assembly for two year terms. The Security Council makes all important decisions relating to wars, revolutions, border clashes, and other tense international situations. It is the Security Council that must decide what action to take, such as sending UN troops or observers. Each of the five permanent members — the United States, France, Britain, the Soviet Union, and China — has veto power. In other words, for the United Nations to send troops anywhere or take any real action in an international crisis, all five permanent members must agree or at least abstain. If only one of the five votes "NO," nothing can be done.

The General Assembly set up a Trusteeship System to take care of the old territories that had been League of Nations Mandates. Under the system,

Common scenes in the more ''modern'' district centers — corrugated tin architecture and lots of trash. This was taken in Colonia, Yap, a few years ago, but has since been cleaned up. (Photo by Carlos Viti)

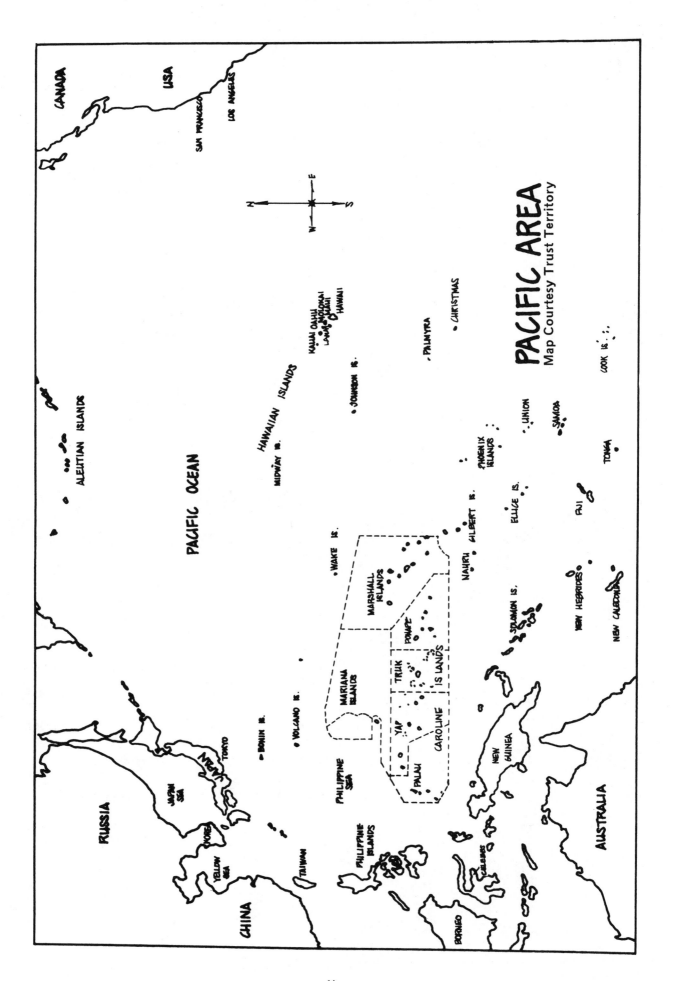

PACIFIC AREA
Map Courtesy Trust Territory

countries such as the United States, New Zealand, Australia, and others would continue to operate and administer the territories as United Nations Trust Territories. These countries would report regularly to the Trusteeship Council of the United Nations. They were also expected to prepare the territories for self-rule. That is the meaning of "trust" in Trust Territory. The administering country is holding the territory in trust for the people of the territory. That country is supposed to get the people ready for the day when they will be politically and economically prepared to rule themselves. Thus trust means to prepare for self-rule.

The United States did not want the Micronesian islands to become a regular Trust Territory. The islands had cost many American lives in World War II, and the United States felt they were strategically important. That means the United States felt the islands were important for the military defense and security of the United States. Instead of becoming a regular Trust Territory, the islands became a Strategic Trust Territory. They were established as such by the Security Council, not the Trusteeship Council or General Assembly. This is very important, for the United States has a veto on the Security Council. This means the United Nations can do nothing about the islands without the approval of the United States. Effectively, this means the United States can do anything it wants in the islands and keep them as a Strategic Trust Territory as long as the United States feels necessary. If the United Nations tries to get the United States to do anything it doesn't want with the islands, it has to do so through the Security Council where the United States can veto the move.

Neat, clean, and well kept thatch village on the outer island of Kapingamorangi, Pohnpei. (Photo by Carlos Viti)

2. Early Years of the Trust Territory

The United States did do anything it wanted. It built a big base on Kwajalein in the Marshalls and a secret Central Intelligence Agency base on Saipan in the Marianas. It tested atomic bombs on Marshallese atolls, moving the islanders from their homes and poisoning the islands of Bikini and Eniwetok with radioactive waste. It kept everybody out of Micronesia, just as the Japanese had done.

The Strategic Trust Territory was a contradiction. Because it was a Trust Territory, the United States was supposed to get it ready for self-rule. But because it was a Strategic Trust Territory, the United States

Youth on an outer island — Kapingamorangi, Pohnpei. (Photo by Carlos Viti)

really didn't have to. The prevailing attitude of Americans and other developed countries in those days was one of not much concern for the future of primitive territories. It was just assumed that the people would always need a big brother to look after them. The attitude of the islanders was mixed between awe at the power and wealth of the United States, gratitude at liberation from the harsh

Japanese, and inferiority at their own ability to care for themselves in the modern world they barely understood. They felt the United States knew best, and islanders should do what they were told.

Until 1961, the United States did little for the islands. Nothing was done to develop the economy, education was very limited, and only minimal services maintained. The islanders were basically left to their subsistence lifestyles. That may or may not be a bad way to live, but what was bad was the total lack of opportunity to develop and change if they wanted to. In 1961, a United Nations Visiting Mission was finally allowed to make an inspection of the islands. Their report strongly criticized the United States for failing to live up to the trust part of Trust Territory — it had done almost nothing to prepare the islands for self-rule. Of course the United States could have ignored the report. But attitudes were changing by then, and the bad publicity caused much pressure from world public opinion. The United States decided it was time to change its policy toward the Trust Territory.

3. Money and Change Come to the Trust Territory

Kennedy replaced Eisenhower as President of the United States in 1961, and the Trust Territory budget went from $7.5 million a year to $15 million a year. Money began pouring into Micronesia. Education was increased, airports built, hospitals constructed, roads improved. Most importantly, local government bureaucracies were greatly expanded. People began moving to the main centers to get government jobs. Subsistence fell off as a money economy replaced it. Customs, traditional skills, and culture began to erode. The cost of living and lifestyle became more expensive. Money became, for many in the Trust Territory, the primary source for survival, rather than just supplementary to subsistence.

Unfortunately, no local economy was developed at the same time that would support the more modern lifestyle of cement houses, cars, motor boats, and store-bought food. It was all supported from the top — by the U.S. money which supported the local governments. The United States supported local governments, local governments supported the economy. Without the U.S. grants, the whole system would collapse. And instead of trying to develop private business other than retail stores — businesses

Youth in the district center of Kolonia, Pohnpei. (Photo by Carlos Viti)

that produce products for export and bring cash into the economy — Micronesians preferred the security of government jobs. And many of the local political and economic leaders felt their positions of wealth and power depended on maintaining strong ties with the United States.

So ironically, although the new money coming in made the standard of living more modern, it actually made the islands even more dependent on the United States. Although they had better educated leaders and more developed political systems, the islands were actually less able to become independent than before the money began coming in. Some people believe this was done purposely by the United States. If it could keep the islands dependent on the U.S. money, then the United States would always be in control. Others feel it was only the result of typical American misguided helpfulness. Americans often think enough money will solve any problem.

4. The End Nears

In 1970 the islanders began the process of choosing a future status and negotiating with the United States for an end to the Trusteeship. In the meantime, the Trust Territory has fragmented into four different groups. Because different island groups in the Trust Territory are very different in language and culture, they began to go their separate ways. For reasons to be discussed in the next chapters, the Northern Marianas has become a U.S. Commonwealth. The Marshalls and Belau have their own separate governments in free association with the United States. The remaining groups — Yap, Truk, Pohnpei, and Kosrae — stuck together as the Federated States of Micronesia (FSM), also in free association with the United States. Free association is a form of partial independence. The islands control their own internal affairs and set up their own local governments. The United States provides defense and money, in return for the right to control the area militarily. The United States also decides what a military mat-

As if caught in a time warp, a Yapese man walks down the street in Colonia, Yap. His traditional dress of three separate cloths (one red, one blue, one striped) and a strand of hibiscus contrasts with the pickup trucks as does the thatch hut with the tin building. (Photo courtesy **Glimpses Magazine***)*

ter will be.

Again, some feel the United States was happy with the breakup. It made it easier to obtain favorable terms for the United States' continued presence in the islands. A united Micronesia seeking full independence may have been tough, and embarrassing, for the United States to handle. But Micronesian loyalties don't extend very far from their own island or cluster of islands. Any sense of unity would only have developed with a strong effort by government leaders. That never happened.

The negotiation process has taken 16 years. First each island group approved a choice of status by plebiscite. Then each of the four groups negotiated a specific agreement with the United States. That agreement then had to be approved by island legislatures as well as the people in general referenda. Except in Belau, all passed without problems. Then the agreements were sent to the U.S. Congress. For the FSM and the Marshalls, this caused some problems because the US Congress amended the Compacts of Free Association. The amendments eliminated some of the sections to prevent the creation of tax havens for U.S. citizens, force the islands to buy goods from the U.S., and limit the control over the 200 mile zones. Compromises were worked out, and the island governments approved the Compacts as amended. They were then signed by President Reagan, and sent to the Trusteeship Council of the United Nations. There the agreements establishing the Commonwealth of the Northern Marianas and the freely associated states of the Marshalls and the FSM were accepted, and in late 1986 the United States fully implemented those agreements. The separate governments had been operating in a de facto status since the late 1970s. Only Belau remained unresolved, and although it is operating in de facto free association status, by the end of 1986 it was the only remaining entity of the Trust Territory.

However the U.S. has yet to send the agreements to the UN Security Council. Now, the very reason the U.S. wanted to establish the Trust Territory through the Security Council in the first place will cause problems. The Soviet Union is very critical of the agreements, and considers free association to be false independence. They could veto the change in status and try to keep the islands, officially at least, under the control of the Security Council. But the United States might ignore the veto or simply inform the Security Council that the Trust Territory has been terminated. The Trust Territory of the Pacific Islands was the only strategic Trust Territory, the only one set up by the Security Council, and is the only one remaining. All the others have obtained full independence or some form of self-rule. Soon, the Trust Territory of the Pacific Islands should pass into history as well.

CHAPTER REVIEW

Vocabulary: United Nations, General Assembly, Security Council, Trusteeship System, Trusteeship Council, trust territory, trust, strategic trust territory, United Nations visiting mission, free association

Questions:

1. What was the idea and purpose of the trusteeship system?

2. What is the importance of the U.S. veto in the Security Council as far as the Trust Territory of the Pacific Islands is concerned?

3. What policy did the United States follow in the early years of the Trust Territory of the Pacific Islands?

4. What effects did money have on the Trust Territory of the Pacific Islands?

For Further Reading:

Baker, Bryon and Wenkam, Robert. *MICRONESIA — THE BREADFRUIT REVOLUTION*. Honolulu: East-West Center Press, University of Hawaii, 1971.

DeSmith, Stanley A. *MICROSTATES AND MICRONESIA*. New York: New York University Press, 1970.

Hughes, Daniel T. and Lingenfelter, Sherwood G. *POLITICAL DEVELOPMENT IN MICRONESIA*. Ohio State University Press, 1974.

Murray, James N. Jr. *THE UNITED NATIONS TRUSTEESHIP SYSTEM*. University of Illinois Press, 1957.

Nevin, David. *THE AMERICAN TOUCH IN MICRONESIA*. New York: W.W. Norton and Co., 1977.

Chapter 13: The Northern Marianas

1. Geography

The Northern Marianas are a chain of 14 volcanic islands running north-south in the northwest Pacific. The chain, about 375 miles (600 km) long, is located about 1500 miles (2400 km) east of the Philippines and starts about 1000 miles (1600 km) south of Japan. Guam, the southernmost and largest of the Mariana Islands, is politically separate and not included. Only seven of the islands are permanently inhabited. Most of the people live on Saipan, the largest and most developed. Saipan is the capital of the group. Rota has much farming and produces many fruits and vegetables. Relatively flat Tinian has a beef and dairy ranch. It also may be the sight of a future U.S. military base. It was a base during the war, from which planes took off to drop the atomic bomb on Japan. Less than 200 people live on the northernmost populated islands of Alamagan, Anatahan, Agrihan [highest mountain in Micronesia at 3166 feet (949.8 m)], and Pagan. The population of Pagan, about 50, was evacuated in 1981 following the eruption of the island's active volcano. The Paganese are now living on Saipan but hope one day to be able to return to Pagan. The total land area of the islands is about 200 square miles (520 km²). The climate is warm and the rainfall varies. Saipan's temperature varies less year round than any other place in the world.

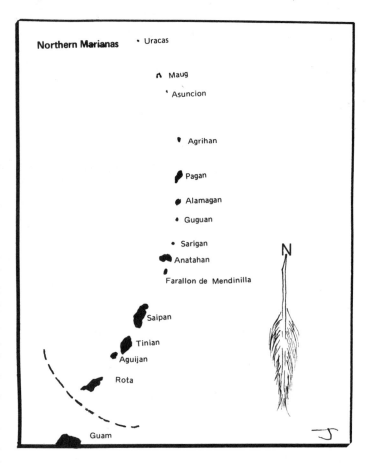

2. People and Culture

The original Chamorro inhabitants of the Northern Marianas were forcibly moved to Guam by the Spanish during the Spanish-Chamorro wars (see Chapter 11). About a hundred years later some Chamorros, by now mixed with Mexican and Filipino blood, were allowed to resettle. Also moving to Saipan were Carolinians from Truk and Yap whose outer island atolls had been destroyed by typhoons. The Germans took over from Spain but

One of Saipan's modern luxury hotels serving a fast-growing tourist industry. (Photo courtesy Pacific Daily News)

did very little. The Japanese, coming next, extensively developed the main islands as sugar plantations. Thousands of Japanese were living in the islands at the start of World War II. Saipan was captured by the Americans after one of the bloodiest battles of the war. The Northern Marianas then became part of the U.N. Trust Territory. The United States, of course, was in control.

Today the population of 20,000, mostly living on Saipan, is divided into two ethnic groups. The Chamorros are the large majority. Carolinians make up a significant minority. There are also many stateside Americans living and working there. Because of a hotel construction and tourist boom, there are also several thousand alien workers from Korea, China, and the Philippines.

Like Guam, the culture is heavily influenced by Spanish Catholic Church customs. Unlike Guam, there is much more Japanese than American influence. Saipan is not quite as developed as Guam, and cultural controls of the extended family are much stronger. Also, the presence of the Carolinians helps add a more traditional Micronesian flavor to the community.

But the Marianas are changing. The people want a more modern lifestyle. They are proud of the development that has taken place. They look to Guam as an example, hoping to achieve the good things Guam has without the cultural breakdown and crime. They want to be more Americanized and modern, and have consistently worked toward that goal. Their lifestyle is still much slower and more relaxed than Guam's, but it is changing.

One custom of the Chamorros, both on Guam and the Northern Marianas, is the chewing of betelnut. Chamorros prefer the dry, hard nut which, when chewed, induces a slight stimulation.

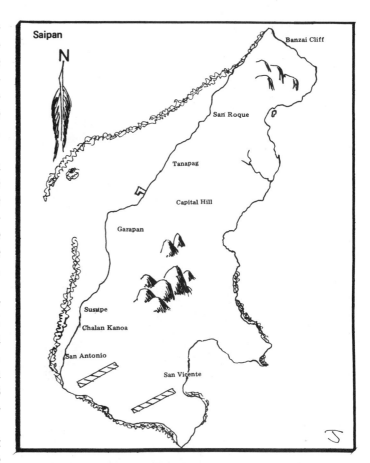

tial for agricultural development, with Rota and Tinian already growing much food.

Like Guam, the Northern Marianas is undergoing a boom. The number of tourists has increased to over 100,000 per year, and many new hotels are being built. There are also several garment assembly factories on Saipan.

The main potential for the future is a military base which the United States may build on Tinian. Such a base would pump needed dollars into the economy. At present, the lifestyle of the islands is completely dependent on U.S. grants.

3. Economy and Resources

The Marianas, like the rest of the Trust Territory, depend largely on U.S. money to support their local government. The local government in turn is the main employer and supports the rest of the economy.

Tourism is the largest private industry. There are several luxury hotels on Saipan, and many Japanese visit the island. They come to enjoy the beaches and warm weather, and also to view the battlegrounds and memorials of World War II. The balance of trade is very poor, with beef, dairy products, and sweaters the only exports. More food should be grown for local consumption to reduce imports. There is poten-

4. Political Status

For several reasons, the people of the Northern Marianas voted to separate from the rest of the Trust Territory. First was their desire to stay close to the United States. The rest of the Trust Territory wanted free association, but the Northern Marianas preferred commonwealth with the United States. Time and again they have shown a desire to stay permanently connected to the United States. They even tried to join Guam once, but Guam refused. The people like the development and progress that have

5. Major Problems

Suicide Cliff, where Japanese jumped to their deaths to avoid capture by Americans in World War II. Others jumped off Banzai Cliff over the ocean below. (Photo courtesy Pacific Daily News)

taken place in the Northern Marianas. They feel that the only way to maintain the current modern lifestyle and guarantee continuation of progress is to stay tied to the United States.

Secondly, as the most developed district of the Trust Territory, the people felt more sophisticated, and did not want to be connected to or controlled by islands such as Truk or Belau. Those islands are at least 10 years behind the Marianas in development.

Finally, it was the Northern Marianas' desire to keep any economic benefits from the potential military base on Tinian. If still politically connected with other islands, they might lose much money in programs for the rest of the islands. But if they are separate, rent from such a base might support their entire economy.

So the people of the Northern Marianas voted to become a U.S. Commonwealth. They are now permanently connected with the United States. The Commonwealth Covenant was fully implemented by the United States in November, 1986, after being partially implemented since 1978. The people are now full U.S. citizens, and the islands are no longer a Trust Territory. The local government consists of an elected governor and a two-house elected legislature.

Developing the economy is a key problem for the islands. The current tourist boom is helping, but there are concerns that too many aliens are being hired rather than locals trained to do the work. Also, the power and water systems have many problems and may not be able to function well enough to provide adequate service as the economy grows. Suggestions have been made to privatize power and water, which are currently owned by the government. Privatization of the telephone system led to vastly improved service. The overall efficiency of the government has also been often criticized, and the U.S. federal government is currently investigating charges of bribery and corruption among Northern Marianas government officials.

Other problems include the feelings of the Carolinian minority that they are not always treated fairly by the Chamorro dominated government. The people of Rota had been upset by a lack of capital development on their island, but several projects have now been completed there. There is also concern by stateside residents that they will not have all the rights of locals though all are now full U.S. citizens. Related to that are disagreements in interpretation of the Commonwealth Covenant regarding the limits of U.S. sovereignty over the islands. For example, the Northern Marianas government wants the right to sign fishing treaties with foreign countries. Finally, a protest movement has developed over U.S. Air Force plans to build a radar site on Saipan. Many feel that it will make Saipan a target in a nuclear war. Others feel it is part of the deal that the Northern Marianas made with the United States to make the islands available for military use.

In December, 1986, a bad typhoon struck Saipan, leaving the island without power or water and destroying many homes. Recovery will take some time, but will be aided by U.S. disaster relief funds.

CHAPTER REVIEW

Vocabulary: Saipan, Carolinians, betelnut, commonwealth

Questions:

1. Why are the Northern Marianas separate from Guam?

2. What is the Northern Marianas' attitude toward the United States and modernization?

3. Why did the Northern Marianas separate from the other islands of the Trust Territory?

For Further Reading:

Alkire, William H. *AN INTRODUCTION TO THE PEOPLES AND CULTURES OF MICRONESIA*. Addison-Wesley Publishing, 1972.

Carter, John (ed.). *PACIFIC ISLANDS YEAR BOOK*, 15th edition. Sydney: Pacific Publications, 1984.

Hezel, Francis; and Berg, M.L. (eds.). *WINDS OF CHANGE*. Trust Territory of the Pacific Islands, 1979.

Stanley, David; and Dalton, Bill. *SOUTH PACIFIC HANDBOOK*. Chico, California: Moon Publications, 1982.

Chapter 14: Belau (Palau)

1. Geography

Belau is a grouping of several hundred volcanic islands and a few coral atolls located about 400 miles (640 km) east of Mindanao of the Philippines. It is the westernmost part of Micronesia. Only about eight of the islands are inhabited — four of the larger volcanic complex and four of the outer island atolls. Hundreds of tiny rock islands lie within the barrier reef of the volcanic complex. Many are no more than limestone "mushrooms" with a few trees on top.

The largest island of Belau is Babelthuap, second largest in Micronesia. The smaller island of Koror is the capital and developed center. It is right next to Babelthuap and connected to it by a long cement box girder bridge. Two other islands are connected to Koror by causeway. The airport is on Babelthuap, and plans are to build a new national capital next to it.

Rainfall is plentiful and the islands are very fertile. The rock islands are very beautiful and a major tourist attraction. Americans and Japanese love to swim, snorkel, and water ski among the rock islands and dive on the rich reefs. Some of the islands have marine lakes in the middle, connected to the sea by tunnels through the limestone. On Babelthuap the villages are all along the mangrove covered shoreline. The people must be careful, for in the mangrove swamps are still some saltwater crocodiles. Even less plentiful are the dugongs, rare sea cows hunted almost to extinction. The main islands are hilly but not very steep. The total land area is about 175 square miles (455 km 2).

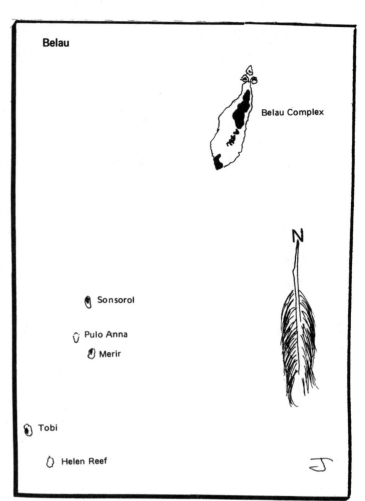

2. People and Culture

Belau had its share of beachcombers and traders. They would often take sides in wars between Koror and one of its main rival villages on Babelthuap. European navies became involved, once destroying many canoes and men's houses on Babelthuap, and once executing a Koror chief for the murder of a European trader. The Spanish did little to support their claim to the islands until very late. The Germans started to develop the area but were not around very long. The Japanese exploited the islands heavily. They mined almost all the phosphate deposits. They brought in forced labor from other Micronesian islands. This development was, of course, for the benefit of the Japanese. In World War II there was a big battle on Peleliu, and many war relics remain.

The Belauan culture is very strong, but the people are also very forward looking. The islands are the most developed and advanced after the Marianas. In contrast to the islander stereotype, Belauans have a reputation for being ambitious and hard working. They may be the most efficient of all Micronesians. Thousands of Belauans have left to get jobs in Yap, Guam, Saipan, Hawaii, and even the mainland United States. They have been successful in establishing sizable communities in those places. No other Micronesian group has done that. Almost 2000 Belauans live on Guam.

The capital island of Koror is modern and developed. The rest of the islands are still in varying levels of village subsistence lifestyle. Those who want salaried jobs go to Koror and eventually leave. There is still much farming and fishing.

There are two ethnic groups in Belau. The vast majority of the 18,000 people are ethnic Belauans, and speak a language completely different from any other Micronesian language. A small minority of a few hundred are Carolinian. They originate from the outer island atolls of Sonsorol, Tobi, and Pulo Anno.

They speak a dialect close to the language of the outer islands of Yap and Truk and the Carolinians of Saipan. It is not even close to Belauan.

Belauans chew green betelnut, wrapping it in a leaf and adding lime. They are proud of their Abai, or traditional men's houses. Story boards, sold to tourists, are replicas of the stories carved for decoration on the beams of the Abai.

3. Economy and Resources

Like many other islands, the government is the economy. U.S. money supports the local government. Plans have been made to reopen the failed tuna cannery and copra processing plant in an effort to increase exports and create jobs. Tourism helps bring in badly needed cash. Belau has a healthy share of visitors attracted by the beauty of the rock islands and the surrounding reefs. Also much marijuana is being grown illegally, with most of it being smuggled to Guam and the U.S. The Belauan variety is reputed to be of extremely high potency and is very much in demand. Some effort has been made to reduce this undesirable cash source.

The hope lies in the future. The establishment of a 200-mile (320 km) fishing zone and the resultant sale of licenses can bring in some money. Plans for a supertanker offloading port at Kayangel Atoll, which would have changed drastically the islands' economy and lifestyle, were abandoned due to environmental and cultural concerns.

Finally, the United States had plans for a military base in Belau. Such a base would have brought in much money, created jobs, and perhaps supported the local economy from rent money. As of now the United States has no immediate plans to build any base in Belau, but wants the option to do so should the need arise.

The Belauan local economy cannot support the

Koror — capital of Belau. Some of the Rock Islands can be seen at the upper right. (Photo courtesy Pacific Daily News)

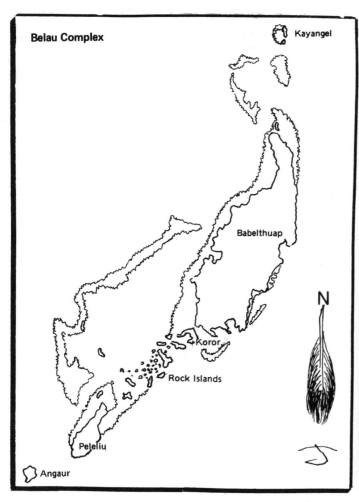

An Abai, traditional men's house. (Photo courtesy MRTC)

present lifestyle without U.S. grants. Imports are too high, jobs too scarce.

4. Political Status

Following the example of the Northern Marianas and the Marshalls, Belau went its own separate way. Originally part of the Federated States of Micronesia, Belau pulled out when the other islands refused to make Belau the capital of the FSM. In addition to being angry about not getting the capital, the Belauans felt that they didn't want their destiny controlled by the other islands of Yap, Truk, Pohnpei, and Kosrae. Finally, similar to the Marianas, they didn't want to share any potential rent money from a U.S. base with the other, more populous districts. Keeping all the economic benefits from such a base could very well support their entire economy.

Belau decided to draw up its own free association compact with the United States. In this semi-independence, Belau would control its own internal affairs, and the United States would provide military protection. The United States would also provide

money, and be allowed to build a base if it so desired.

There have been many problems for the new government. A constitution was rejected by the legislature but passed by the people in a plebiscite. The great disparity in wages — with workers paid low wages while government officials became rich — caused a violent one-day strike. The compact of free association, which for Belau was to last 50 years, has had its problems winning approval. The Belauan constitution forbids any nuclear material in Belau, and the non-nuclear provision can only be overridden by a 75% vote of the Belauan people. For the United States to defend Belau, as agreed to in the compact, it must have the right to at least transit Belauan waters with nuclear powered ships or ships that may carry nuclear weapons. Five separate plebiscites were held over three years, and the votes were in favor by 62%, 66%, 72%, 66%, and 67%, thus failing to reach 75%.

Following the last of these plebiscites, the President of Belau, Lazarus Salii, laid off about 900 government workers. Belau had to continue to operate under Trust Territory funding. That had been exhausted in anticipation of large amounts of U.S.

Youth hanging around outside a pool hall in a village on Babelthuap. (Photo by Carlos Viti)

money guaranteed under the compact. With the failure of the compact, the government was broke and unable to pay many of its workers until the start of the next fiscal year, when it would receive some additional money. The United States refused to provide any money to help Belau through the crisis, saying it was Belau's fault that they had used up their budget too quickly. Some critics of U.S. policy in the islands feel this was done purposely to put such financial pressure on Belau that they would be forced to do something to approve the compact. Whether by plan or not, the resulting layoffs caused a crisis in which Belauans against the compact were put under heavy pressure. The legislature agreed to amend the constitution of Belau to eliminate the 75% requirement, and the people passed the amendment in yet another plebiscite. After the amendment was carried, a final plebiscite on the compact itself was

held, and the people approved it by a 73% majority. That has not quite been the end of things, for anti-compact groups sued in the Belauan courts saying the amendment was no good since it had not been done according the amendment procedure laid out in the constitution. The suits were withdrawn, partially due to compromises between President Salii and anti-compact leaders and partially due to violence and intimidation. By September, 1987, the Belauan government had certified the compact as approved and was awaiting action by the U.S. Congress. Operating in de facto free association status, with an elected legislature and elected president, the islands are officially the only remaining part of the Trust Territory. Future political status and future financial aid from the United States is still uncertain, for there is much criticism within the United States over the developments in Belau.

5. Major Problems

The most important problem for Belau is finding a way out of the future status complication. Upon that hinges the future economic development as well, and such things as building a new capital on Babelthuap. During all this political turmoil, violence has played a continual role. Stateside lawyers working on the compact have had their boats, cars, and even homes burned by arsonists. And in an event that shocked the entire Pacific, the President of Belau before Salii, Haruo Remeliik, was assassinated. More recently, the father of a lawyer working on the suit to overturn the amendment was shot and killed while he waited at his son's office. Whether the situation has finally stabilized, and the United States will officially implement the compact and the United Nations accept the implementation, remains to be seen.

CHAPTER REVIEW

Vocabulary: Koror, rock islands, story boards, abai

Questions:

1. Why are Belauans considered ambitious?

2. Why did Belau decide to separate from the Trust Territory?

3. What is the hope for Belau's economic future?

4. What has been the problem related to the compact of free association with the United States?

For Further Reading:

Alkire, William H. *AN INTRODUCTION TO THE PEOPLES AND CULTURES OF MICRONESIA.* Addison-Wesley Publishing, 1972.

Carter, John (ed.). *PACIFIC ISLANDS YEAR BOOK,* 15th edition. Sydney: Pacific Publications, 1984.

Hezel, Francis; and Berg, M.L. (eds.). *WINDS OF CHANGE.* Trust Territory of the Pacific Islands, 1979.

Stanley, David; and Dalton, Bill. *SOUTH PACIFIC HANDBOOK.* Chico, California: Moon Publications, 1982.

Chapter 15: The Marshall Islands

1. Geography

The Marshalls consist of two chains of atolls and coral islands. They run several hundred miles north to south. Twenty-four of the atolls and islands are inhabited. The total land area is only 66 square miles (171.6 km²). They are all flat. The lagoons of the atolls are quite large, and many of the islands are long and skinny. Each atoll may have dozens of islands, but only a few are inhabited. The islands are not very fertile. Little taro is grown, and the main food crops are coconuts and pandanus. Breadfruit is eaten in season. The northern islands of the group have limited rainfall, and water shortages are common. There are no rivers on the islands. Almost all of the islands are much less than one square mile.

2. People and Culture

Due to their habit of attacking ships, the Marshallese developed a dangerous reputation and were avoided for a long time. Eventually, however, some traders were able to settle in, and from then on the Marshalls were visited often by outsiders. Whalers, traders, and beachcombers were numerous. Perhaps the heaviest influence on the Marshallese was the missionaries. Many customs and traditions of ancient Marshallese faded under the pressure of the strict Protestant missionaries. Clothing was introduced, and dancing abolished. Many recipes for local medicine were lost.

Other customs and skills dropped out due to progress. Once the Marshallese were great navigators who built large sailing canoes and sailed easily and often between the various atolls. Now they wait for government ships to travel from atoll to atoll. They build smaller canoes, but only for fishing inside the lagoons.

Today the people make many handicrafts to sell to tourists passing through Majuro airport. Stick charts are a tourist favorite. They were part of Marshallese navigation lore. The charts were used as training aids.

Many customs do survive. The traditional chief system is still very powerful. Extended families are much stronger than on some islands. And of course one main ingredient of their culture today is religion.

The Germans tried to develop Jaluit when they had the islands. The Japanese used the islands for military bases. There was a big battle for Kwajalein during World War II.

There is one ethnic group — the Marshallese — who number about 35,000. They speak their own distinct language. There are two slightly different dialects, one for the Ralak Chain and one for the Ratak Chain.

Majuro is the capital and most developed island. On most of the islands the people live a village subsistence lifestyle.

3. Economy and Resources

The Marshalls produce quite a bit of copra. This is the main cash crop for the islanders. There is also a sizable handicraft industry. But the mainstay of the economy is the existing U.S. military base on Kwajalein Atoll. The rent money from this base, plus the jobs created for the Marshallese, should serve as a stable base for the Marshallese economy. In addition, the large expanse of water covered by the islands' 200-mile (320 km) economic zone gives a great potential for selling fishing licenses. Tourism has not been developed as there is not very much to offer tourists on the flat atolls.

Lately the Marshallese have been seeking loans for development projects that the United States has failed to finance. They have borrowed money from Britain for a power plant, and from other countries to purchase smaller commuter airline planes. Taiwan and Japan have also provided aid. A fish processing plant has been constructed on Majuro for exportation of certain fish products to Japan. New copra boats have also been provided, and improvement of Majuro's water system is planned. The Marshallese feel that by seeking aid and loans from other countries they become less dependent on the United States.

4. Political Status

The Marshallese, blessed with an already existing U.S. military base, decided it was not economically sound to remain tied to the other islands of the Trust Territory. They did not want to share the rent

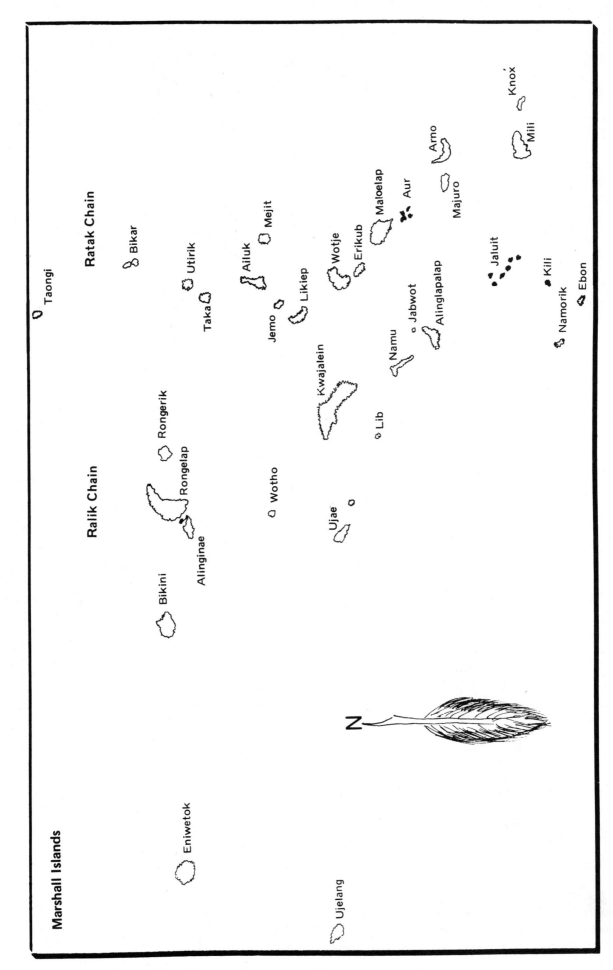

Marshall Islands

Ralik Chain

Ratak Chain

Taongi

Bikar

Utirik

Taka

Ailuk

Mejit

Jemo

Likiep

Wotje

Erikub

Maloelap

Aur

Amo

Knox

Mili

Majuro

Jaluit

Kili

Namorik

Ebon

Eniwetok

Bikini

Alinginae

Rongelap

Rongerik

Wotho

Ujae

Kwajalein

Lib

Namu

Jabwot

Alinglapalap

N

Ujelang

Main Street, Majuro. This road goes all the way to the end of the atoll at Laura Village, for a total of 32 miles. In some places, the land is barely wide enough for the road. For an aerial view of Majuro, see the atoll photo in Chapter Two. (Photo courtesy **Glimpses Magazine***)*

money they get from the base. They also have enough copra and other economic potential to attempt to make it on their own. They decided on a separate free association compact with the United States. Operating in de facto status since the late 70s, the Marshalls' compact was fully implemented in October, 1986. The islands are no longer part of the Trust Territory, and as part of the deal Marshall Islanders will be allowed free entry into the United States. The compact is to last for fifteen years, during which time the United States will provide money and defense for the right to use Kwajalein and the right to deny entry into the islands by any foreign military.

5. Major Problems

Main problems, besides further development of the economy, include food and water shortages on some islands; transportation problems due to the large distances between atolls; and lack of good communications with the outside world.

Of embarrassment to the United States are the still radioactive atolls of Bikini and Eniwetok. The United States used those atolls to conduct atomic tests in the 1950s. The islanders tried to move back to their homes once. The United States even built concrete houses for them. But the ground water was still "hot," and the coconuts and other food grown on the islands contaminated. The people were again moved off and many are suing the United States.

The Bikini islanders are unhappy with the com-

pact because it establishes a $75 million claim fund for damages resulting from the testing, and forbids the islanders from suing for any more than that. It is still unclear whether an attempt will be made to clean up Bikini, which may cost $50 million, or whether the Bikini islanders will simply buy someplace else to live. Most are younger than 40 and have never lived on Bikini. The people of Eniwetok were allowed to resettle on the half of their atoll that was not used for tests. In a related event, the people of Rongelap, who suffered fallout when the wind shifted during a test conducted on Bikini in the 50s, asked to be moved off their island becuause they believed it to be still contaminated. U.S. officials disagreed, but the entire population was transferred by the environmental group Greenpeace to an island on Kwajalein.

Also embarrassing is Ebeye. Ebeye is an island on Kwajalein Atoll. Many Marshallese work at the U.S. base on Kwajalein. But they are not allowed to live there or stay overnight. After work the Marshallese take a ferry to a town on Ebeye. Ebeye is considered by many to be the worst slum in the Pacific. There are more than 5000 people living on one tenth of a square mile of land. Relatives of workers go to Ebeye because it is more developed than their home islands. There are stores, theaters, bars, electricity, and other modern amenities. But it is incredibly overcrowded, the sewer system breaks down often, and disease is rampant. The Marshallese would like to

Washing clothes in the back yard of a Majuro home — a common chore for Marshallese women. (Photo courtesy **Glimpses Magazine***)*

settle on other islands in the atoll or be allowed to stay on Kwajalein. Kwajalein is very clean and modern, similar to a U.S. suburb. The United States claims the Ebeye problem is the Marshallese' fault. There are too many people on Ebeye who really don't belong. The Marshallese say they can't turn away relatives. It is not a happy situation.

Current plans call for development of a causeway to connect several reef islands that stretch for five miles north of Ebeye, thus allowing the population to spread out more. New water, sewer, health, and power systems are to be constructed also.

In 1982, a demonstration was begun by the Marshallese who are natives of Kwajalein and traditionally own the atoll's islands. They are not happy with the terms of the rental agreement for the U.S. base, and are upset at not being allowed to move off Ebeye to live on some of the atoll's unused islands. They

began a protest occupation of Kwajalein itself and Roi Namur, another island on the atoll. There have been several such protests since.

It is hoped that the causeway expansion will satisfy the Kwajalein islanders at least somewhat, but the key issue is the distribution of the rent money. The United States only pays rent to foreign governments, not foreign citizens. The Marshall Islands Government is responsible for giving the land-owners their share, and that is where the disagreements arise.

Another problem in the Marshalls and all rapidly changing islands has been serious malnutrition among some children. Parents, especially in the developed capital of Majuro, feed their children too much junk food instead of the nutritious local diet. Modern is supposed to be better, but often is not.

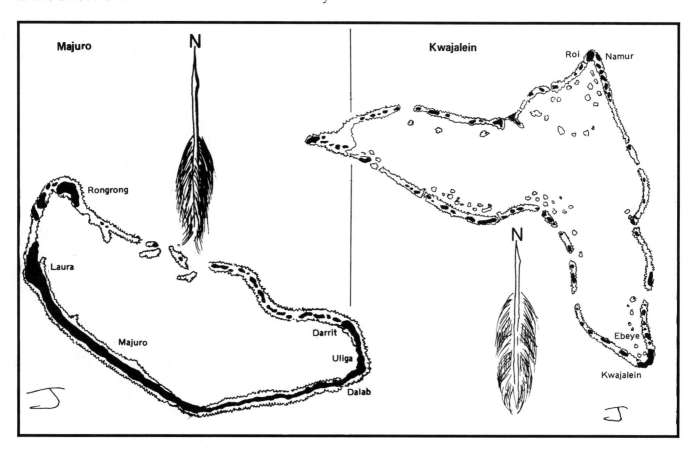

CHAPTER REVIEW

Vocabulary: Majuro, Kwajalein, Bikini, Eniwetok, Ebeye

Questions:

1. What are the Marshall Islands like physically?

2. Why did the Marshalls decide to separate from the Trust Territory?

3. What is the problem with Bikini and Eniwetok?

4. What is the problem with Ebeye?

For Further Reading:

Alkire, William H. *AN INTRODUCTION TO THE PEOPLES AND CULTURES OF MICRONESIA.* Addison-Wesley Publishing, 1972.

Carter, John (ed.). *PACIFIC ISLANDS YEAR BOOK,* 15th edition. Sydney: Pacific Publications, 1984.

Hezel, Francis; and Berg, M.L. (eds.). *WINDS OF CHANGE.* Trust Territory of the Pacific Islands, 1979.

Stanley, David; and Dalton, Bill. *SOUTH PACIFIC HANDBOOK.* Chico, California: Moon Publications, 1982.

Chapter 16: The Federated States of Micronesia

The remaining islands of the Trust Territory — Yap, Truk, Pohnpei, and Kosrae — have grouped themselves together as the Federated States of Micronesia. Not surprisingly, they have few resources and no potential U.S. bases. Each of the four states is very different, and we will discuss the geography, people and culture, and economy and resources of the states separately.

1. Yap

Yap State consists of one volcanic complex of four islands and 11 inhabited outer island atolls. The total land area is about 50 square miles (130 km²). Yap proper is located about 550 miles (880 km) southwest of Guam. The Yap volcanic complex has rolling hills, with picturesque villages along the shoreline. There is plenty of rain and much subsistence agriculture.

Yap is the most traditional island in Micronesia, perhaps in all the Pacific. European traders for years were frustrated at the Yapese indifference. The Yapese could not be bribed or tricked into making copra. They were just not interested enough in the metal tools, cloth, and other trinkets offered in payment. The only thing the Yapese valued was their unique stone money. These were huge flat discs of stone with holes in the middle. They were quarried in Belau, several hundred miles to the west, and brought to Yap by sailing canoe. The more trouble experienced in bringing a piece back to Yap and the more people who died trying to get it home, the more value it had. The huge stones were carried on poles stuck through the holes and then set up in villages. Once set in place, the larger stones were never moved. They were also never stolen. The owner of a disc could use it by simply transferring the ownership to another person in exchange for land or whatever was needed. The ownership changed, everybody knew who the new owner was, but the stone stayed put. This was true even if the new owner lived in a different village across the island. The stones are still used today by the Yapese for purchasing land and other traditional transactions.

An American named O'Keefe was the first to get the Yapese to make copra. He did it by helping them transport more stone money from Belau in his Chinese junk. Today the Yapese know the difference between O'Keefe's money and money brought by

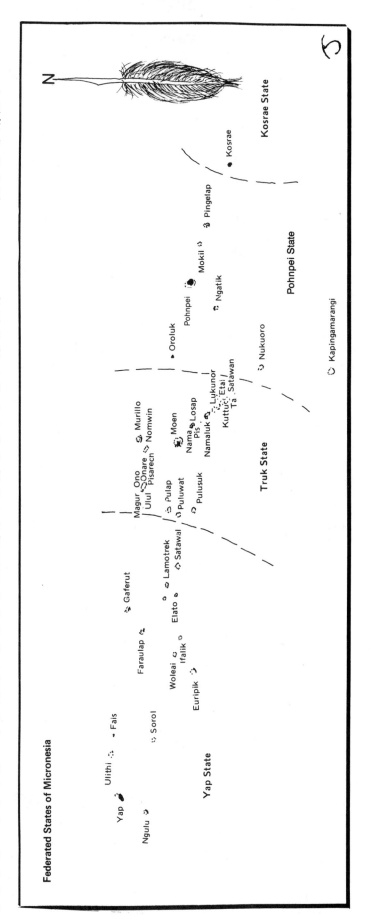

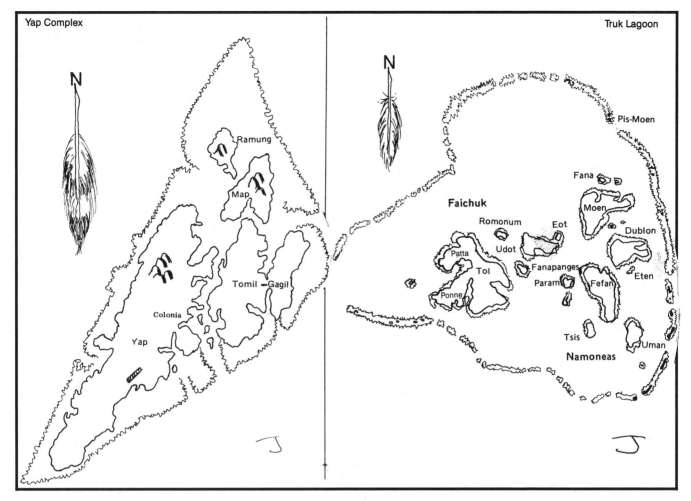

N

Ramung

Map

Tomil — Gagil

Colonia

Yap

N

Pis-Moen

Fana

Faichuk

Romonum

Moen

Eot

Udot

Dublon

Patta

Fanapanges

Eten

Tol

Param

Fefan

Ponne

Tsis

Uman

Namoneas

canoe. Stone money brought over by O'Keefe was obtained too easily. It is not worth as much as earlier pieces.

The indifference to change and the modern world has helped Yap maintain its traditions. The people wear western clothes when in the main center town of Colonia, but many still dress traditionally in the villages. The men wear a complicated system of loin cloths and hibiscus fiber. The women wear grass skirts. Yapese also chew the green betelnut like the Belauans do.

There is also a strict caste system on Yap. People are born into their caste. According to many outside observers, low-caste Yapese are discriminated against in many ways, including the lack of opportunity for good jobs. Many low-caste Yapese who manage to get away from Yap and get an education never return.

The people living on the outer island atolls are not Yapese. True Yapese are from Yap proper and speak a language different from any other in Micronesia. Outer islanders are Carolinian and speak dialects similar to outer island Truk and Saipan Carolinian. The outer islands traditionally "belong" to Yap, specifically to the Yapese district of Gagil. In years past, canoes came from all the outer islands, even some in Truk, bringing tributes of food.

Even today when they come to Yap, outer islanders usually stay in one small slum area. Outer island men wear a one-piece loin cloth. The women wear a wrap-around lava lava. Total population of the state is about 12,000; 8000 on Yap proper, 4000 on the outers.

Yap State relies more on subsistence than any other state. There is no real economy outside of government jobs supported by U.S. grants. Tourism is developing slowly. There are only two hotels, and Yapese don't really like outsiders walking through their villages gawking. Copra is the only cash crop. There is a potential for fishing, but it is not yet developed. The outers are almost completely subsistence, with Ulithi being the only outer island with any type of minimal development.

2. Truk

Truk State consists of a cluster of volcanic islands surrounded by a single barrier reef and 24 inhabited outer island atolls. It is located 600 miles (960 km) southeast of Guam. The Truk Lagoon is unique geographically. The islands are peaks of a sinking

Commuting in the Truk Lagoon. Many Trukese go to jobs every-day on Moen, the capital island, and return to their home islands by motor boat after work. These trips take anywhere from half an hour to two hours, depending on the distance from Moen. The Truk Lagoon is 40 miles wide. (Photo courtesy **Glimpses Magazine**)

An often repeated scene on many outer islands throughout the Pacific — a ship's motor boat taking passengers and supplies back and forth between the ship and the beach. The field trip ship is the only link to the outside world for many Pacific islands. This ship is anchored off Lamotrek, Yap, but could be almost any-where. (Photo by Mark Skinner)

extinct volcano. In a few million years, the mountains will disappear, leaving the barrier reef and reef islands. The Truk Lagoon will then be another atoll, like the Marshalls. Total land area of the state is about 45 square miles (117 km²). The high islands of the Truk Lagoon are lush and fertile. Rainfall is plentiful.

Truk always had a fierce reputation and was avoided by whites. The islands of the Lagoon warred with each other constantly. Missionaries became established in the slightly mellower outer islands before finally converting the people of the Lagoon. The Japanese developed the Lagoon area extensively,

growing sugar cane and even rice. They built a huge naval base, the headquarters for the Japanese Navy in World War II. American planes sank over 60 ships in the Lagoon during a series of raids. Today those wrecks are a protected underwater park, and draw scuba divers from all over the world.

Moen, the capital island of Truk, is developed. There are many cars, paved roads, electricity, and other modern amenities. In general the people of the Lagoon have given up their traditional ways for a money economy.

There are four areas within Truk State. The

Stone money bank - Yap. (Photo courtesy MRTC)

A typical homesite on Pohnpei island, but away from the town area of Kolonia. (Photo courtesy **Glimpses Magazine**)

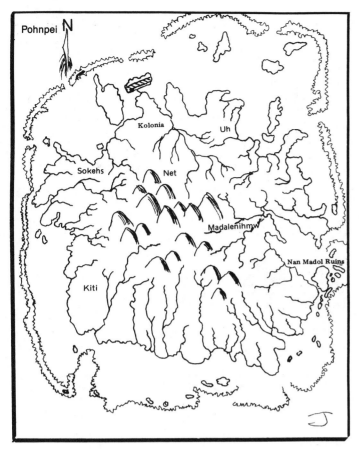

Mortlocks, too, have considered some form of political autonomy. Economically, there is some tourism from scuba divers, but otherwise the islands are totally dependent on U.S. money. Development was set back even further by a devastating typhoon that struck the Lagoon in December, 1987. Due to its large population and lack of economic potential, Truk is a big headache for the FSM.

3. Pohnpei

Pohnpei State consists of one large volcanic island and six inhabited atolls. It is located about 450 miles (720 km) east of Truk.

Pohnpei is one of the most beautiful islands in the Pacific, even though it has no beaches. The shoreline is covered with vast mangrove swamps that exist due to the many rivers. Pohnpei gets over 200 inches (500 cm) of rain per year, making huge rivers and numerous waterfalls. The area of the state is 145 square miles (377 km²), most of it on Pohnpei island. The island is fertile and there is much local agriculture. The island produces a lot of food for local consumption, including huge yams.

Pohnpei was beset with many beachcombers. Most were supported by different chiefs, and served

Lagoon is the most populated. To the southeast are the Mortlock Atolls. Mortlockese speak a dialect close to Lagoon Trukese, but consider themselves different people. Mortlockese are forward looking, and many have moved to Moen to get jobs that don't exist on their atolls. North of the Truk Lagoon are the Hall Islands. They have also given up many of their traditional ways. To the west of the Lagoon are the Westerns and Namonwitos. These atolls are more traditional. The islanders still navigate and sail canoes over hundreds of miles. They speak a dialect much different from Lagoon Trukese. They still wear traditional loin cloths and lava lavas. The Western Trukese feel they have much more in common with the outer islanders of Yap.

The total population of Truk State is 48,000 — the most populated of the FSM. This is a serious problem, for Truk has no resources. It was the major drain on the Trust Territory budget, and is now the major drain on the budget of the FSM. Since government is the only real economy, Truk depends heavily on U.S. grants. Imports are high, and except on most outer islands subsistence has fallen off.

Truk State has many problems. Lack of unity is one. Even within the Truk Lagoon there is disagreement. The Faichuk area, in the west of the Lagoon, feels it has not received its fair share of the U.S. dollars. It has voted to become a separate state, but the FSM government has delayed that for now. The

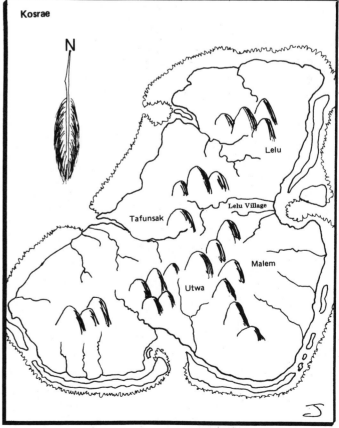

Yap. Men's house in village away from the town area of Colonia. Some pieces of stone money are leaning against the porch area. (Photo courtesy MRTC)

as the chiefs' agents in trading with visiting whalers. However they did contribute to many problems in Pohnpei, spreading disease, causing fights, interfering in local politics, and often making drunken nuisances of themselves. The population of Pohnpei declined rapidly from smallpox, syphilis, and other introduced diseases. During the German years, the district of Sokehs rebelled and killed some German administrators. The Germans retaliated by executing the chiefs of Sokehs and exiling all the people to other parts of Pohnpei, leaving the district empty.

Pohnpei has numerous ethnic groups. Pohnpeians are beginning to be outnumbered by other islanders living there. There is also much mixed blood, both from all the whites who lived there and from the ethnic groups intermarrying. Mortlockese, originally from Truk State, have a sizable community on Pohnpei. The Germans let them occupy and settle into the empty Sokehs area when typhoons destroyed their atolls in the Mortlocks. Some later returned to the Mortlocks, but many stayed in Pohnpei.

Outer islanders from Pingelap and Mokil, atolls to the east of Pohnpei, have villages on Pohnpei. Their languages are different from Pohnpeian, though Pingalapese is close. Far to the south of Pohnpei are two atolls populated by Polynesians: Nukuoro and Kapingamorangi. Their languages and customs are Polynesian, and with some difficulty they can communicate with Samoans and Tahitians. More of these Polynesians live in the village of Porakeit on Pohnpei than on their home islands. Many Kosraeans have also settled on Pohnpei, left over from the days Kosrae was part of Pohnpei and many of the people moved in to get jobs.

The state has some interesting customs. There is a royalty and nobility system, and the people must use a separate language when addressing a person of title. Pohnpeians also drink sakau, the mouth-numbing mild narcotic known as kava in Polynesia and yaqona in Fiji.

Economically, Pohnpei still relies too much on imports, but has much local agriculture. Tourism is growing. People come to see the waterfalls and the mysterious, ancient ruins of Nan Madol, an entire city made of huge basalt rock crystals. The rivers of Pohnpei may one day provide it with ample hydroelectric power, cutting out reliance on imported oil. Pohnpei is the capital of the FSM, and development is increasing rapidly around the district center town of Kolonia. The population of the state is almost 30,000.

In the vote for acceptance of the compact of free association, Pohnpei was the only state of the FSM to vote against by a narrow 51% to 49% margin. Since the other three states voted for the compact, Pohnpei was obligated to remain in the federation. However the other states are worried that Pohnpei may one day try to pull out of the FSM, as some of

The ruins of Nan Madol: artificial islands, canals, and structures made of basalt rock crystals piled carefully together like logs. Many mysteries remain regarding this ancient city. (Photo courtesy MRTC)

Pohnpei's leaders are not happy being connected with the other islands.

4. Kosrae (Ko-shy)

Kosrae State, the easternmost island of the FSM, used to be part of Pohnpei. Kosrae is one volcanic island of about 40 square miles (104 km²) located 350 miles (560 km) southeast of Pohnpei. It is very fertile. The island was hit hard by whalers, and the pirate Bully Hayes was shipwrecked there. Resultant diseases and fighting reduced the population from several thousand to a few demoralized hundred. Into this depressing situation came the Protestant missionaries, who literally saved the Kosraeans and rebuilt their culture. The people recovered but lost many of their ancient customs and traditions. Today the island is very religious, with no bars and no dancing. The total population is only 6700, and though imports are rising, the island produces much food. The airport was recently completed, and in 1986 Kos-

rae was added to the route of Continental Air Micronesia's 727 island hopper between Hawaii and Guam which also stops at Truk, Pohnpei, Kwajalein, and Majuro. (The other leg of the route connects Yap and Belau to Guam.) Kosrae is a very beautiful island with many rivers and waterfalls. Lelu is the main town and developed area. There is also an abandoned basalt rock crystal city at Lelu similar to Nan

Looking across to the main town of Lelu, Kosrae. (Photo by Marshall Kirby courtesy of MRTC)

Madol. Plans are being considered to develop the island more for tourism, but fear of rapid cultural changes has kept things moving at a cautious pace. The new jet service will definitely increase travelers to the island and open it up for more development, and the Kosraeans are worried about keeping that development under control.

These four very different groups make up the FSM. They stuck together out of necessity. The more economically viable districts, those with bases or possible future bases, pulled out, leaving these four to fend for themselves. They have no real resources and no future U.S. bases. There is not much on which to base an economy. Under the compact of free association, the United States will handle defense and the islands will receive money. The money from the United States will be the main support of the economy. The compact is to last for 15 years. The United States wants the deal simply to keep military control of the area and make sure no other country moves in.

During the 15 years the economy is supposed to be developed. The only real potential for economic growth at this point is fishing. License deals have been worked out with countries such as Japan and Taiwan. This brings in a little cash. Tourism also helps, and there are a few agricultural exports like copra and Pohnpei's gourmet pepper, but the main support of the economy is the government which is supported completely by U.S. grants. It could be argued, though, that as long as the United States wants military denial rights in the islands, it should pay for those rights. That, then, becomes a viable economy, for the FSM is in effect capitalizing on a resource — its location.

A store in Lelu, Kosrae. (Photo by Marshall Kirby courtesy of MRTC)

The people elect a legislature which then chooses a president. The compact was fully implemented by the United States in November, 1986. All FSM citizens now have the right to enter freely into the United States and stay as long as they want. What effect this will have on the islands' emigration, which had been growing steadily, is unclear. Some believe that many people, especially young men, will leave to look for jobs in Guam, Hawaii, or the U.S. mainland.

Besides the economy, the major problem facing the FSM is holding the federation together. The many different ethnic groups, languages, and loyalties have already led to many problems. They are sure to lead to others.

The total land area of the FSM is 300 square miles (780 km²). The total population is about 95,000.

CHAPTER REVIEW

Vocabulary: stone money, caste system, loin cloth, lava lava, Colonia, Truk Lagoon, Mortlocks, Westerns, Faichuk, Sokehs, sakau, Nan Madol, Kolonia, Yap, Truk, Pohnpei, Kosrae

Questions:

1. Why are these four states sticking together?

2. What are some of the differences among the four states?

3. What economic potential is there in the FSM?

For Further Reading:

Alkire, William H. *AN INTRODUCTION TO THE PEOPLES AND CULTURES OF MICRONESIA.* Addison-Wesley Publishing, 1972.

Carter, John (ed.). *PACIFIC ISLANDS YEAR BOOK,* 15th edition. Sydney: Pacific Publications, 1984.

Hezel, Francis; and Berg, M.L. (eds.). *WINDS OF CHANGE.* Trust Territory of the Pacific Islands, 1979.

Stanley, David; and Dalton, Bill. *SOUTH PACIFIC HANDBOOK.* Chico, California: Moon Publications, 1982.

Chapter 17: Nauru

1. Geography

Nauru is a single raised coral island just south of the equator about 1000 miles (1600 km) northeast of New Guinea. Its total land area is only nine square miles (23.4 km²). It is surrounded by a fringing reef that drops off to deep ocean. There is thus no off-shore lagoon area, but there is a brackish freshwater lagoon in the island's interior. Around the coast and around the lagoon are fertile belts where coconuts, pandanus, and bananas are grown. The middle of the island is barren. Nothing much can grow there because the ground is almost pure phosphate. Rainfall is irregular, and there are no rivers. The island's highest point is about 200 feet (60 m) above sea level on top of the flat central plateau.

2. People and Culture

Nauru's isolation played an important part in its history. The people developed as a very distinct group different from other Micronesians. The strong South Equatorial Current made Nauru a difficult landfall, often sweeping canoes west into empty ocean. The population of the island was held steady by the frequent dry spells which limited the food supply of the fertile belts. However there was usually plenty of fish offshore, and this was supplemented by raising milkfish on the reef and in the central lagoon.

Beachcombers, some good and some bad, became important to Nauru. They acted as go-betweens with passing ships and also added variety to the gene pool.

Civil wars beginning in 1878 almost wiped out the population. European traders and beachcombers supplied guns, and the fighting was non-stop. When the Germans moved in and took possession in 1888, they confiscated all the weapons and put an end to the fighting. Two missionaries, one Protestant and one Catholic, settled in and converted the population. Original Nauruan dancing was barred, and traditional clothing was replaced by dresses and pants. However, the missionaries are also credited with putting the Nauruan language into writing. Phosphate, valuable as fertilizer, was discovered about 1899, and soon a British company was allowed to begin mining. After World War I Australia took over Nauru, and the Australians continued mining.

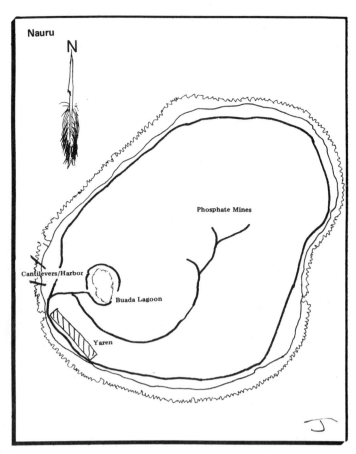

Phosphate from Nauru was vital for Australian agriculture. The Nauruans were paid almost nothing for their island's resources.

During World War II, Nauru was occupied by the Japanese. The Nauruans were treated brutally by the Japanese, most being sent to Truk or other islands in Micronesia to work as forced laborers. Many died. After World War II, Nauru became a U.N. Trust Territory administered by Australia. After independence in 1968, the Nauruans began to get full control of their phosphate.

There are about 5000 Nauruans living on Nauru, and they have their own distinct Micronesian language. There are about 3000 outsiders who live on Nauru and work in the phosphate industry. Most of them are from Kiribati and Tuvalu.

Today a favorite pastime of Nauruans is driving around the island. This takes about half an hour at most. They also like to catch and train the huge frigate birds. Nauruans can afford many cars, stereos, TVs, radios, and other consumer items. But most Nauruans still enjoy a simplified lifestyle. After work and on weekends, they go fishing, work in their gardens, play sports, and attend church. The southwest shoreline area is the most developed, containing government offices, modern stores, the airport, and the harbor.

Aerial view of Nauru — all nine square miles of it. (District Committee Publisher Nauru photo)

3. Economy and Resources

Nauru is the richest nation in the Pacific and one of the richest in the world. Phosphate pays for everything. Nauruans who own land with phosphate are paid huge royalties. For others there are good-paying government jobs and private service industries. The government is financed completely by money from phosphate exports. It spends almost $90,000,000 per year. The government receives half the profit per ton of phosphate.

To insure against the day, near the turn of the century, when the phosphate will be gone, Nauru has made many investments. It owns an airline and several ships. It owns an apartment complex in Australia, hotels in Samoa and the Marshalls, an office building on Saipan in the Northern Marianas, a hotel on Guam, a building in Texas, an office in Hong Kong, and phosphate plants in India and the Philippines. Nauru uses Australian money and invests in Australian banks. This makes Australia happy, as it helps shore up the Australian dollar.

4. Political Status

Nauru is independent. It is one of the few small island nations that can afford independence. The president is elected by the parliament which is elected by the people. Australia provides any defense needs.

Nauruan citizenship is very carefully defined by the Nauruan constitution. Persons with only one Nauruan parent are not automatically granted citizenship. This is to prevent Nauruan wealth from being diluted or flowing out of Nauru due to mixed marriages.

5. Major Problems

With the phosphate due to run out in a few years, the major problem for Nauru is to make good investments to keep the money coming in when the phosphate is finally gone. There is some concern among Nauruans as to whether the investments that have been made will bring in enough money to support the current standard of living. Also the population is increasing rapidly, resulting in housing and employment shortages. The necessary importation of food, water, and fuel is very expensive. The government has considered constructing an OTEC power plant to cut down on imported oil and improve the balance of trade even more, but so far has not done so. The recent decline in the value of the Australian dollar has also hurt Nauru's economy. Finally, there is the problem of what to do with the worked-out phosphate fields. A Commission of Inquiry has been formed to find the best way to rehabilitate the now useless land.

The phosphate works with the wasteland of mined-out fields behind. (Photo by Terrence Debao)

CHAPTER REVIEW

Vocabulary: phosphate

Questions:

1. Describe the island of Nauru.

2. Why is the island so wealthy?

3. What are the Nauruans doing to prepare for the future?

4. What is Nauru's relationship with Australia?

For Further Reading:

Alkire, William H. *AN INTRODUCTION TO THE PEOPLES AND CULTURES OF MICRONESIA.* Addison-Wesley Publishing, 1972.

Carter, John (ed.). *PACIFIC ISLANDS YEAR BOOK,* 15th edition. Sydney: Pacific Publications, 1984.

Hezel, Francis; and Berg, M.L. (eds.). *WINDS OF CHANGE.* Trust Territory of the Pacific Islands, 1979.

Stanley, David; and Dalton, Bill. *SOUTH PACIFIC HANDBOOK.* Chico, California: Moon Publications, 1982.

Viviani, Nancy. *NAURU, PHOSPHATE AND POLITICAL PROGRESS.* Honolulu: University of Hawaii Press, 1970.

Chapter 18: Kiribati (Kiribas)

1. Geography

Kiribati consists of the Gilbert, Phoenix, and some of the Line Islands. The total land area is about 310 square miles (806 km²). The islands are scattered, covering over 2000 miles from east to west in the central Pacific. The ocean area is estimated at 2,000,000 square miles (5,200,000 km²). All 35 of the islands are low, flat atolls or coral islands except the raised coral island of Banaba. The northern Gilberts are more fertile, the southern Gilberts relatively dry. The Phoenix and Line groups were uninhabited when stumbled upon by explorers and whalers. These islands were claimed and used by the United States and Britain, who did some guano mining. Guano is bird manure used for fertilizer. When the Gilberts became independent, the United States and Britain gave up claims to the Phoenix and most of the Line group, transferring them to Kiribati. Ocean Island, or Banaba, is now also part of Kiribati. It is a raised coral, phosphate-rich island similar to Nauru. The indigenous name for the Gilbert Islands is Tungaru. However since the nation includes more than just Tungaru, the people decided to use the name Kiribati, pronounced Kiribas, which is the way the local people for years have pronounced the British name "Gilbert."

People and Culture

The Gilbertese were known as fierce warriors. They used shark-teeth spears, and constructed suits of armor from coconut rope. Their bodies were completely covered from head to foot. The islands were hit hard by blackbirders, losing many people to the slave ships. The British took the islands as a colony, connecting them with the Polynesian Ellice group, now known as Tuvalu. The Japanese took over some of the islands in World War II, and Tarawa was captured by the Americans in a bloody battle. The Gilberts separated from Tuvalu and became independent in 1979.

There are about 63,000 people in Kiribati. They are Gilbertese and speak their own Micronesian language. Banabans speak a dialect close to Gilbertese. Only the capital atoll of Tarawa is very developed. Most of the people live village lifestyles, with subsistence farming and fishing. Copra is the cash crop.

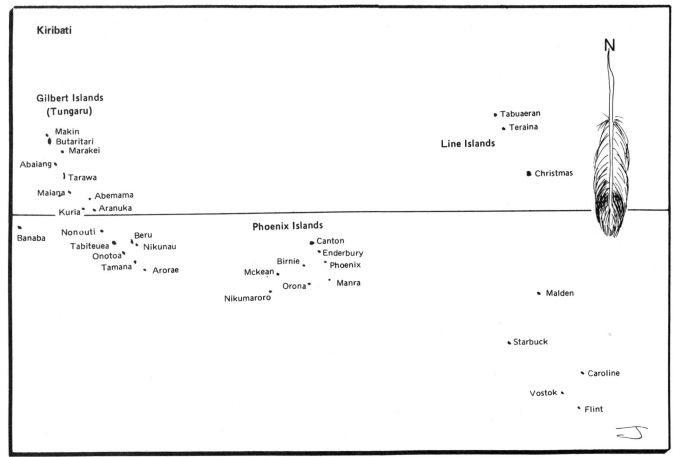

Kiribati

Gilbert Islands (Tungaru)

Makin
Butaritari
Marakei
Abaiang
Tarawa
Maiana
Kuria
Abemama
Aranuka

Banaba
Nonouti
Tabiteuea
Onotoa
Tamana
Beru
Nikunau
Arorae

Phoenix Islands

Mckean
Birnie
Orona
Nikumaroro
Canton
Enderbury
Phoenix
Manra

Line Islands
Tabuaeran
Teraina
Christmas

Malden

Starbuck

Caroline

Vostok
Flint

N

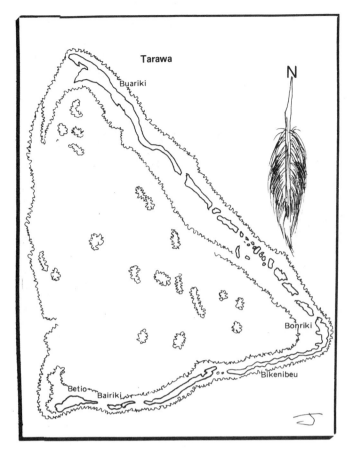

to resettle there instead of crowding into Tarawa. There is great fishing potential, especially with the 200-mile zones. Japan, South Korea, Taiwan, the United States, and even the Soviet Union have made license agreements with Kiribati. There used to be phosphate on Banaba, but it is all mined out. At present imports outweigh exports. Some of the deficit is made up by a small tourist business which is developing slowly. Another important source of money is the pay sent home by some 800 Gilbertese working as sailors on ships, the product of a local maritime academy. There are also about 500 Gilbertese working on Nauru who send home cash. There is now a government fishing company, and fish is sold to the Star Kist cannery in American Samoa. Postage stamp sales also help a little. The rest of what Kiribati needs is supplied by aid from Britain. However in 1986, for the first time, the government was able to balance its budget without British aid. This was due mostly to the fees from fishing licenses.

3. Economy and resources

4. Political Status

Copra and fish are the major exports. The government has developed copra plantations on some of the Line Islands and is encouraging people

Kiribati is an independent republic and a member of the Commonwealth of Nations. The people elect an assembly which then chooses a president.

Bairiki, Tarawa — one of the three developed islands of the capital atoll. (Kiribati Ministry of Natural Resources Development photo)

Net fishing on the beach at Abemama Atoll. (Kiribati Ministry of Natural Resources Development photo)

Drying copra in the sun in Kiribati. (Kiribati Ministry of Natural Resources Development photo)

5. Major Problems

The main problems of Kiribati are economic. In addition, there are problems relative to administering such widely scattered islands. There is also an overpopulation problem on Tarawa, as people move in from the undeveloped atolls to get jobs. It is hoped development of the Phoenix and Line Islands will relieve some of this pressure, as I-Kiribati (people of Kiribati) move there to work on copra plantations.

The Banabans are not very happy about being part of Kiribati. They had sought independence. For years their island's phosphate was mined by combined British, Australian, and New Zealand interests. The Banabans were paid an incredibly low royalty considering the value of their phosphate. Nauruans were getting four to five times as much for their phosphate. When Banabans refused to sell more land for mining, the colonial government just took what it wanted. The Banabans sued Britain, and in 1981 accepted $10 million plus interest. The phosphate had already run out in 1979, and the Banabans feel that with the money due them for past exploitation they could afford independence. The island itself is torn up from the mining, and most Banabans live on Rabi Island in Fiji, where they are Fijian citizens. Britain has offered to rebuild Banaba, and Banabans have been granted special rights in the Kiribati constitution. But the bitterness remains.

Another problem is the difficulty of enforcement of the vast 200-mile fishing zones. In addition, the license deals must be renewed yearly, and sometimes problems develop. Japan reduced its aid to Kiribati when the license fee was raised, and a renegotiation of the Soviet pact fell through when the Russians requested the right to enter Kiribati lagoons. Related to the Soviet deal is concern by the United States, which feels that the Russians really only want the right to hang around in Kiribati waters to make it easier for them to spy electronically on the U.S. base at Kwajalein in the Marshalls.

The road for Kiribati will not be easy, but through increased development of copra and fishing resources, it should make some progress toward self-sufficiency.

CHAPTER REVIEW

Vocabulary: Gilbert, Tungaru, Phoenix, Line, guano, Banaba, Tarawa

Questions:

1. What kinds of islands are in Kiribati?

2. Discuss Kiribati's current economic situation and future potential.

3. How did Kiribati get all those extra islands?

4. Why are the Banabans unhappy?

For Further Reading:

Alkire, William H. *AN INTRODUCTION TO THE PEOPLES AND CULTURES OF MICRONESIA.* Addison-Wesley Publishing, 1972.

Carter, John (ed.). *PACIFIC ISLANDS YEAR BOOK,* 15th edition. Sydney: Pacific Publications, 1984.

Hezel, Francis; and Berg, M.L. (eds.). *WINDS OF CHANGE.* Trust Territory of the Pacific Islands, 1979.

INVESTMENT IN THE GILBERT ISLANDS. Tarawa: Ministry of Natural Resources Development.

Stanley, David; and Dalton, Bill. *SOUTH PACIFIC HANDBOOK.* Chico, California: Moon Publications, 1982.

UNIT FIVE: MELANESIA

Melanesia occupies the southwest portion of the Pacific, south of the equator, west of the date line, and east of Australia. These islands are quite different from Micronesia and Polynesia in many ways. Melanesia means black or dark islands. This refers to the skin color of the people, who tend to be the darkest of all Pacific islanders. Melanin is the name for skin pigment. Melas is the Greek word for black.

The islands tend to be quite large, with several classified as continental islands. This means more space, more variety of land forms, and more chance for natural resources.

Melanesia has more diseases, especially malaria. This disease is not found in Micronesia or Polynesia.

There are also more people in Melanesia than in Micronesia and Polynesia combined — almost four and a half million. There are also more languages and ethnic groups — about 1000. A unique language, Pidgin, has developed as a common speech for many of the tribes in Melanesia. Pidgin consists of a Melanesian syntax and grammar with a heavily accented and idiomatic English vocabulary.

Though the island nations of Melanesia are still under-developed, their problems are slightly different from those of other islands.

Chapter 19: Papua New Guinea

1. Geography

Papua New Guinea (PNG) is the largest nation, in both area and population, of all the Pacific nations we will study. Located just north and east of Australia, PNG consists of the eastern half of New Guinea Island plus the rather large offshore islands of New Britain, New Ireland, Bougainville, and several smaller islands. The western half of New Guinea island is part of Indonesia. New Guinea is the second largest island in the world after Greenland.

The main islands of PNG are continental, with the rest being volcanic and atolls. Total land area is about 178,000 square miles (462,800 km²). Being continental islands, they have much variety of land forms and vegetation. New Guinea has mountains up to 14,000 feet (4200 m), long river valleys, highland plateaus, coastal plains, rain forests, swamps, rolling hills — every type of terrain imaginable. It rains quite a bit, over 200 inches (500 cm) per year in some places. The temperature is tropical, but highland areas tend to be cooler. The land is usually very fertile. There is so much diversity in geography within islands and from island to island that there is not enough space to talk about it here.

2. People and Culture

PNG was isolated for much of the post-contact era, especially the interior of New Guinea. The land was too rugged and the people too savage for the Europeans to attempt to do much away from the coastal areas and offshore islands. There was one disastrous attempt to colonize New Ireland. Most of the Europeans died of infection, diseases like malaria, or were killed by islanders. In the 1880s Germany made a protectorate of the northeastern coast of New Guinea and the large offshore islands, while at the same time Britain made a protectorate of the southeastern quarter of New Guinea. The Germans established plantations and trading stations in their holdings, but these were never profitable. During World War I an Australian force captured German New Guinea.

In the 1920s and 1930s explorers began penetrating the New Guinea highlands, becoming aware for the first time of the hundreds of tribes and relatively large population (over 2,000,000) living there. During World War II the Japanese occupied all but the southeastern coast of New Guinea. Their plans for an amphibious landing at Port Moresby were stopped by the carrier battle of the Coral Sea. They attempted an overland invasion, crossing the rugged Owen Stanley range, but were turned back by combined Australian and American forces. The fighting took place in some of the worst terrain and conditions imaginable. Often the allies were guided and assisted by local tribesmen. Meanwhile, the large

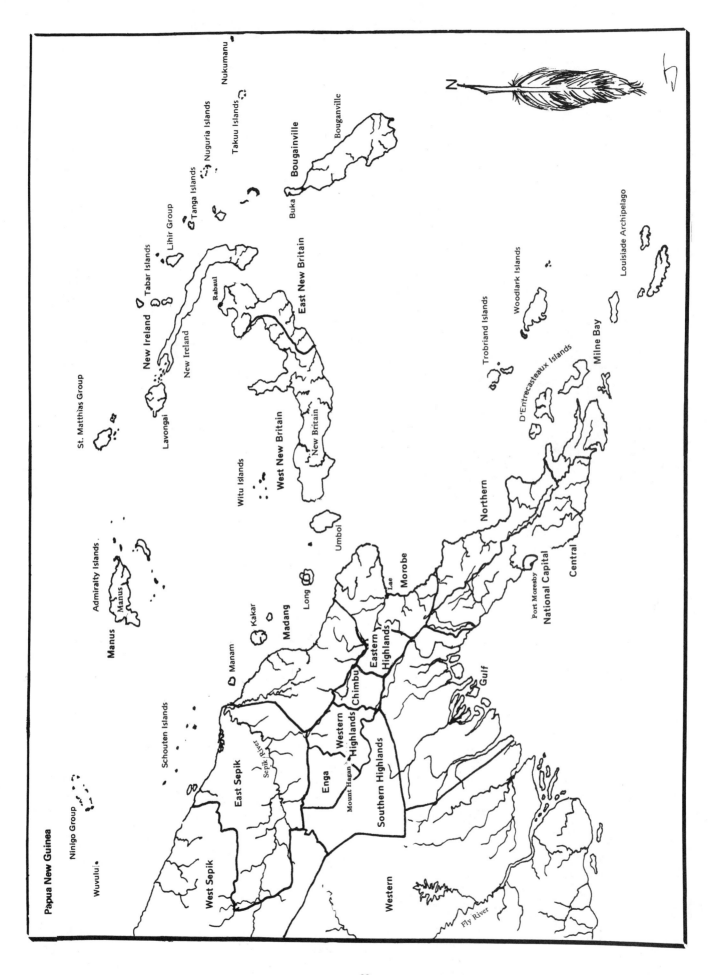

Papua New Guinea

Ninigo Group

Wuvulu

West Sepik

East Sepik

Sepik River

Schouten Islands

St. Matthias Group

Manus

Admiralty Islands

Manus

Manam

Kakar

Madang

Long

Umboi

Witu Islands

West New Britain

New Britain

New Ireland

New Ireland

Lavongai

Tabar Islands

Lihir Group

Tanga Islands

Nuguria Islands

Takuu Islands

Nukumanu

Rabaul

East New Britain

Buka

Bougainville

Bougainville

Enga

Mount Hagen

Western Highlands

Chimbu

Eastern Highlands

Southern Highlands

Western

Fly River

Gulf

Morobe

Lae

Northern

Central

National Capital

Port Moresby

Trobriand Islands

Woodlark Islands

D'Entrecasteaux Islands

Milne Bay

Louisiade Archipelago

N

Rush hour in Port Moresby, the capital and most developed city of Papua New Guinea. (PNG Government Office of Information photo)

Japanese base at Rabaul was made useless by American air raids. The allies then drove up the coast of New Guinea, cutting off and isolating many pockets of Japanese troops until the end of the war.

Today, although a money economy is growing, many people still live a village subsistence lifestyle. PNG's three million plus people are divided into over 700 tribes, each with its own separate language. English is the official language but Pidgin is widely used. Each tribe also has its own colorful dress and unique tribal dances. Sometimes there might be a

A village in the highlands of the Central Province. (PNG Government Office of Information photo)

different tribe and a different language just in the next valley. This ethnic diversity leads to a lot of tribal warfare. There is a payback system among the tribes. A murdered man's relative must kill someone from the enemy tribe. Then that person's relatives must kill someone from the first tribe. Back and forth, some of these payback feuds have gone on for longer than the people can remember — perhaps even for thousands of years. The government has tried to stop them, but some killing still goes on. PNG people have also been accused of cannibalism as recently as the 1980s.

The raising and possessing of pigs is very important, as they are often used as a bride price and are the center for ceremonial feasts. The top cuspids of boars are often knocked out. The lower tusks then continue to grow up and curl back, sometimes growing painfully into the boar's lip. These curved tusks are highly valued.

The main subsistence staples for most of the people are yams, sweet potatoes, and the sago palm. Protein comes from fish in the coastal areas and river valleys, and of course pigs. The people also like to chew green betelnut with lime.

Traditional leadership roles often depend on wealth of land and productivity of gardens. The vil-

The Panguna copper mine on Bouganville. (PNG Government Office of Information photo)

lager who can outdo everyone in giving big feasts becomes chief.

Though many people in PNG are Christian, many ancestor worship and spirit religions survive. These religions often require preserving the bones or even complete bodies of deceased ancestors. The building of huge spirit houses is also important in many areas. These houses represent the finest achievements of traditional architecture. PNG also gave birth to cargo cults. The islanders could not understand how white men could have so many good things which helped them live so easily without ever doing any real work. How could writing on papers and standing behind store counters produce all the wealth that the white man enjoyed? It took many hours of backbreaking labor in the gardens for a PNG man to get rich. Cargo cults sought the secret of white man's riches. They developed rituals and even cleared runways for planes filled with the goodies of civilization which the planes would bring just for the islanders. The planes and ships never came, but many cargo cults continued to seek the answer to the mystery of the wealth of the modern world.

The coastal areas and main towns of Port Moresby, Lae, Rabaul, and others are relatively developed and modern. Many of the small villages are rather remote and isolated. They still tend to be quite primitive.

3. Economy and Resources

PNG's economy can be summarized in one word: potential. The nation has many resources and agricultural products. Copra, coffee, rubber, natural insecticide, and cocoa are the main export crops. Although natural gas has been discovered, production is not yet developed. Copper exports from Bougainville mines had given PNG a favorable trade balance, but a sharp drop in the world price for copper has reduced earnings greatly. A new and expensive mine for gold and copper was developed in the highlands close to the Indonesia border, and PNG is trying to increase production to make up for the reduced price. New products being developed include timber, tea, and sugar. PNG is also trying to become self-sufficient in food. Food imports have been rising even though almost 88% of the population still lives a subsistence lifestyle. Tourism has been increasing slowly, and there is a large diversity

Picking coffee — one of Papua New Guinea's many export crops. (PNG Government Office of Information photo)

of things for visitors to see. In spite of its economic potential and increased development, PNG still needs aid from Australia to cover its government budget.

4. Political Status

After World War II Papua New Guinea became a U.N. Trust Territory administered by Australia. It became fully independent in 1975. It is a member of the Commonwealth of Nations. The people elect a parliament which then chooses a prime minister.

5. Major Problems

PNG is not without problems. The main ones are economic. Developing raw materials like natural gas and copper is hard without capital and modern technical assistance. Most of the capital investment to develop PNG's raw materials comes from Australia.

As a result, Australians control much of the economy. Fear of too much foreign control has actually slowed development which in turn has led to severe unemployment problems. Falling copper prices have also hurt, which along with the reduction of Australian aid has caused a budget deficit for the PNG government, necessitating cutbacks in services.

Unity is also a major problem. With more than 700 tribes and languages, many of them traditional enemies, it is hard to get cooperation and a sense of nationhood. Tribal fighting continues in the more remote areas. Such fighting is a traditional way of ending disputes. In recent times land problems, elections, bar fights, stealing, and sexual affronts seem to be causing more disputes than ever. In one incident a tribal fight erupted in the streets of a provincial capital.

Urban drift is another problem. Thousands head for the towns and cities to get jobs. They leave their extended families and villages, and the culture begins to break apart. In the cities the people lack both the economic support and social control that the extended families provide. Unemployment, street crime, and general loss of purpose are growing city problems. Crime in Port Moresby has

Papua New Guinea has more than 700 different tribes, each with its own colorful dress — (top) Wigmen of the Tari Basin; (center) Dancers from the Western Highlands; (lower left) Mekeo dancers from Central Province; (lower right) dancers from the Marshall Lagoon area. (PNG Government Office of Information photos)

(left) Biami villager fishing with bow and arrow; (above) the Asaro Valley Mudmen. (PNG Government Office of Information photo)

become especially bad. Gangs of young unemployed roam the city at night, stealing anything they can. A vicious gang rape prompted public demonstrations and forced the government to take stronger action. Police were increased, troops brought in from the highlands, gates put up on roads into the city, and a curfew was established. To make matters worse, corruption and white collar crime are also serious problems. Finally, people wanted by the police can hide in their home villages, where the villagers often refuse to hand them over.

There is also a secessionist movement on Bougainville. The people of that island feel they could afford independence if they could keep all the copper profits for themselves.

Papua New Guinea is one of the three Pacific island groups that has malaria. Major efforts are being done to control this mosquito-borne disease.

PNG is the only Pacific nation or territory with a land border, as the western half of New Guinea is the Indonesian territory of West Irian. In the 1980s, Indonesian development policy in West Irian began causing some serious problems. Malays from Java and other crowded Indonesian islands were resettled in Irian Jaya, taking land that traditionally belonged to West Irian tribes. These tribes are eth-

nically Papuan, and, especially near the border, are related to tribes in PNG. Reports out of West Irian are sketchy, but the Papuans have been fleeing across the border into PNG, claiming atrocities by Indonesian troops. The Indonesian army is conducting a campaign against the OPM — a movement by indigenous Melanesians of West Irian to free their territory from Indonesian control. Indonesian pursuit of the rebels has been ruthless, and Indonesia claims the rebels are using camps on the PNG side of the border as bases for attacks into West Irian. Naturally sympathetic to the West Irians, the PNG government became angered at reports of a road built by Indonesia which apparently crosses the border at several points. There was also a fly-over of PNG airspace by Indonesian jets, and reports of Indonesian troops attacking refugee camps in PNG territory. However the border is located across extremely rugged terrain and is not well defined.

The main problem for PNG is what to do about all the refugees, which may number as many as 11,000. They are living a poor lifestyle in the crowded camps, but most do not want to return, fearing reprisals by Indonesia. Relations with Indonesia are severely strained. Some in PNG even fear an invasion of PNG by Indonesia, and are wondering if Australia would come to the rescue. Meanwhile the United Nations has agreed to help determine the status of the refugees. Indonesia, with a tight control of the press, has given very little information on the state of affairs in West Irian. It is possible that there are as many as 32,000 Indonesian troops in the territory, and perhaps as many as 200,000 West Irians have been displaced from their homes. In mid-1987, PNG and Indonesia did sign a friendship treaty in an effort to defuse some of the tension.

Papua New Guinea is a fascinating new country. Still primitive but becoming modern, it is potentially the richest and most powerful nation in the Pacific.

CHAPTER REVIEW

Vocabulary: payback, Port Moresby, urban drift, secession, Pidgin, cargo cults

Questions:

1. Why does PNG have such a unity problem?

2. Why is PNG potentially rich and powerful?

3. What is the problem PNG has in developing resources?

4. Why does PNG have a problem with Indonesia?

For Further Reading:

Carter, John (ed.). *PACIFIC ISLAND YEARBOOK*, 15th edition. Sydney: Pacific Publications, 1984.

Lea, DeAmity; and Irwin, Pub. *NEW GUINEA, THE TERRITORY AND ITS PEOPLE*. Melbourne: Oxford University Press, 1967.

Ryan, John. *THE HOT LAND*. Melbourne: McMillan, 1970.

Stanley, David; and Dalton, Bill. *SOUTH PACIFIC HANDBOOK*. Chico, California: Moon Publications, 1982.

THIS IS PAPUA NEW GUINEA. Port Moresby: Papua New Guinea Government Office of Information, 1980.

Chapter 20:
The Solomon Islands

1. Geography

Located east of PNG, the Solomon Islands are a double chain of six large continental islands and many smaller ones. The land area is 11,500 square miles (29,900 km²). The climate is tropical, the islands are rugged and heavily wooded, and rainfall is about 100 inches (250 cm) per year.

2. People and Culture

The Solomons have an interesting history. They were visited early by the European explorer Mendana. There was much bloodshed between Mendana's Spanish and the islanders. After Mendana left, no Europeans could find the islands again. Navigation was poor in those days. Many different explorers tried to find them, though. Since Mendana had found some gold, the rumor had developed that these islands were so incredibly wealthy that they must have been the source for the vast wealth of King Solomon of Israel — the king in the Bible. Thus the name Solomon Islands, even though King Solomon never got close to the islands.

It wasn't until 200 years after Mendana that Europeans found the islands again. Missionaries made some attempts to convert the islanders in the mid 1800s, but many were killed. There was very little missionary success until the early twentieth century. Britain took the islands over as a protectorate in the 1880s, partially to stop the abuses of blackbirding. The labor trade had been heavy in the Solomons, with many islanders going to Australia and Fiji. Though most had gone voluntarily and were eventually returned, some had been kidnapped and many died before ever seeing home again. Others remained where they had been sent, and their descendants still live in Fiji. The British government helped get many of the islanders returned. Also the British put an end to the war canoe raids by the more aggressive tribes, and tribal fighting was greatly controlled. Thus secure from surprise canoe raids, islanders began to move their villages to the shoreline where more food resources were available. In the early 1900s several European and Australian companies established large plantations in the islands.

In World War II the Solomons were the scene of heavy fighting. American troops wrested Guadalcanal from the Japanese after a bitter battle. There were many sea battles in "The Slot," the channel between the two rows of islands. Future American President John F. Kennedy was almost killed when a Japanese destroyer rammed his PT boat in "The Slot."

After World War II, a movement known as "Marching Rule" spread through many of the Solomons. This movement was basically anti-government, anti-church, and anti-European influence. It organized commune-like villages which had their own strict rulers, police, and courts. The movement was also part cargo cult, expecting deliveries of material wealth of the West. It lasted for six years, 1944-1950, and was eventually broken up by the British colonial government using armed police. Marching Rule villages had built forts and tried to keep government agents out. Many of its leaders spent time in jail.

Traditional leadership in the Solomons is not hereditary, but is based on the "big man" system. The man who can give the biggest feast with the most food becomes big man, or chief.

Solomon islanders are famous for their intricate traditional wood carving. There is also a unique system of money made from feathers. In some villages there are shark-worshipping cults with interesting rituals of shark calling and feeding.

There are 250,000 people in the Solomons, speaking 87 different local languages. English is the official language; Pidgin is widely used. Most of the people are Melanesians, but there are some Polynesians on outlying atolls. There are also some Europeans, some Chinese, and a small Gilbertese community. Most Solomon Islanders are Christian, but many continue ancestor worship as well.

There is very little economic development in the Solomons. Most of the people live village subsistence lifestyles. Honiara, the capital on Guadalcanal, is the only real town.

3. Economy and Resources

The Solomons do have some resources. Fish is the main export, followed by timber, copra, palm oil, rice, cocoa, and gold. There are deposits of bauxite (for aluminum) and phosphate, but these have not yet been mined. Development of the economy has been slow, but the balance of trade has remained roughly equal. This is due to the large level of subsistence living which so far has kept demands for imports rising at a manageable rate. Tourism in the islands is negligible, but stamp sales bring in about $1 million per year. Australians are involved heavily in the development activity that does exist, and much is financed by outside aid. Since the 1970s, the government has been buying back plantations previously owned by foreigners. To pay for its operations, the Solomon Islands government still needs aid grants from Britain.

4. Political Status

The Solomons are an independent country and a member of the Commonwealth of Nations. The people elect a national assembly which then chooses a prime minister. The Solomons became independent in 1978.

5. Major Problems

The Solomon Islands have become the malaria capital of the world, with the highest number of reported cases. This is a major problem, a deterrent to development, and a deterrent to tourism. Efforts have been increased to deal with the problem, usually by more spraying of DDT to kill the mosquitoes. However effective control still eludes health authorities.

Unity is another problem, as tribal rivalries still occasionally erupt into violence. On Malaita one tribe has tried to declare independence. They are traditional and non-Christian, and have clashed often with the Christian tribe that controls the Malaita local government.

Urban drift has created some serious problems in Honiara. Young men come to the town and live with relatives who have jobs. By custom, the relatives can't turn them away, and must feed and shelter them. The young men then spend their time hanging around, drinking, and fighting. They do not look for work, but there aren't many jobs available anyway. Not surprisingly, crime is on the rise in Honiara.

In June of 1984 the Solomon Islands government captured an American tuna boat fishing in its 200-mile zone. The boat owners refused to pay any fine, as the United States at that time maintained tuna was a migratory fish and not subject to the 200-mile zone limitations. The Solomon Islands impounded the boat and threatened to sell it. President Reagan then placed an embargo on all imports from the Solomons. The United States was the biggest customer for Solomon Islands fish, and the embargo meant a loss of $1 million. However the Solomons claimed they were able to sell their fish elsewhere. After lengthy negotiations, the boat owners paid S$770,000 plus a S$60,000 fine and the boat was released. The incident strained relations between the United States and the Solomon Islands government. However it was one of the developments that helped change the U.S. attitude toward paying for tuna licences. In the face of growing Soviet interest, the United States began to see good relations with the small Pacific nations as more important than a principle of fishing rights on the high seas. Also, the incident was embarrassing, making the United States look like a rich bully refusing to pay due compensation to a poor, small Pacific island nation.

In early 1986 the Solomon Islands were struck by Typhoon Namu, the worst in over a century. Entire shoreline villages, built on man-made islands on the reef, were washed away. Mud slides buried other villages. The total death toll may never be known. Almost every home in the islands was either completely destroyed or severely damaged. Crops were practically wiped out. Recovery will be difficult and take quite a while.

Government shipyard at Tulagi. Before World War II Tulagi was the capital. After the war, the British colonial administration moved into the buildings left behind by the Americans at their base at Honiara, Guadalcanal, which became the capital. (Photo by Jimmy Cornell.)

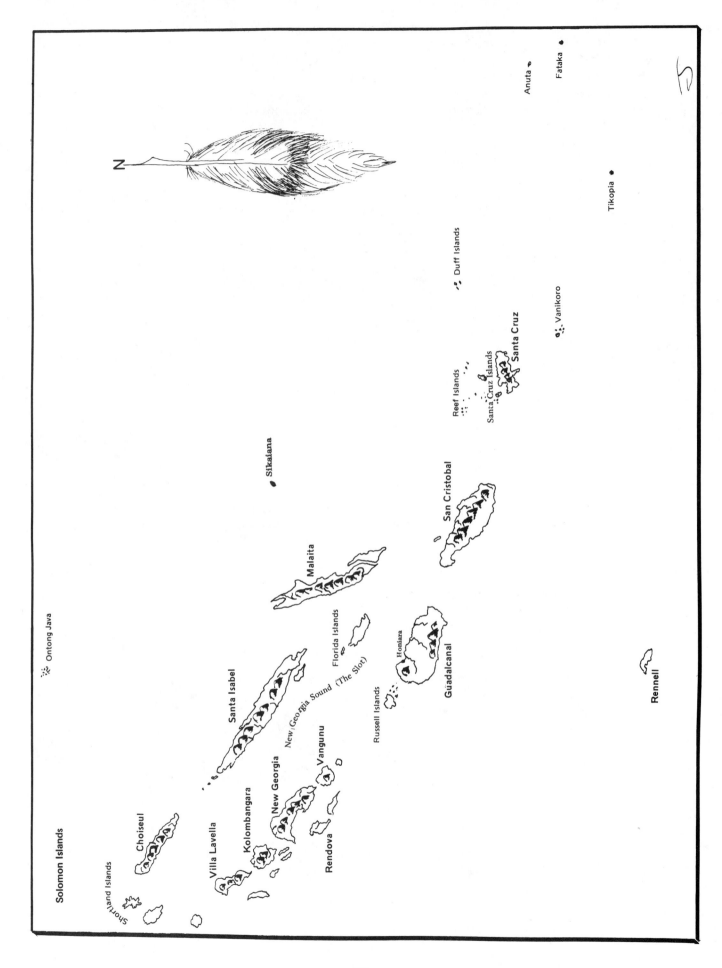

Solomon Islands

Shortland Islands
Choiseul
Ontong Java
Santa Isabel
Villa Lavella
Kolombangara
New Georgia
Vangunu
Rendova
New Georgia Sound (The Slot)
Florida Islands
Russell Islands
Honiara
Guadalcanal
Malaita
Sikaiana
San Cristobal
Reef Islands
Santa Cruz Islands
Santa Cruz
Duff Islands
Vanikoro
Tikopia
Anuta
Fataka
Rennell

N

108

The arrival of the monthly supply ship, the **Compass Rose**, *at Ughele, Rendova. (Photo by Jimmy Cornell.)*

CHAPTER REVIEW

Vocabulary: The Slot, Guadalcanal, Honiara, Marching Rule, big man

Questions:

1. What is the lifestyle like for most Solomon Islanders?

2. What was the Solomon Islanders' attitude towards Europeans and change?

3. What happened in the Solomons during World War II?

4. What was the Marching Rule movement?

5. Why did the Solomon Islands have a conflict with the United States?

For Further Reading:

Carter, John (ed.). *PACIFIC ISLANDS YEAR BOOK.* Sydney: Pacific Publications, 1984.

Kent, Janet. *THE SOLOMON ISLANDS.* Harrisburg, Pa.: Stockpile Books, 1972.

SOLOMON ISLANDS HAND BOOK. Honiara: Solomon Islands Information Service.

Stanley, David; and Dalton, Bill. *SOUTH PACIFIC HANDBOOK.* Chico, California: Moon Publications, 1982.

Chapter 21: Vanuatu

1. Geography

Vanuatu, known formerly as the New Hebrides, is located east of Australia and south of the Solomons. The main islands are large enough to be classified continental, with many more being volcanic and atolls. There are about 80 islands in all, 60 inhabited. The total land area is 4600 square miles (11,880 km²). Rainfall is plentiful and the islands have lush tropical vegetation. There are active volcanoes in Vanuatu, including some that are underwater. The islands are mountainous with peaks up to 5900 feet (1800 m).

2. People and Culture

Vanuatu has the historical distinction of being the only Pacific island area to have two colonial rulers — at the same time. Both Britain and France shared colonial administration of the islands in what was called a condominium. Each duplicated the other. There were two court systems, police forces, school systems, administrations, etc. The dual system is blamed for much confusion and little accomplishment during its existence.

Earlier in their history, the people of Vanuatu, like the Solomons, had little positive contact with whites. Sandalwood was discovered, and the sandalwood traders clashed often with the islanders. Many islanders died in the forests cutting sandalwood for their chiefs. Blackbirders also raided the islands heavily, sharply reducing their population. Western diseases, such as measles, reduced it even more. Missionaries were not readily accepted. Many, blamed for the various troubles caused by whites, were killed.

World War II affected the islands greatly. Espirito Santo was a big American base. The islanders saw all kinds of planes and ships bringing in tons of food, vehicles, appliances, and other supplies. After the war the islanders developed the cargo cults. These are local native religions such as the John Frum Movement. These are serious religions and their followers believe that one day John Frum will come to Vanuatu bringing planeloads of goods just for the islanders. At times they have almost turned violent, but usually they are just uncooperative. They blame the whites, the missionaries, and even the govern-

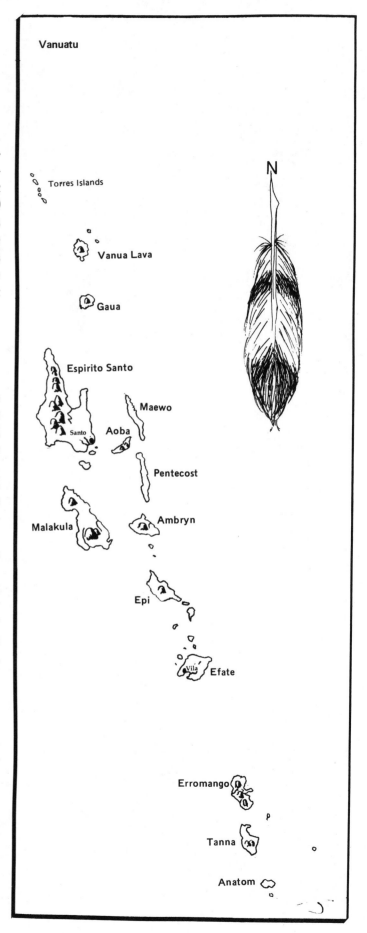

Vanuatu

Torres Islands

Vanua Lava

Gaua

Espirito Santo

Maewo

Santo   Aoba

Pentecost

Malakula   Ambryn

Epi

Vila   Efate

Erromango

Tanna

Anatom

ment for preventing islanders from getting all of the goods of the modern world.

The population of Vanuatu is 130,000. Most are Melanesians, but there are small minorities of Polynesians, Vietnamese, Chinese, and Europeans. Like Papua New Guinea, the many different tribes have unique attire and ritual dances. One world famous Vanuatu custom is land diving. Men jump head first off high platforms with vines tied to their feet. The vines are measured to stop them just short of the ground.

There are over 100 local languages, but the official languages are English, French, and Bislama, the Vanuatu form of Pidgin.

3. Economy and Resources

Vanuatu has been working hard to improve its balance of trade. In 1984 the balance was in surplus, but has since slipped back into a deficit. Main exports include copra, fish, beef, coffee, cocoa, and timber. Favorable tax laws have made Vanuatu a banking and finance center, attracting many financial institutions.

There was a tourist boom in the mid 80s, aided by hotel and airport expansions and visits by cruise ships. Totals are less than 100,000 per year though, and have dropped recently. The main tourist market for Vanuatu is Australia. Over 80% of the people still live mostly from subsistence farming and fishing, and this keeps imports down.

Vila, on the island of Efate, is the only real developed town, although there is a small European-style town on the largest island of Espirito Santo. Most of the rest of Vanuatu consists of villages or plantations. Reducing foreign control of the economy is a major goal of the government. Upon independence, all land owned by foreigners was returned to the original Vanuatu owners. Most of these plantations and ranches were then leased back to the French, British, or Australians who had owned them. Although the government reported a budget surplus in 1984, Vanuatu still relies on aid grants from France, Britain, Australia, New Zealand, Canada, and Japan to cover both government operations and economic development projects. Recently Vanuatu signed a fishing treaty with the Soviet Union. The treaty allows port visits but no shore facilities. It means an additional source of cash for the government.

Main Street, Vila, Vanuatu's capital. (Photo courtesy Vanuatu Visitor's Bureau)

Fresh produce market, Vanuatu. (Photo by Mack Nowack, courtesy Vanuatu Visitors Bureau)

Big Nambas tribesman of Malekula standing on ceremonial grounds. (Photo courtesy Vanuatu Visitors Bureau)

4. Political Status

Vanuatu is an independent country. The independence has not come easily. The unique condominium situation of the country led to much political factionalism, often along lines of those who preferred French and those who preferred English. In the late seventies there were boycotted elections and other problems related to the political divisions in the islands. Upon independence in 1980, groups on both Tanna and Espirito Santo were dissatisfied with the election results. They claimed voting irregularities, and the group on Espirito Santo seized control of the island and tried to secede from Vanuatu. The Vanuatu government requested help from Papua New Guinea. Troops from PNG were sent to Santo, and the rebellion was crushed. The leader of the separatist movement was jailed, and PNG troops occupied the island for several months.

The people elect a parliament which chooses a prime minister. An elected President is the Head of State.

5. Major Problems

Vanuatu faces serious economic problems: improving the balance of trade, improving development, and reducing foreign control of the economy. It is also infected by the malaria mosquitoes.

The government has been able to overcome most of the problems related to the rebellion on Espirito Santo. There has been no more trouble from dissident elements. National unity, a natural problem with so many tribes, seems to be improving. Still of concern are relations with France. The Vanuatu government had blamed France for encouraging the rebellion's leaders, and Vanuatu continues to be critical of France's policy towards its Pacific territories, especially New Caledonia. In late 1987, Vanuatu expelled its French ambassador for statements he had made in the press.

Vanuatu has received much criticism lately for making friendly relations with the African country of Libya. Libya has a bad reputation among many of the countries of the world, who blame it for sponsoring much terrorism. The United States, Australia, and France are especially concerned, and fear Libya is helping Vanuatu support violent dissident groups in New Caledonia and Irian Jaya. These countries also are not happy with Vanuatu's dealings with the Soviets.

In February, 1987, Vanuatu was struck by a bad typhoon. Winds of over 100 miles per hour buffetted the main island of Efate. Many homes were destroyed, and about 30 people killed.

CHAPTER REVIEW:

Vocabulary: Espirito Santo, cargo cults, John Frum Movement, Efate, condominium, land diving, Vila

Questions:

1. Explain how the condominium government worked.

2. What caused the rebellion on Espirito Santo and what happened?

3. What are Vanuatu's relationships with the Soviet Union and Libya?

For Further Reading:

Beasant, John. *THE SANTO REBELLION*. Honolulu, Hawaii: University of Hawaii Press, 1984.

Carter, John (ed.). *PACIFIC ISLANDS YEAR BOOK*, 15th edition. Sydney: Pacific Publications, 1984.

Lini, Walter. *BEYOND PANDEMONIUM; FROM THE NEW HEBRIDES TO VANUATU*. Wellington, New Zealand: Asia Pacific Books, 1980.

Stanley, David; and Dalton, Bill. *SOUTH PACIFIC HANDBOOK*. Chico, California: Moon Publications, 1982.

Chapter 22: New Caledonia

1. Geography

New Caledonia is located east of Australia. It has one main continental island and several smaller volcanic islands and atolls. The main island is cigar shaped, 300 miles (480 km) long by 30 miles (48 km) wide. The total area of the group is 7370 square miles (19,903 km²). New Caledonia is just inside the tropics and has a slightly cooler climate than other areas in Melanesia. The main island has a mountain range down the middle and numerous rivers that run to either coast. The east coast is heavily forested, the west is a drier plain used mostly for cattle.

2. People and Culture

Like other Melanesian islands, New Caledonia resisted European intrusion. First visited by Cook, the islands were taken over by France. The French made a penal colony out of the main island, sending numerous unwanted prisoners there. Many of their descendants still live in New Caledonia. A few hardy European settlers moved to the island. Many were killed and sometimes eaten by the islanders. There were many uprisings against the whites and much bloodshed on both sides. The last major uprising was in 1917.

There are about 150,000 people in New Caledonia. Of these only 45% are indigenous Melanesians. The rest are French, Polynesians, and Asians. The Melanesians refer to themselves as Kanaks, and they speak about thirty different local languages. Almost all the French, Polynesians, and Asians live in or near Noumea. There are are almost no mixed marriages between the French and the Melanesians.

Noumea is a modern city, but most Melanesians still live in relatively isolated rural villages. The French live in the city. In the villages the lifestyle is subsistence farming and fishing.

3. Economy and Resources.

New Caledonia has the strongest economy in Melanesia. It is loaded with deposits of nickel, and is one of the world's leading nickel producers. Noumea, the capital city, is advanced and developed. The cost of living in the city is high, but so are the wages. There are many jobs available, which attract many

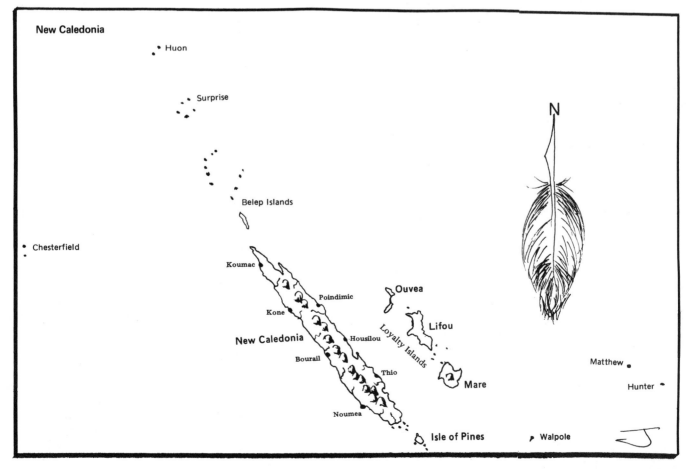

Downtown Noumea, capital of New Caledonia. (Photo courtesy Pacific Daily News)

French and Polynesians from French territories to move to New Caledonia. Demand for nickel has dropped considerably in recent years, however, lowering the price and reducing export earnings. Thus the economy of New Caledonia is not as comfortable as it once was, and the balance of trade is actually negative.

New Caledonia has good agriculture which provides most local food needs. Coffee and copra are exported. Tourism is also big business, as many visit the island each year. The importance of tourism has grown recently as a way to help make up for the decline in the nickel industry. However recent violence in the territory has hurt the tourist business. Except for the nickel mines and a few ranches, all the industry, development, and modern lifestyle is located in or near Noumea. A few French families control most of the businesses and the government.

4. Political Status

New Caledonia is an Overseas Territory of France. The people are French citizens. They may vote in French presidential elections, and they elect a voting representative to the French parliament in Paris, France. Their local government is controlled by France. A High Commissioner is appointed by the government in Paris. The local legislature traditionally has had very little power.

People from New Caledonia may move to France or any French territory, and other French citizens from France or other French territories may move to New Caledonia.

5. Major Problems

New Caledonia has very serious problems with racial equality and harmony. The Melanesians feel they are being exploited. They are not being paid any money for the nickel that is mined from what were their tribal lands. There are very few Melanesians in high government or business positions. The modern, developed lifestyle of Noumea benefits mostly the French. The French control the economy and much of the voting for representatives to Paris. The Melane-

Savannah-like plains of New Caledonia's west coast, perfect for cattle raising. By contrast, the east coast is steeper and more lush. (Photos courtesy New Caledonia Government Office of Tourism)

sians are now outnumbered by outsiders.

All this has led to an independence movement. There have been some violent demonstrations, and an independence leader has been assassinated. The French claim they are helping the Melanesians by building a stable economy and improving education and health in the villages. Many Melanesians feel this is only token development — and is too little too late. They see little Nauru as an example of what islanders can do if allowed to control their own lands and resources. France does not want to let New Caledonia go. They consider it as much a part of France as the Riviera. The French living in New Caledonia also want to stay part of France.

There has been much violence, confusion, and political turmoil in the last few years. Elections have been boycotted by the Kanaks, who want voting limited to those people who have at least one parent born in New Caledonia. This would eliminate many of the French voters and most of the Polynesians and Asians. There have been shootings and bombings, at least 20 deaths, and France has about 7000 soldiers stationed in the territory. The Kanak independence groups have declared a provisional independent government. France has tried to come up with several plans to settle the situation. The territory was recently divided into four regions, each region with its own council. The Kanaks won control in three of the regions, the French in the fourth of Noumea. A status referendum was held in September, 1987, with the choices being either continuing as a French Territory or total independence. The Kanaks organized a boycott of the voting, angry

Traditional conical-shaped hut of Melanesian villages in New Caledonia. (Photo courtesy New Caledonia Government Office of Tourism)

because there was no choice of a semi-independent status such as free association as had been promised earlier by France. Despite the boycott, some 59% of eligible voters (French citizens with at least three years residence in New Caledonia) voted, choosing continued control by France by an overwhelming 98%. This does not at all satisfy the Kanaks, and the situation is far from settled. Meanwhile the United Nations has added New Caledonia to its list of colonies that do not have self-determination. The likelihood for more violence in the territory remains high.

CHAPTER REVIEW

Vocabulary: penal colony, Noumea, nickel

Questions:

1. Why do so many French and Polynesians from French territories move to New Caledonia?

2. What does it mean to be an Overseas Territory of France?

3. What is the conflict between the Melanesian Kanaks and the French?

For Further Reading:

Carter, John (ed.). *PACIFIC ISLANDS YEAR BOOK*, 15th edition. Sydney: Pacific Publications, 1984.

Stanley, David; and Dalton, Bill. *SOUTH PACIFIC HANDBOOK*. Chico, California: Moon Publications, 1982.

Chapter 23: Fiji

1. Geography

Fiji is located in the south central Pacific — straddling where the International Date Line is supposed to pass. In fact, the date line was zigzagged to the east partially as a convenience for Fiji, so that all of the islands of the group would be operating on the same day. Fiji consists of more than 300 islands. They range from small coral atolls to larger volcanic islands to the two large main islands of the group, Viti Levu and Vanua Levu. These two are continental, with Viti Levu being just about the same size as the Big Island of Hawaii. The total land area of the group is about 7000 square miles (18,272 km²). About 100 of the islands are permanently inhabited.

The larger islands are mountainous, with peaks up to over 4000 feet (1200 m). There is plenty of rainfall and many rivers on the larger islands. Due to the prevailing winds only the eastern sides of the islands are heavily forested. The mountains block the rain-bearing winds and keep the western sides drier and less wooded.

2. People and Culture

Fiji was a meeting place and melting pot of many different peoples from Melanesia and Polynesia. The Fijians are considered Melanesian, but most of their historical contact was with the Polynesian groups of Tonga and Samoa.

The Europeans quickly labeled the Fijians as savage cannibals. It was not a healthy place for ship-wrecked sailors. But eventually a beachcomber community began to develop, many being deserters from whalers. Some of them were quite vicious themselves, meddling in local wars, killing and raping almost at will. Sandalwood was discovered, and in a few years was all cleaned out. Then the Europeans came to trade for sea slug, which was in great abundance on Fijian reefs. Missionaries came too, but had little success until the late 1800s.

In the 1850s one of the Fijian chiefs, Cakobau (Thakombau), had become quite powerful. He began to claim the title of chief of all Fiji, though there still were several other powerful chiefs not under his control. Deep in debt to some American traders, Cakobau offered to cede (give) Fiji to Britain if the British government would cover his debts. Britain refused at first, but many British began settling in Fiji.

Busy side street and canal in Suva, Fiji. (Photo by Phyllis Koontz)

They developed plantations of first cotton, then sugar. Cakobau made an effort at establishing some kind of centralized authority over the islands, but rivalries among the chiefs made his government ineffective. This disturbed the growing European community, who preferred the stability of a strong government. The local British residents began encouraging Britain to take over the islands. Concerned about possible French and American interests in Fiji, Britain finally agreed with the British settlers. In 1874 a treaty was drawn up giving Fiji to Britain as a colony. It was signed by Cakobau and all the other important chiefs, and Britain began administering the islands.

Fiji had been one of the destinations for black-bird labor. Britain stopped the importation and thus helped to put an end to much of the blackbirding in the Pacific. To replace that supply of labor, Britain began to bring in workers from India.

There are 700,000 people in Fiji. Of these, only 45% are Fijian. Half the population is Indian. The remaining 5% is divided among Europeans, other Pacific islanders, and Chinese. The island of Rotuma is Polynesian, and the island of Rabi is populated by Micronesians from Banaba, Kiribati.

The Fijians have an interesting custom of fire-walking. Several dancers walk barefoot over white-hot coals without getting burned. They also drink yaqona (kava), the mouth-numbing drink, but theirs is a weaker solution than that drunk on Pohnpei. The main cities of Suva and Lautoka, on Viti Levu, are modern and developed. Most of the rest of Fiji is rural plantation, small farms, and small villages. Many people grow cash crops for market, but there is also much subsistence farming and fishing. Away from the cities, the Indians tend to live on individual farms. The Fijians prefer living in villages as they have for centuries.

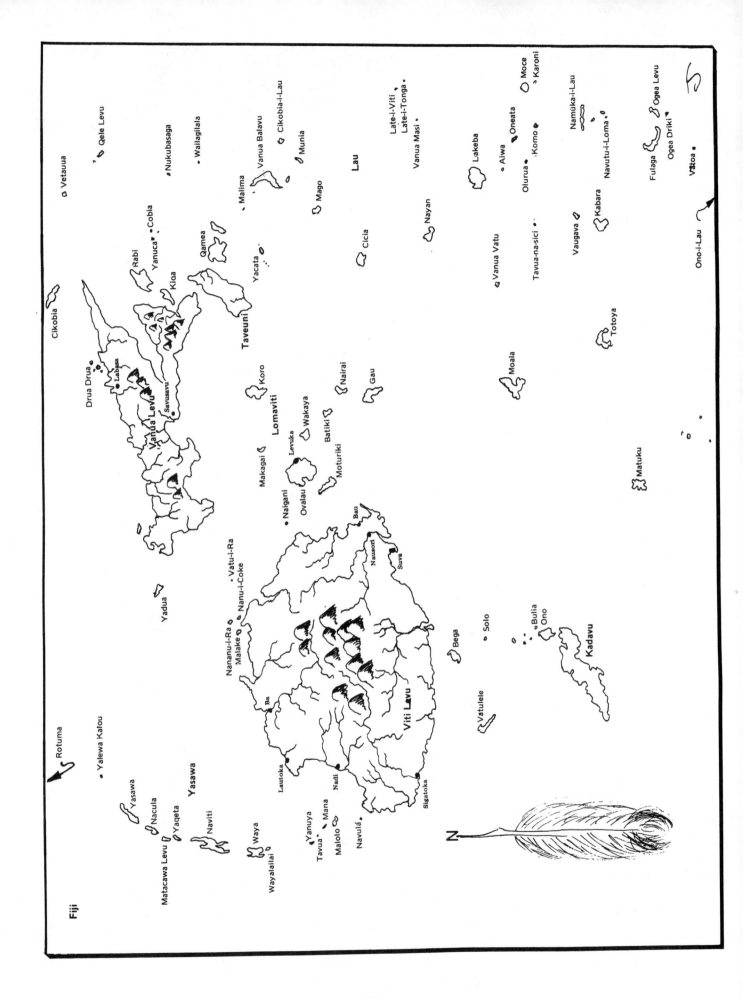

Fiji

Rotuma

Yasawa

Yalewa Kalou

Yasawa
Matacawa Levu
Nacula
Yaqeta
Naviti

Waya
Wayalailai
Yanuya
Tavua
Mana
Malolo
Navula

Cikobia

Drua Drua
Labasa
Vanua Levu
Savusavu

Rabi
Yanuca
Cobia
Kioa

Qamea
Taveuni

Yacata

Yadua

Nananu-i-Ra
Malake
Vatu-i-Ra
Nanu-i-Coke

Ba
Lautoka
Nadi

Sigatoka

Makagai
Levuka
Ovalau
Naigani
Koro
Lomaiviti
Wakaya
Batiki
Moturiki

Nairai
Gau

Bau
Nausori
Suva

Viti Levu

Bega

Vatulele

Vetauua

Qele Levu

Nukubasaga

Wailagilala

Malima

Cikobia-i-Lau
Munia
Mago
Vanua Balavu

Lau

Cicia

Nayan

Moala

Totoya

Matuku

Late-i-Viti
Late-i-Tonga
Vanua Masi

Lakeba

Vanua Vatu
Tavua-na-sici

Vaugava

Moce
Karoni

Oneata
Olurua
Komo
Aiwa

Namuka-i-Lau

Navutu-i-Loma

Kabara

Fulaga
Ogea Levu
Ogea Driki
Vatoa

Ono-i-Lau

Solo
Bulia
Ono

Kadavu

N

Fijian women weaving mats at the Fiji Cultural Center. (Photo by Phyllis Koontz)

Fijian policemen in Suva. (Photo courtesy Institute for Polynesian Studies)

3. Economy and Resources

Fiji has a very active economy based on agriculture and tourism. Sugar is the main export crop. Molasses, coconut oil, ginger, timber, and fish are also exported. Gold is mined and is Fiji's second best export earner. Exploration is currently going on for oil and other minerals. Imports, however, are still much greater than exports. World sugar prices have dropped, and this hurts the economy. However there has been a reduction lately in food imports. Also Fiji has built an expensive hydroelectric power generating dam on Viti Levu. It is to supply all of the power needs for the island, and will greatly reduce the need for fuel imports. Tourism is increasing and helps make up for some of the trade deficit. Visitors to Fiji now number over 200,000 per year. Indians, Europeans, and Chinese control the economy. Fijians own most of the land, though much of it is leased to Indians. To help meet government spending, Fiji receives grants from Australia, New Zealand, and others.

Fiji is the home of the main campus of the University of the South Pacific. Many Pacific island governments contribute financial support and send students to the institution.

4. Political Status

Fiji became independent in 1970. It is a member of the Commonwealth of Nations. The people elect a house of representatives which chooses a prime minister. The House had 52 members, and by law 22 must be Fijian, 22 must be Indian, and the other eight general members. There are two major political parties in Fiji, the Alliance Party and the National Federation Party. Due to the events of 1987, in which the military seized control of the government, the whole design of the government may change.

An Indian riding a load of sugar cane.

A farm in the interior of Viti Levu, Fiji. (Photos by Bob Richards)

5. Major Problems

The same economic problems plague Fiji that plague most of the islands. Imports outnumber exports and resources are not fully developed.

In 1983, Hurricane Oscar struck Fiji, doing approximately $110 million in damage. It was the worst storm to hit Fiji in many years.

Just as big a problem is racial harmony. The Indians and the Fijians do not get along on several points. There is little mixing between the races. Recent efforts to desegregate the primary schools have met with opposition by both Indians and Fijians. The Indians feel discriminated against because the law prevents them from buying much land and they have little control of the government. Recently however, many Indians have been granted longer leases, thus easing their fear of eviction by Fijian landowners. The Fijians fear the Indians' economic control and population advantage.

All this came to a head in the elections in 1987. The Alliance Party, dominated by ethnic Fijians, had controlled Fiji's government since independence. The party had a pro-Western foreign policy, allowing visits by U.S., British, and Australian warships. A small group of ethnic Fijians leading the National Federation Party opposed this, and wanted Fiji to follow more of a non-aligned policy. They went to the ethnic Indians for support, promising the Indians to change the Fijian constitution to allow them to own more land. They won the subsequent election, and Fiji had its first government run by an Indian-dominated cabinet. But after one month the Fijian army, which consists mostly of ethnic Fijians, staged the Pacific's first ever coup d'etat. The new prime minister and his cabinet were arrested and the government replaced by Fijians. The move was supported by Fiji's traditional chiefs. The Indian population was outraged, and staged several demonstrations and strikes. The Fijian leadership was just unwilling to see the country taken over by the non-indigenous Indians. After a few months, compromises were worked out between the two parties, and a change in the constitution was planned. Just when a new coalition government was about to be formed, the military again took over the government. Colonel Rebuka, leader of the military, said he could not accept the compromise and wanted to make sure that Fijians would always control the government. He hinted at withdrawing from the Commonwealth and declaring a republic, totally scrapping the Fijian Constitution. The leaders of both parties and most judges have come out opposed to this, but as of October, 1987, Rebuka remained in control. The resulting instability has drastically hurt Fiji's economy, as Indians have closed up their shops and refused to cut sugar cane. Tourism has also dropped off considerably.

The reaction to this incident by the rest of the Pacific nations and territories was mixed. Most criticized the coup as un-democratic. However the "Melanesian Block" — PNG, the Solomons, and Vanuatu — supported the Fijian take-over. In the case of Vanuatu this was particularly ironic, for Vanuatu has the type of foreign policy that the newly elected Fijian government was preparing to follow. Apparently more important to Vanuatu is the concept that the Pacific islands should be under the control of native islanders. Australia has been very upset by the two coups, and after the latest one considered sending navy units to Fiji to protect the Australian lives and property there.

CHAPTER REVIEW

Vocabulary: Viti Levu, Suva, Lautoka, Vanua Levu, coup d'etat

Questions

1. How did Fiji become a British colony?

2. Why are there Indians in Fiji?

3. What are some of the problems between the Indians and Fijians?

4. What happened in the elections of 1987 and afterward?

For Further Reading:

Carter, John (ed.). *PACIFIC ISLANDS YEAR BOOK*, 15th edition. Sydney: Pacific Publications, 1984.

Stanley, David; and Dalton, Bill. *SOUTH PACIFIC HANDBOOK*. Chico, California: Moon Publications, 1982.

Scarr, Derek. *FIJI — A SHORT HISTORY*. Laie, Hawaii: Institute for Polynesian Studies, Brigham Young University, 1984.

Ravuvu, Asesola, *THE FIJIAN WAY OF LIFE*, Suva, Fiji: University of the South Pacific, 1984.

Veramo, Jo. *GROWING UP IN FIJI*. Suva, Fiji: University of the South Pacific, 1985.

UNIT SIX: POLYNESIA

The Polynesian Triangle is an area of the Pacific that lies inside an imaginary triangle. The three points of the triangle are Hawaii to the north, New Zealand to the southwest, and Easter Island to the southeast. This triangle is not completely accurate, for Polynesian Tuvalu and Norfolk are outside of it, and part of Melanesian Fiji lies within. The rest of the islands inside the triangle comprise Polynesia, which is mostly south of the equator and east of the date line. Since New Zealand is usually well covered in regular world geography texts, and since it is more a Pacific rim nation, it will not be covered in this text.

Polynesia has some interesting differences from Micronesia and Melanesia. The people are generally taller than Micronesians and lighter-skinned than Melanesians. One significant difference is the uniformity of language. Almost all Polynesians can understand each other. There are several languages, but even these are close enough to be mutually intelligible if spoken slowly. This is especially true if a Polynesian of one language spends time in another area. He quickly learns which letters to change, and then realizes the words are generally the same. *Aloha* in Hawaii is *Alofa* in Samoa. *Tahiti* in Tahitian is *Kahiki* in Hawaiian.

Otherwise, Polynesian islands tend to repeat the same story of other islands. The problems are economic and developmental, and changing lifestyles are breaking down traditional cultures.

POLYNESIAN LANGUAGE CHART

COMPARISON OF POLYNESIAN WORDS:

English:	love	taro	bird	old	man	ancestor	fish	yes	canoe
N.Z. Maori:	aroha	taro	manu	tawhito	tane	tupuna	ika	ae	waka
Samoan:	alofa	talo	manu	matua	tane	tupu	i'a	ioe	va'a
Tahitian:	aroha	taro	manu	tahito	tane	tupuna	ia	ae	va'a
Hawaiian:	aloha	kalo	manu	kahiko	kane	kupuna	ia	ae	waa
Tongan:	aloofa	talo	manu	tefito	tangata	tubu	ika	io	vaka
Marquesan:	kaoha	kalo	manu	tehito	kane	tupuna	ika	ae	vaka

COMPARISON OF POLYNESIAN PHRASES:

English:	Hello	Thank you	How are you?	Goodbye
N.Z. Maori:	Kia ora	Whakapai	Pehea Koe?	Kia ora
Samoan:	Talofa	Fa'afetai	Faa pefea?	Tofa soifua
Hawaiian:	Aloha	Mahalo	Pehea 'oe	Aloha
Tahitian:	'Ia orana	Mauruuru roa	Maita'i anei oe?	Parahi
Tongan:	Malo e lelei	Malo	Fefe Hake?	'Alu a e

SOURCE: Micronesian Area Research Center, University of Guam.

Chapter 24: American Samoa

1. Geography

The two Samoas, Western and American, are located in the middle of the South Pacific. American Samoa is the eastern group, consisting of seven volcanic islands and atolls. The total area is 76 square miles (197 km²). The main island of Tutuila is about 52 square miles (135 km²). About 62 miles (100 km) due east of Tutuila are the three islands of the Manu'a group. Far to the east is the uninhabited Rose Atoll, and far to the north is another atoll, Swain's. The volcanic islands are steep and heavily wooded. Pago Pago Bay of Tutuila is considered the best sheltered deep-water harbor in the Pacific.

2. People and Culture

The Samoan islands were the scene of intense rivalry between Britain, the United States, and Germany in the late 1800s. All three wanted to control Samoa, mainly because of the good harbor at Pago Pago. Then the Samoans themselves began having wars among several chiefs, each wanting to be the supreme chief of Samoa. The outside powers became involved, each country backing a different chief's claim. After the typhoon described in Chapter Nine, Britain withdrew its claim, Germany obtained Western Samoa, and the United States took the eastern part, now known as American Samoa.

Traditionally Tutuila had been an island of refuge for Samoan chiefs in exile from the main Samoan islands of Savaii and Upolu, now Western Samoa. As such, the island was out of the mainstream of Samoan politics. The Manu'a islands were independent unto themselves and had their own high chief. Swain's Island was populated by people more associated with the Tokelau group, but had been acquired by an American citizen. Rose was uninhabited. After the decision between the United States and Germany, the United States was able to get the chiefs of Tutuila, and eventually Manu'a, to sign treaties of cession, giving the islands to the United States.

American naval governors began administering the islands in 1900. Very little was done, however, until the appointment of a civilian governor, H. Rex Lee, in 1961. Lee embarked Samoa on an intensified program of modernization and development. At the same time, a new constitution for the islands proclaimed the importance of protecting Samoan culture. A huge government bureaucracy was created, and the drive toward development began to stagnate.

There are 37,000 Polynesians in American Samoa. The Fa'a Samoa, Samoan way of life, is still consid-

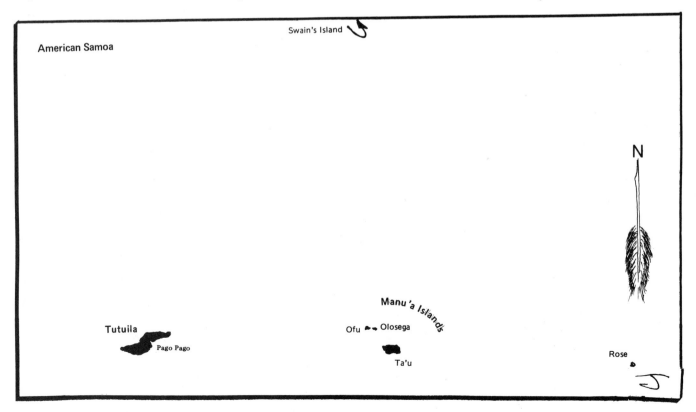

American Samoa

Swain's Island

N

Manu'a Islands

Tutuila   Ofu ▸◂ Olosega

Pago Pago   Ta'u   Rose

ered very important. Under this system, the extended family chiefs, or Matai, control all the land of the family. They decide who lives where, and who farms which piece of land.

The capital and main town area along the Pago Pago shoreline are modern with all the amenities of a small city. Most of the jobs are here, and Samoans from the Tutuila villages commute to work on an efficient bus system.

In the villages, the Fa'a Samoa and church services are still the focus of life. Ritualistic kava drinking ceremonies are an important part of local custom, as are council meetings and long speeches. There also is still some subsistence farming and fishing. However money is becoming more important and many seek salaried jobs. More and more homes are being built with modern materials and supplied with electricity. Many Samoans have refrigerators and TV sets with video recorders, even in the villages.

3. Economy and Resources

Measured by balance of trade, American Samoa has a prosperous economy. There are tuna canneries in Pago Pago, and a fleet of tuna fishing boats. These provide many jobs, though most of the cannery workers are from Western Samoa and most of the sailors are Korean. Tuna exports give American Samoa a favorable balance of trade.

Measured by whether the economy can support the current lifestyle, it is not prosperous. Most American Samoans have government jobs or work in stores and service industries that survive because of the government payrolls spent in them. Less than half of the yearly government budget is raised from local sources; the rest is supplied by grants from the United States. Without the grants supporting the local government, the current expensive lifestyle would collapse.

4. Political Status

American Samoa is an unincorporated Territory of the United States. The people are U.S. nationals, not citizens. They may enter the United States freely to live and work but they may not vote in U.S. elections unless they obtain full citizenship. The American Samoa government has a two-house legislature. One is elected by popular vote, the other by the Matai who are chosen by their families. For years the people did not want to elect their own governor, fearing that one family would gain too much power. Finally

in 1978, they began electing a governor by popular vote. Previous governors were appointed by the United States.

The current political status has been seen by most American Samoans as quite good. They have many advantages of association with the United States, but maintain almost complete control over their own islands. There seem to be no movements toward any status change.

5. Major Problems

The rapid development of American Samoa in the 1960s has led to many problems. The old and valued social system is breaking down. Crime and juvenile delinquency are now major problems, especially in Tutuila. The old people see the culture dying, the young see the new way as better opportunity. Many move to Hawaii or the mainland U.S. searching for salaried jobs and education. There are some 20,000 American Samoans in Hawaii, and another 65,000 in the U.S. mainland. Once away from Samoa, young Samoans are free from the tight control of the Matai. Unfortunately, they are not used to this lack of control, and many end up getting into various kinds of trouble. Meanwhile other islanders, especially from Western Samoa, move into Pago Pago for the jobs that are available.

Recently American Samoa was concerned because the United States sought to extend the U.S. minimum wage law to the territory. The adoption of the $3.35 per hour standard threatened to chase the tuna canneries away since they would not be able to compete due to the increased labor cost. The United States relented, the law was not applied to American Samoa, and the canneries stayed.

The economy, though strong, is not strong enough to support the government. There is much

Pago Pago Bay and Harbor — at one time desired by the United States, Germany, and Britain. (Photo by Bob Richards)

dependency on the United States. The future status is unclear, but the islands will probably remain tied to the United States for a long time.

In January of 1987 a typhoon struck the Manu'a group, destroying over 90% of the homes on the island of Tau.

Like the cultures of many islands, the Fa'a Samoa is under great pressure as American Samoa tries to find a way to fit comfortably into the 20th century.

Downtown Pago Pago. The buses are called Aiga (family) buses. Cranes for the harbor are visible behind the buildings. (Photo by Phyllis Koontz)

Meeting fale of a village outside Pago Pago on Tutuila. (Photo by Phyllis Koontz)

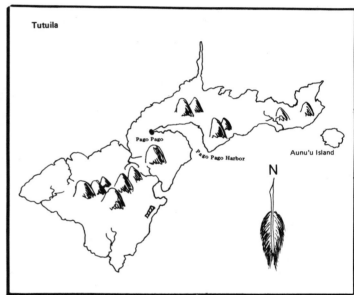

CHAPTER REVIEW

Vocabulary: Tutuila, Pago Pago, Fa'a Samoa, Manu'a, Matai System

Questions:

1. How did American Samoa end up in the control of the United States?

2. How does the Matai System work?

3. What is Samoa's relationship with the United States? What is the status of American Samoans?

4. Why is the American Samoan economy strong but not strong enough?

For Further Reading:

AMERICAN SAMOAN ANNUAL REPORT TO THE SECRETARY OF THE DEPARTMENT OF INTERIOR. Pago Pago: Office of Samoan Information, 1981.

Carter, John (ed.). *PACIFIC ISLAND YEAR BOOK*, 15th edition. Sydney: Pacific Publications, 1984.

Chirstensen, Chris. *AMERICAN SAMOA IN THE SOUTH SEAS*. Honolulu: R. Bloom Co., 1973.

Stanley, David; and Dalton, Bill. *SOUTH PACIFIC HANDBOOK*. Chico, California: Moon Publications, 1982.

Chapter 25: Western Samoa

1. Geography

Western Samoa is located in the middle of the South Pacific just west of American Samoa. There are a total of nine volcanic islands with a combined area of 1133 square miles (2934 km²). Most of that area is on the two main islands of Savaii and Upolu. These islands have steep volcanic peaks in the center and plains along the coast. The rainfall is plentiful and there are many rivers and waterfalls. The soil is fertile and the islands are heavily wooded, especially in the less populated mountain areas.

2. People and Culture

The Samoan system of titles of nobility is very complicated, but occasionally one chief, through alliances and wars, can acquire the title of Tupu-o-Samoa, or king of all the islands. When the last king died in 1841, rivals for his title began a series of wars that lasted for years. These continual contests played into the hands of the growing European community. Samoans began selling more and more of their land to the Europeans and Americans to get money to finance their wars. Europeans always preferred to have one paramount island leader to deal with, and different European factions began supporting different chiefs. Ironically, the Tupo-o-Samoa was mostly a title of ceremony and prestige, and not one that could exercise political or administrative control over the villages. Eventually the white community began pressuring their different home countries to take charge and bring stability to Samoa. Britain, the United States, and Germany all became involved, and after the typhoon described in Chapter 9, Germany gained control.

The islands became a colony of Germany in 1899. The Samoans did not like the German administration of their islands. They began the Mau Movement, which basically sought independence for Samoa. The Germans were unsympathetic, and some Mau leaders were exiled to the Marianas.

After World War I control passed to New Zealand. New Zealand did not do a very good job at first. The New Zealand administrators looked down on the Samoan traditional leaders. They were insensitive and refused to consult the Samoans on any issues. This led to a continuation of the Mau

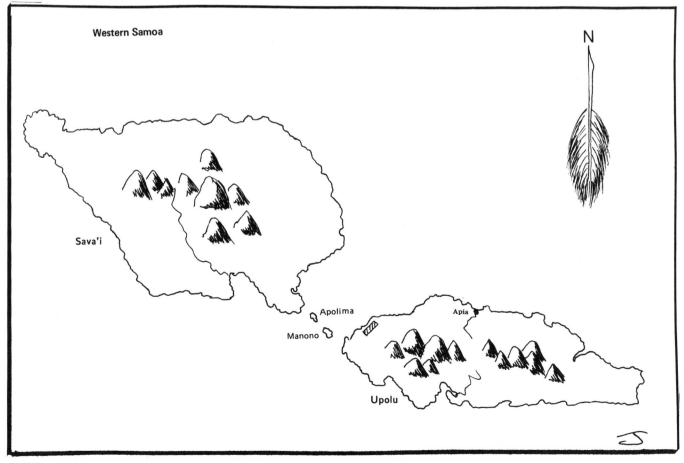

Western Samoa

N

Sava'i

Apolima

Manono

Apia

Upolu

Movement, in which the Samoans, aided by some Europeans, began to prerssure New Zealand for more self-government. Relations between the Mau leaders and New Zealand became worse and worse, and one demonstration ended when the police opened fire. Eleven people died. Things only began to improve after the New Zealand elections of 1936, when the Conservatives were replaced by the more sensitive Labour Party. Western Samoa became a UN Trust Territory after World War II, administered by New Zealand, which by then was preparing them for self-rule. In 1962, they became independent.

There are 165,000 people in Western Samoa. All are Polynesian and speak Samoan. The extended family system of control by the Matai is even stronger here than in American Samoa. The Matai control the land and the government. Development has been slow. Only Apia, the capital, is a city. The Matai want to preserve the Fa'a Samoa, but there is much pressure for change, especially from the young. Preserving the culture is actually government policy. The constitution of Western Samoa declares that the nation is based on the Fa'a Samoa and God. The people are about two-thirds Protestant and one-third Catholic.

Kava drinking and other ceremonies are very important to the Samoans. There are many different titles for different types of chiefs, some whose main job is to make long speeches. In the villages most people live in thatched, open-sided "fale." Privacy is maintained by the Samoan etiquette of never deliberately looking into an open fale. More and more houses, however, are being built with wood and tin.

Samoan youth in cloth lava lava standing in front of his fale. (Photo by Bob Richards)

3. Economy and Resources

Western Samoa's main exports are copra, cocoa, and bananas. Timber has recently been developed for export. There is some manufacturing of clothing and canning of fruit. Local farming and fishing help keep down imports, but they still greatly outnumber exports by about three to one. Some of the difference is made up by tourism, which currently is about 40,000 visitors per year and increasing. Money sent home by Western Samoans working abroad also helps. The rest is supplied by outside aid, mostly from New Zealand.

Outside Apia, most of the people live a village subsistence lifestyle. There is not much job opportunity in Western Samoa. Many who want jobs move into Apia, where growing numbers of unemployed have become a major problem. Others leave for New Zealand or American Samoa, though new restrictions on immigration by New Zealand are slowing down the migration there. Currently the government is trying to improve agricultural exports to reduce the trade deficit. There is also a planned airport expan-

Downtown Apia, Western Samoa. (Photo by Phyllis Koontz)

sion to enable bigger jets to land, thus bringing in larger numbers of tourists.

4. Political Status

Western Samoa is independent. It was the first Pacific colony to gain its independence from western powers. Its legislature is elected only by the Matai. The Matai are chosen by their families. There is a ceremonial high chief, known as Head of State, who is appointed by the Fono, or legislature. He appoints a new prime minister after reviewing a secret vote by a new legislature. The prime minister then becomes head of government.

In 1984, after an austerity program of budget cuts, the government announced a surplus of funds in the bank. By 1985, the government announced that foreign debts had been paid. However foreign aid was still very important and necessary to finance government operations and capital projects. The government was still in need of some $25 million per year from Australia and New Zealand.

Village in Western Samoa. (Photo by Bob Richards)

5. Major Problems

The main problems of Western Samoa are economic and cultural. The balance of trade needs to be improved, and unemployment is too high. This, together with the tight control of the Matai, has caused many young Samoans to leave. There are about 40,000 Samoans living in New Zealand, and many in American Samoa. This is a drain on Samoa's human resource. It is taking away many of the brightest and most ambitious people. These are people Samoa cannot afford to lose. They are the ones needed to help Samoa adapt to the 20th century.

In 1981 government workers went on strike for higher wages. The strike lasted quite a while, but eventually the strikers won. This was a hint that the tight, slow-development control by the Matai is beginning to crack at a grassroots level.

During the El Nino weather phenomena of 1983, Western Samoa experienced an extended dry season resulting in a series of bad forest fires. The fires were in inaccessible terrain and burned up much in valuable timber reserves.

Western Samoa is a perfect example of how the 20th century creates pressures on island cultures. The Samoans have been very successful in preserving their Fa'a Samoa. Yet that success has slowed down development and chased many young Samoans away. If they give in to the pressure for development, the traditional cultural controls will weaken and problems such as crime will increase. It is the dilemma of all islands. How can an island modernize and preserve the traditional culture at the same time? Western Samoa, as are most islands, is caught in the middle.

Throw net fishing in Western Samoa. (Photo by Bob Richards)

CHAPTER REVIEW

Vocabulary: Savaii, Upolu, Apia, Mau, fale, Fono

Questions:

1. What powers do the Matai have?

2. What does the constitution of Western Samoa say about culture and religion?

3. To what problems has the tight Matai control contributed?

4. Compare and contrast Western Samoa with American Samoa.

For Further Reading:

Carter, John (ed.). *PACIFIC ISLANDS YEARBOOK,* 15th edition. Sydney: Pacific Publications, 1984.

Foy, James W.; and Cumberland, Kenneth B. (eds.). *WESTERN SAMOA; LAND, LIFE, AND AGRICULTURE IN TROPICAL POLYNESIA.* Christchurch, N.Z.: Whitcombe & Tombs, 1962.

Lockwood, Brian. *SAMOAN VILLAGE ECONOMY.* New York: Oxford University Press, 1971.

Stanley, David; and Dalton, Bill. *SOUTH PACIFIC HANDBOOK.* Chico, California: Moon Publications, 1982.

Chapter 26: Tuvalu

1. Geography

Tuvalu is a chain of nine atolls and coral islands located south of the Gilberts. Only eight of the atolls are permanently inhabited. The land is all flat with tropical atoll vegetation. There are only ten square miles (26 km²) of dry land in the entire chain. Rainfall varies from season to season and year to year, but is fairly heavy — close to 100 inches (250 cm). The main atoll of Funafuti has slightly less than one square mile of land.

2. People and Culture

Tuvalu was known for many years as the Ellice Islands. Many white beachcombers and traders made Tuvalu their home, intermarrying with the locals. Missionaries were accepted, and the islanders all became Christian. Britain took the group first as a protectorate, then as a colony, including them with the Micronesian Gilberts. Tarawa, in the Gilberts (Kiribati), was developed as the center for the colony,

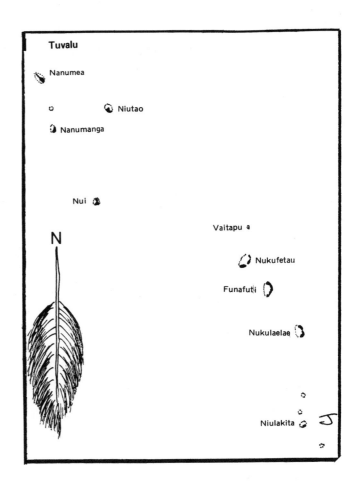

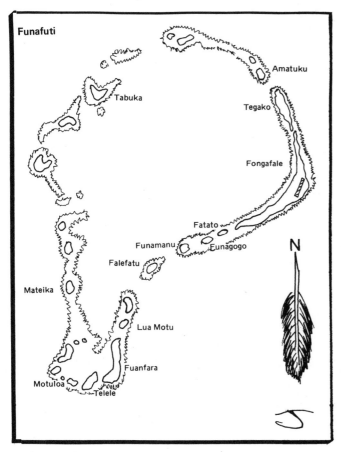

and many Tuvaluans went there for jobs. The two groups separated in 1975, and Tuvalu became independent in 1978.

The population is about 9000. Most of the people are Polynesian and speak Tuvaluan, a Polynesian language closely related to Samoan. The island of Nui is populated by Gilbertese-speaking people, who consider themselves a minority within Tuvalu. Jobs are scarce and exist mostly in Funafuti. On the other islands, most of the people live a village lifestyle. They depend on their own farming and fishing for most of their food. Funafuti is the only town area and has the only hotel.

3. Economy and Resources

Copra is the main cash and export crop. It nowhere near makes up for imports. Selling stamps to collectors brings in some money, as do salaries sent home by Tuvaluans working overseas, mostly on Nauru. Due to its out-of-the-way location and lack of air service, hotel facilities, and attractions, Tuvalu has not had much of a tourist industry. Britain provides much aid and quite a bit of money in development grants. Tuvalu also has a cash reserve which is invested.

The country was not happy when it did not receive any share of the profits from phosphate mining on Banaba, which became part of Kiribati. Many Tuvaluans worked there until the mines were closed. As part of the former Gilbert and Ellice Islands Colony, of which Banaba was a part, Tuvalu felt it should have received something. The British grants have helped replace that potential source of capital. There is a maritime training school in Tuvalu, and about 300 Tuvaluans are working on ships around the world. Japan gave Tuvalu a commercial fishing boat, and both South Korea and Taiwan pay for licenses to fish inside Tuvalu's 200-mile zone. Australia and New Zealand also provide aid for development projects.

4. Political Status

Tuvalu is an independent country and a member of the Commonwealth. The legislature has representatives elected by atoll. The heavily populated atolls get two representatives and the lightly populated get one each. The executive is a prime minister chosen by the legislature.

5. Major Problems

The main problems are economic. The economy depends quite a bit on Britain. The fishing potential must be developed more if the economy is to become viable. Related to that is unemployment, which forces many Tuvaluans to leave to seek jobs elsewhere. The breakdown of cultural controls due to the development that has taken place is similar to that of other islands.

CHAPTER REVIEW

Vocabulary: Funafuti, Ellice

Questions:

1. What are the islands like geographically?

2. Describe the economy. What keeps it going? What potential is there?

3. Why do you think Tuvalu separated from the Gilberts?

For Further Reading:

Carter, John (ed.). *PACIFIC ISLANDS YEARBOOK*, 15th edition. Sydney: Pacific Publications, 1984.

Stanley, David; and Dalton, Bill. *SOUTH PACIFIC HANDBOOK*. Chico, California: Moon Publications, 1982.

Tuvaluan man in canoe in Funafuti Lagoon. In the background is Fongafale — the capital and most developed island of Tuvalu. (Photo by Jimmy Cornell)

Chapter 27: Tokelau

1. Geography

Tokelau is located just north of Samoa. The group consists of only three small, flat, coral atolls. The total land area is about four square miles (10.4 km²). The islands have the typical limited atoll vegetation. Rainfall is relatively heavy. Each atoll has several reef islands circling a lagoon. The atolls are Atafu, Nukunono, and Fakaofo.

2. People and Culture

The Tokelau Atolls were heavily visited by blackbirders. They were one of the last groups of islands to become known to Europeans who did not really visit them until the 1840s. As an out-of-the-way, isolated group, they attracted many beachcombers and traders. The islands were not taken under any European power's protection or control until 1889. At that time, Britain claimed jurisdiction. Later they became part of Britain's Gilbert and Ellice Islands Colony. In 1925 their control was transferred to New Zealand, who administered them from their colony of Western Samoa.

There are only 1700 people on the three atolls. They are Polynesian, speaking Tokelauan, which is closely related to Samoan. Their traditional and cultural organizations are similar to those of Tuvalu. Due to the large number of European beachcombers who settled in Tokelau, many of the islanders are of part-European descent. Light skin and occidental features are not uncommon.

3. Economy and Resources

Tokelau's entire economy is based on copra — the only cash crop. The people live a village subsistence lifestyle, growing or catching a considerable portion of their own food. Besides copra, handicrafts, stamps, and coins, the only other source of income is money sent home by the many Tokelauans who have gone overseas to work. Some of these have gone to Samoa, though many are in New Zealand. This migration was helped by the Tokelau Resettlement Scheme. The people were encouraged to move to New Zealand in order to relieve overcrowding on Tokelau.

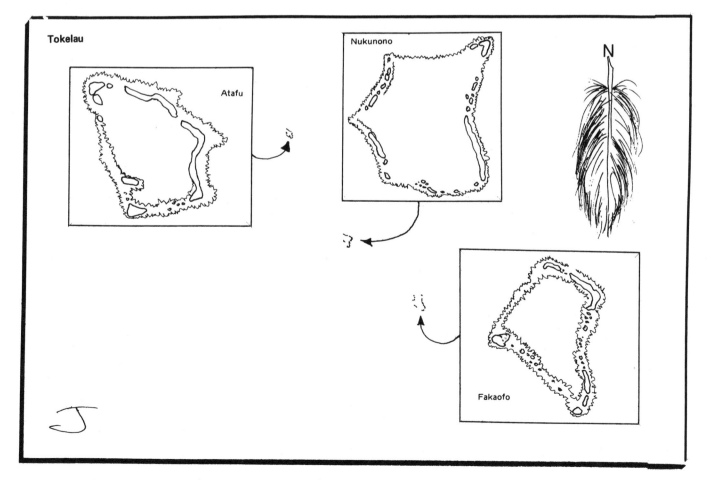

New Zealand provides about $3 million per year to fund the budget of the Tokelau Public Service. The Tokelau Public Service provides the only salaried jobs on the islands, and employs about 175 teachers, school aids, doctors, nurses, and other administrative officials. Each island has an elementary school and a small hospital. In addition New Zealand and other organizations provide development funds for public works projects on the islands.

4. Political Status

The islands are a dependency of New Zealand. The people are New Zealand citizens, with the right to live, work, own land and vote in New Zealand. There is no main island or administrative center. Each island has a separate local government consisting of village councils and chiefs. The administrative office is located in Apia, Western Samoa. The administrators are appointed by New Zealand, but are usually islanders.

There is talk of moving the administration to Tokelau, but this is considered difficult at the present time due to the islands' transportation and communication problems. Each atoll sends representatives to a General Fono (council), which rotates its regular meetings among the three atolls. New Zealand follows a policy of allowing the islanders to take more and more responsibility for self-government. The islanders themselves are in the process of discussing and considering what type of political development they want. However there are no specific plans at this time for any major status change.

5. Major Problems

Tokelau has nothing on which to base an economy — nothing to justify development. It can support a limited number of people at a subsistence level only. There are no airports, no ports or docking facilities. Shipping service connecting the islands with Apia is monthly only. There are no high schools, and students must continue their education in Western Samoa. The court system for the islands, which have no serious crime, was located on Niue, but is being transferred to New Zealand.

About the most frustrating problem the islands have is their isolation caused by poor transportation and communication facilities. It is hoped that a more regularly scheduled ship service will help with transportation. Recently a United Nations Development

Program grant installed equipment on the atolls for the upgrading of Tokelau's telecommunications.

The islands are difficult and expensive for New Zealand to maintain. But for the people, Tokelau offers a chance to live a traditional, quiet, Polynesian lifestyle. This is good for those who want it. Usually the young prefer to leave. This splits families and causes sadness. Such migration is often necessary due to overpopulation and lack of available land. The islands have a population ceiling above which they can't support the people. Tokelau will probably continue as it is indefinitely.

Tokelau women making handicrafts. (South Pacific Commission photo from Handicrafts of the South Seas)

CHAPTER REVIEW

Vocabulary: Tokelau Resettlement Scheme, dependency, Atafu, Nukunono, Fakaofo

Questions:

1. What does Tokelau consist of?

2. Explain Tokelau's relationship with New Zealand.

3. Why do many people leave Tokelau?

4. Do you think Tokelau will ever become developed? Why or why not?

For Further Reading:

Carter, John (ed.). *PACIFIC ISLANDS YEAR BOOK*, 15th edition. Sydney: Pacific Publications, 1984.

Stanley, David; and Dalton, Bill. *SOUTH PACIFIC HANDBOOK.* Chico, California: Moon Publications, 1982.

Chapter 28: Niue

1. Geography

Niue is located in the South Pacific between Tonga and the Cook Islands. It is a single, raised-coral island of about 100 square miles (260 km²). The island rises to an upper plateau about 200 feet (60 m) above sea level. The soil is fertile, but thin and rocky. There are no rivers, as the ample rainfall sinks into the limestone. There are some underground freshwater pools in caves. Situated just inside the tropics, the island's climate is relatively mild.

2. People and Culture

Niue is one of the lonelier and more isolated Pacific islands. There are no nearby inhabited neighbor islands. Niue seems to have been settled by two groups: the first coming from Samoa, the second from Tonga. European missionaries were unsuccessful at first, but eventually converted the entire island to Christianity. Originally called Savage Island, Niue was avoided by outsiders at first. Eventually blackbirders, like Bully Hayes, hurt the island, depleting the population of men. Niue began to request protection from Britain. Britain at first refused, but finally took over in 1900. A year later, the island came under New Zealand control as part of the Cook Islands.

The population is about 3000. The people are Polynesian. The language is a cross between Tongan and Samoan. The island's social system is unique in that there are no hereditary chiefs. Family elders are involved only in land disputes.

The main town of Alofi is the only developed area. The people live in villages, all of which do have electricity.

3. Economy and Resources

The economy is based on agriculture. Subsistence farming is important, but there are many crops grown for export. Copra, handicrafts, honey, passion fruit, and limes are the main exports. Much of the island is planted in coconut trees. Cattle are raised for local consumption. Exports are, however, heavily outnumbered by imports. Tourism is not very developed yet, however, there is one hotel. The island does have jet service. New Zealand supplies

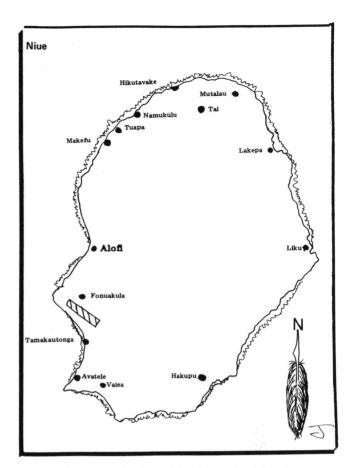

grants, loans, and other aid to keep the island's economy solvent. As in other islands, much money comes in from Niueans working overseas.

4. Political Status

Niue is self-governing in free association with New Zealand. This means Niue controls internal affairs, while New Zealand provides defense, aid, and takes care of foreign affairs. The people are New Zealand citizens. The legislature is elected, and it chooses a premier.

5. Major Problems

Niue's main problems are economic. There are limited resources and few jobs. Imports are much too high, outnumbering exports by about ten to one. This has caused many Niueans to migrate to New Zealand, where 10,000 live today. One Niuean leader has accused the free association agreement as being the cause of such migration since economic development was insufficient and free entry to New Zealand is too tempting. Today, the island looks empty, with many houses boarded up. Those who leave seldom return. The Niue government has decided to install

Buildings on Niue. (Photo courtesy Pacific Publications from South Seas Guide)

a cable television system, believing that might keep people home and attract others to return.

At present, the island is a financial burden for New Zealand, which currently supplies 90% of the Niue budget. Agriculture was dealt a blow by storms in 1979. Most passionfruit trees were wiped out and may never recover. Over 80% of the salaried jobs on the island are governmental. In 1983, there were fewer than 300 tourists. Niue needs 3000 per year to have enough to create an economic impact without the ill effects that sometimes accompany tourism.

The primary goal for Niue is to maintain a viable population and become self-sufficient economically. Currently the island seems a long way from achieving such a goal.

CHAPTER REVIEW

Vocabulary: Alofi

Questions:

1. What is the island of Niue like geographically?

2. Explain the relationship between Niue and New Zealand.

3. Explain Niue's economic situation and the resulting problems.

For Further Reading:

Carter, John (ed.), *PACIFIC ISLANDS YEAR BOOK*, 15th edition. Sydney: Pacific Publications, 1984.

Stanley, David; and Dalton, Bill, *SOUTH PACIFIC HANDBOOK*, Chico, California: Moon Publications, 1982.

Chapter 29: The Cook Islands

1. Geography

Located in the South Pacific between Niue and French Polynesia, the Cook Islands are a group of 15 volcanic islands and coral atolls, split into a northern group and a southern group. The northern islands are all flat atolls, the southern mostly volcanic. Geography varies from island to island, with some of the volcanic ones being very fertile. The islands are quite spread out. It is almost 1000 miles (1600 km) from the northernmost island to the southernmost. The Cooks thus cover quite a large area of ocean for so few islands. Mountainous Rarotonga and Aitutaki are considered among the most beautiful islands in the Pacific. The total land area is 92 square miles (240 km²). Rarotonga, the largest island, has 26 square miles (67 km²).

2. People and Culture

The Cooks never were a group of islands until the Europeans combined them administratively. Each island was independent of the other. Protestant missionaries practically took over various islands, wielding strong influence over the different chiefs. Thus, missionaries were able to pass many morality laws and actually controlled entrance to the islands. The British made the islands a protectorate to prevent other countries from moving in. Later the Cooks were transferred to New Zealand's control and became the Cook Islands colony.

There are about 16,000 people in the Cooks. They are Polynesian with a Maori language and culture. New Zealand Maori and Tahitian are very close languages. Rarotonga, the capital, has the only real modern development. Many people still do much subsistence farming and fishing. Most of the rest of the islands have the usual village lifestyle. Traditional chiefs still have great influence and leadership.

3. Economy and Resources

The economy of the Cooks is not healthy. The balance of trade is poor, as imports greatly outnumber exports. The main exports are copra, bananas, citrus juice, canned fruit, and clothing. Rarotonga has a fruit cannery and clothing factory.

Cook Islands

Penrhyn

Rakahanga

Manihiki

Pukapuka

Nassau

N

Suwarrow

Palmerston

Aitutaki

Manuae

Mitiaro

Takutea

Mauke

Atiu

Rarotonga

Mangaia

Tourism helps make up some of the difference in trade. As a tourist destination, the Cook Islands are to New Zealand what Hawaii is to the mainland United States and Guam is to Japan. The remaining imbalance is made up by New Zealand aid and money sent back by Cook Islanders working overseas, usually in New Zealand. Postage stamp sales also bring in some money.

4. Political Status

The Cook Islands are self-governing in free association with New Zealand. The people are New Zealand citizens. Like the islanders of Tokelau and Niue, they may move to New Zealand to live, work, and vote. The Cooks handle internal affairs; New Zealand provides money, controls defense, and handles foreign relations in consultation with the Cook Islands government. At present, the Cook Islands' government feels completely independent. It is doubtful, however, that the islands would ever take the final step toward complete and official independence, thereby losing New Zealand citizenship and the other benefits of their current status.

The islands have an elected legislature which chooses a president. There is also a chiefs' legislature, which is consulted on land and custom issues.

Elections in the Cooks are always interesting. There are two main parties, the Cook Islands Party and the Democratic Party. In 1978, the Cook Islands Party was in power and used government money to fly in voters from New Zealand. They won, but the Supreme Court of the Cooks ruled the election invalid. The Democratic Party took control. Voting by Cook Islanders living in New Zealand was then made legal, and the Cook Islands Party won back control in 1983. However, a few months later, after a parliamentary crisis, the Democratic Party was back in power. Voter turnout is always high, usually running over 90% in the Cooks and over 80% in New Zealand.

Traditional dancing, Cook Islands. (Photo courtesy Cook Islands Tourist Authority)

Ships in the harbor of Rarotonga. (Photo courtesy Pacific Publications from South Seas Guide)

5. Major Problems

The main problem of the Cooks is the economy. The land resources probably cannot be developed much more, though export agriculture has been increased lately. But given the area of the islands' 200-mile zones, the Cooks should be able to make some money selling licenses for fishing. That may be a potential economic boon in the future.

In January 1987, a typhoon passed through the southern group, sending huge storm waves up onto the main street of Avarua, Rarotonga. Many buildings, including hotels, were damaged. It is hoped that this will not affect the islands' tourist industry too badly. About 20,000 tourists visit the Cooks yearly, staying in the numerous cottage-style hotels.

One problem is the migration of Cook Islanders to New Zealand. Jobs are scarce in the Cooks, so people wanting more cash usually leave. The Cooks lose many of their young and ambitious people, which is a heavy drain on human resources. Developing countries all face this problem, as many of the best people needed at home leave to get jobs elsewhere. There are about 24,000 Cook Islanders living in New Zealand.

Other problems are more physical. Transportation and communication among islands so spread out present very real difficulties.

Overall, the main problem of the Cooks is developing the economy enough to provide jobs to keep people from leaving. They do not, however, want to develop to the point of becoming a busy city like Guam. Late in 1985, the government announced that the population, which had been steadily declining, was finally growing again. If the trend continues, it could be a sign that the Cook Islands are beginning to create a viable economy. Many problems do remain, especially the negative trade balance. Currently imports outnumber exports by about five to one.

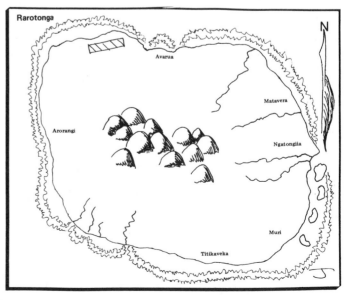

Cook Islanders attending church. (Photo courtesy Cook Islands Tourist Authority)

CHAPTER REVIEW

Vocabulary: Rarotonga, Aitutaki, Avarua

Questions:

1. Why aren't the Cooks a "real" island group?

2. What kind of power and control did the missionaries once have?

3. What is the economic hope for the future of the Cooks?

4. What has been happening to the population of the Cooks and why?

For Further Reading:

Carter, John (ed.), *PACIFIC ISLANDS YEAR BOOK*, 15th edition. Sydney: Pacific Publications, 1984.

Davis, Tom; et al, *COOK ISLANDS POLITICS: THE INSIDE STORY*, Auckland, N.Z.: Polynesia Press, 1979.

Stanley, David; and Dalton, Bill, *SOUTH PACIFIC HANDBOOK*, Chico, California: Moon Publications, 1982.

Chapter 30: Tonga

1. Geography

Tonga is at the west end of Polynesia between Melanesian Fiji and Niue. There are 169 islands in the group, of which 36 are inhabited. The islands include atolls, volcanic and coral islands. They are clustered in three groupings from north to south. The total land area is 258 square miles (671 km²).

Tongatapu, the capital island, is in the southern group. It is a large, flat coral island. There are active volcanoes in the middle group. The northern group has a beautiful lagoon area. There are many interesting sights for the tourist in Tonga. Tongatapu has ocean blowholes, huge protected flocks of fruitbats, and some interesting ancient architecture. The island is about 100 square miles (257 km²) in area.

The islands have typically lush tropical vegetation. Most are fertile with much rainfall. The climate is tropical, but a bit cooler in the south because Tonga is close to the edge of the tropics.

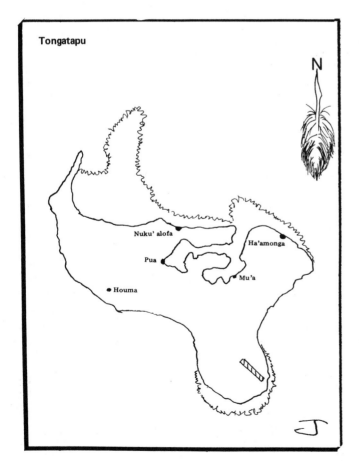

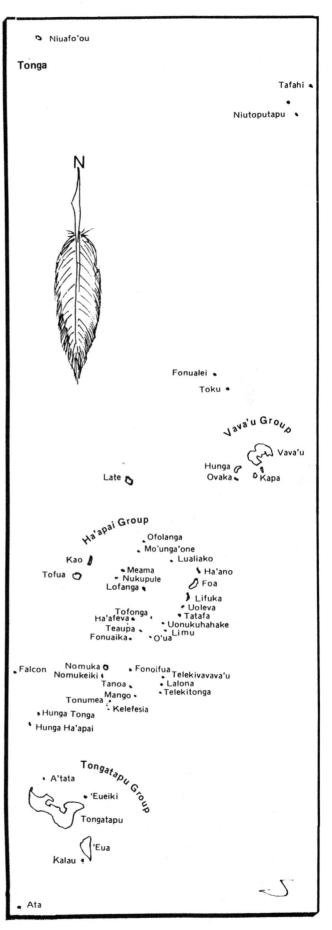

2. People and Culture

People have been living in Tonga for at least 3000 years. At various times in pre-contact days, one chief would manage to gain control of all the islands and become paramount chief or king. When discovered by the Europeans, however, the various island groups within Tonga had fragmented and there were no single rulers who controlled the whole group.

Through the centuries, Tonga always had much contact with Fiji. The two groups had quite a bit of influence on each other.

Captain Cook had named the group the Friendly Islands because of the hospitality he had received. Unknown to Cook, the Tongans were planning to kill him and his crew in order to strip his ship of its metal. They were unable to put their plan into action before Cook left.

In 1806, a young British boy named Will Mariner was captured by the Tongans when they killed most of the crew of the ship he was on. The Tongans stripped the ship of its metal, and Mariner, after being treated poorly at first, was adopted by the local chief. Mariner, himself, became a chief and a land-holder. He stayed in Tonga four years, helping his island father try to conquer the other groups in Tonga. Finally he was able to hitch a ride on a passing ship and returned to Britain.

Tonga's history is unique in that it was the only Pacific island area not to become a real colony of some modern power. The various chiefs of Tonga initiated many civil wars fighting for control of all the islands. In the 1820s, Wesleyan Protestant missionaries arrived. By the 1830s most Tongans were converted to Christianity. This added more rivalries to the civil wars: Christian Tongans vs. non-Christian Tongans. In 1845 the islands were finally united under one chief, Tupou, who became the first king of the present dynasty. The missionaries had much influence over the king. One even became premier. His policies of religious discrimination caused civil unrest and instability. Britain became interested in the group because it feared that this instability would tempt other countries to move in and take over. Tonga became a British protectorate in 1900. The islands kept their local government, and Britain protected their independence. Britain did exercise some control over Tonga's foreign affairs, but Tonga was never considered a true colony, and it was never officially administered by Britain.

One very important and very successful policy of Tupou I was the complete ban on sales of land to

The Royal Palace, Nuku'alofa, Tongatapu. (Photo courtesy Pacific Publications from South Seas Guide)

foreigners. Because of this strict policy, Europeans and Americans were unable to buy land in Tonga. Thus, no large Euroamerican community developed, and Nuku'alofa remained a sleepy village out of the mainstream of Pacific political and economic activity. Also, with no foreign community of any influence in the group, there was no pressure for an outright takeover by some European country. This helped Tonga escape the fate of Fiji, Samoa, Tahiti, and Hawaii, where such communities did exist. All of those groups eventually lost their independence, partially because of the foreigners asking their home countries to step in and take over.

The population of Tonga is about 104,000. The people are Polynesian with their own language. Most Tongans live a village-subsistence lifestyle. There are two classes, nobles and commoners. All land in Tonga officially belongs to the King. Each male Tongan, when he turns 16, is entitled to a piece of land to farm and a house lot in the town or village area. Unfortunately, there is not enough land to go around, so many young Tongan men are placed on a waiting list. The main town of Nuku'alofa is the only built-up area. The rest of the islands have limited development. Tongans are very religious. On Sunday, everything closes down. Stores close, busses and taxis don't run. Everybody goes to church and relaxes at home.

Getting out of church. Note the traditional sashes. (Photo by Bob Richards)

3. Economy and Resources

Copra and bananas are Tonga's main export crops. In addition, fishing is being developed, and some fish is exported to canneries in Fiji. However imports outnumber exports about six to one. Some of this deficit is made up from revenues garnered from the approximately 60,000 tourists who visit Tonga each year. Among the items many tourists buy are huge pieces of traditionally made tapa cloth. Jobs are still scarce, and over 25,000 Tongans have left for New Zealand, Australia, and the United States. These Tongans often send money home to their families. Most of the people in Tonga still rely on subsistence farming and fishing, especially away from Tongatapu. The rest of what Tonga needs is supplied by foreign aid from Australia, New Zealand, Japan, Britain, West Germany, and some international development organizations. Natural oil seepages in the islands have led to many exploratory wells, none of which have found oil. There may be more exploration in the future. If oil ever is found, it may solve most, if not all, of Tonga's economic problems.

4. Political Status

Tonga is an independent kingdom. King Taufa'ahau Tupou IV is in control of the government. He is the president of the privy council and appoints all government positions. There is a legislative assembly. Some of its representatives are elected by the nobles and some by all the people. The King is highly respected by the people and really is in charge of the government.

5. Major Problems

In 1982, a devasting typhoon struck Tonga, causing loss of life and much damage.

Tonga has the same problems of many islands — a sagging economy and out-migration of people. The King is progressive, however, and seeks to develop Tonga while preserving its unique culture and traditions. Nobody in Tonga doubts that he will succeed.

King Taufa'ahau Tupou IV. (Photo courtesy Institute for Polynesian Studies)

Downtown Nuku'alofa. (Photo courtesy Institute for Polynesian Studies)

CHAPTER REVIEW

Vocabulary: Tongatapu, Nuku'alofa, tapa, Taufa'ahau Tupou IV

Questions:

1. Why is Tonga unique in the Pacific?

2. Explain the land system in Tonga.

3. How does Tonga's government work?

4. Discuss Tonga's problems.

For Further Reading:

Carter, John (ed.), *PACIFIC ISLANDS YEAR BOOK*, 15th edition. Sydney: Pacific Publications, 1984.

Gerstel, Donna, *TONGA PICTORIAL; TAPESTRY OF PRIDE*, San Diego: Tofua Press, 1974.

Stanley, David; and Dalton, Bill, *SOUTH PACIFIC HANDBOOK*, Chico, California: Moon Publications, 1982.

Chapter 31: Pitcairn

1. Geography

Pitcairn is a tiny, isolated, volcanic island located in the eastern part of Polynesia. It has only two square miles (5.2 km²) of land. The shore is surrounded by steep cliffs. There is only one area where small boats can land, and it is very tricky. The upper plateau is very fertile and rainfall is heavy. The three nearby uninhabited islands of Oeno, Henderson, and Ducie are included within the jurisdiction of Pitcairn.

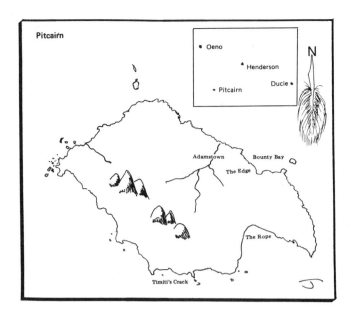

2. People and Culture

Pitcairn was the final hiding place for nine of the famous *Bounty* mutineers. Fletcher Christian and his men came with their Tahitian wives and six Tahitian men. They settled in, burned the *Bounty*, and prepared to live the rest of their lives there. For some, that was not very long. There were not enough women to go around, the white sailors treated the Tahitians poorly, and soon there was trouble. When the killing ended and the island became peaceful, only two mutineers were left alive with ten women and many children. Only one mutineer was alive when the community was finally discovered. The last mutineer, John Adams, had become religious and taught his community a strict morality. He was pardoned by the British Admiralty and never brought to trial.

The mutiny happened in 1789, Christian and the others settled on Pitcairn in 1790, and the community was discovered in 1808. By 1831 the population was getting too high for small Pitcairn, and the islanders were moved to Tahiti. They did not like Tahiti with its freer sexual morality, and they had no natural immunity to diseases there. Many died, and after a few months they were returned to Pitcairn. By 1856, their population, 193, was again too high, and they were all moved to Norfolk Island. A few years later some, homesick for Pitcairn, returned, sharing a total of five surnames. In 1883 the entire population converted to the Seventh Day Adventist faith.

Today, there are only about 45 people on Pitcairn. All of them are descendants of the *Bounty* mutineers, their Tahitian wives, and some American and British sailors who settled on Pitcairn in the early 1800s. The people live mostly by farming and fishing for their own food. They have a unique language which is a mixture of 200-year-old Tahitian and 18th-century sailor's English. Much of that is dying out and being replaced by standard English. There is one central village.

3. Economy and Resources

The only cash economy of Pitcairn is the sale of stamps and the sale of handicrafts to passing ships. British aid helps keep the island solvent.

4. Political Status

Pitcairn is a dependency of Britain. The island is governed by the British High Commissioner to New Zealand who stays in Wellington. The local government consists of an elected island council and an elected magistrate.

5. Major Problems

Pitcairn is just too small and isolated. There is nothing on which to base any kind of cash economy. Because of the nature of the island, there is both a maximum and minimum population limit. Too many and the island does not have enough food. Too few and there are not enough men to man the longboats through the tricky boat landing.

One American millionaire offered to buy or lease Henderson Island, with the money going to the Pitcairn islanders. He wanted to build his own tropical hideaway mansion on Henderson, offered to build new houses for all the islanders on Pitcairn, and offered to set up a light airplane route between Pitcairn and Tahiti. The islanders were not sure about the whole thing. Britain refused the offer.

Another nagging concern has been the lack of an airfield for small planes. Medical emergencies have to await ships, which may not arrive in time. Also, it would be easier to bring in tourists. This would be done very low key and Pitcairn style: a few at a time staying a few days with Pitcairn families. The best place for a runway, however, is also some of the best farmland. At present there is no plan for an airstrip.

One suggestion was made that the Pitcairn islanders declare independence from Britain, then begin charging license fees for fishing in the 200-mile zone around the four islands. Since their population is so small, the fees might be all the money they need.

Pitcairn islanders themselves face the dilemma of life on their small island. For the young children, it is a great place to grow up. There is no crime, no delinquency, no drugs, no alcohol, and no cigarettes. But for teenagers and young adults, there is no education, and there are no opportunities for anything other than a simple lifestyle of farming and fishing.

Fewer and fewer ships are passing by the island, making cash opportunities even smaller. Many Pitcairn islanders have moved to New Zealand, and Pitcairn is trying to convince some to return. At the present time, their biggest problem is maintaining a viable population.

Adamstown, Pitcairn's only settlement. (Photo by Jimmy Cornell)

CHAPTER REVIEW

Vocabulary: *Bounty*

Questions:

1. Who were the ancestors of Pitcairn Islanders?

2. Why was there trouble on the island?

3. Why is there both a maximum and minimum population the island can safely support?

4. What is Pitcairn's relationship to Britain?

For Further Reading:

Ball, Ian, *PITCAIRN, CHILDREN OF MUTINY*, Boston: Little Brown, 1973.

Carter, John (ed.), *PACIFIC ISLANDS YEAR BOOK*, 15th edition, Sydney: Pacific Publications, 1984.

Stanley, David; and Dalton, Bill, *SOUTH PACIFIC HANDBOOK*, Chico, California: Moon Publications, 1982.

Chapter 32: Norfolk

1. Geography

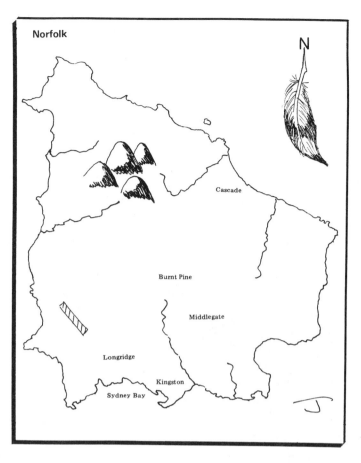

Norfolk is not actually part of Polynesia. However, ancient Polynesians did visit the island, and the current population includes the part-Polynesian Pitcairn descendents. The island is volcanic, located between New Zealand and New Caledonia. The soil is fertile. The island has much open area suitable for cattle. It is the original home for the famous Norfolk Island pine tree, now growing in many other parts of the world. The total area is about 13 square miles (34 km²). Cliffs line most of the coastline. Norfolk is outside the tropics, so the climate is much milder than other islands. Rainfall is about 50 inches (125 cm) per year.

2. People and Culture

Originally (1788) Norfolk was an attempted British farming colony. The colony died out in 1814, and the island next became a prison in 1825. There was much brutality during this period, and the penal colony was eventually closed in 1856. Then came the Pitcairn Islanders brought by Britain that same year. Their population had reached 194, too much for tiny Pitcairn. In a few years some returned to Pitcairn, but the rest remained. Their descendants are there today.

The current population is about 2200. There are two basic groups: the Pitcairn descendants and recent settlers from Australia.

3. Economy and Resources

The mainstay of the economy is tourism. Norfolk receives about 20,000 tourists per year. This, along with low-duty shopping, gives Norfolk a favorable balance of trade. It has created jobs and attracted Australians. There is still much agriculture for local consumption, but much food is imported. All in all, the economy is relatively healthy.

Windswept terrain of Norfolk Island. (Photo courtesy Pacific Publications from South Seas Guide)

4. Political Status

Norfolk is a territory of Australia. The administration is appointed by Australia. There is a locally elected legislature. Australia is beginning to allow the territory to become more self-governing. The people are Australian citizens.

5. Major Problems

The main problems center around future political status and conflict between the Pitcairn people and the newly arrived Australians. Norfolk seems to want more self-rule, but independence is doubtful. Many Australians, both in Norfolk and Australia, want to keep the island as a territory. But the population of Norfolk has resisted attempts to make the island completely a part of Australia. Exactly what future status the island will have remains to be seen.

Old style European architecture is typical of many of the buildings on Norfolk. (Photo courtesy Pacific Publications from South Seas Guide)

CHAPTER REVIEW

Vocabulary: Norfolk Island pine

Questions:

1. Who were the ancestors of today's Norfolk islanders? Why did they come there?

2. Why do many Australians move to Norfolk?

3. What is Norfolk's relationship with Australia?

4. Why is there conflict between the two groups on Norfolk?

For Further Reading:

Carter, John (ed.), *PACIFIC ISLANDS YEAR BOOK*, 15th edition, Sydney: Pacific Publications, 1984.

Hoare, Merval, *NORFOLK, AN OUTLINE OF ITS HISTORY*, St. Lucia, Queensland, Australia: University of Queensland Press, 1961.

Chapter 33: Wallis and Futuna

1. Geography

Wallis and Futuna are two small groups of islands about 120 miles (192 km) apart. They are located between Fiji and Samoa. Wallis is one main volcanic island surrounded by a barrier reef with several flat reef islands. Though volcanic, its hills only go up to 400 feet (120 m). Futuna consists of the two volcanic islands of Futuna and Alofi, about two miles (3.2 km) apart. Futuna is very steep, with mountains over 2500 feet (760 m). The total land area of the two groups is about 48 square miles (124 km²).

2. People and Culture

Wallis and Futuna did not have as much contact with Europeans as other islands. French Marist Missionaries were able to convert the entire population to Catholicism. In 1887, after years of asking, the islands became a French protectorate.

The people are Polynesian, speaking two main dialects. On Wallis, the language is close to Tongan. On Futuna, it more resembles Samoan. The total population is 12,000, 8000 on Wallis and 4000 on Futuna. There are perhaps as many as 9000 people from the territory living in New Caledonia, but with the decline of the nickel industry there many have been returning home.

The lifestyle is mostly subsistence, the only development being around the town area of Mata Utu. Wallis has one traditional king and Futuna has two. Because of fresh water shortages, Alofi has no permanent inhabitants. The people are excellent dancers, and are famous for an exciting sword dance.

3. Economy and Resources

The territory has virtually no exports. The only sources of cash are government jobs and money sent home by Wallisians working in New Caledonia. The main source of livelihood is subsistence farming and fishing. Infestation by the rhinocerous beetle has made copra farming for export impossible. Tourism is not developed. There are only two small hotels on Wallis, and local leaders are hesitant to allow more development in spite of the potential. France has

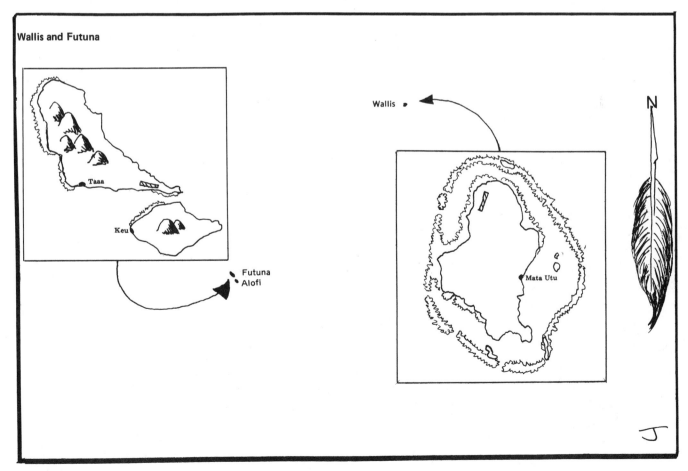

Wallis and Futuna

Taaa

Keu

Futuna
Alofi

Wallis

Mata Utu

N

signed treaties with Japan and South Korea to fish in the 200-mile zone. The money earned, however, amounts to less than 10% of the islands' yearly budget. France operates the local government and pays for all government jobs, public works, health, education, and other necessary services.

4. Political Status

Wallis and Futuna are politically combined as an overseas territory of France. The people are French citizens, vote in French elections, and elect a voting representative to the French Parliament. They also may move to France or any other French territory. The supreme administrator is appointed by France. He is in full control of the government. There is an elected assembly which helps him. He also consults with the three kings and other chiefs.

5. Major Problems

Wallis/Futuna is the most isolated and least developed of France's overseas territories. It has no true economy, and no real development. It also loses much population to New Caledonia. This drains it of the most energetic and ambitious people.

The future of the territory, both economic and political, is unclear. The islanders might actually be happy with the lack of development which has preserved their traditional lifestyle. For the time being Wallis and Futuna will probably remain an isolated, underdeveloped, backwater territory of France. Independence seems unlikely.

CHAPTER REVIEW

Vocabulary: Mata Utu, Wallis, Futuna, Alofi

Questions:

1. What are the sources of cash in Wallis and Futuna?

2. What is the territory's relationship with France?

3. Does there seem to be any economic potential in the islands?

For Further Reading:

Carter, John (ed.), *PACIFIC ISLANDS YEAR BOOK*, 15th edition, Sydney: Pacific Publications, 1984.

Stanley, David; and Dalton, Bill, *SOUTH PACIFIC HANDBOOK*, Chico, California: Moon Publications, 1982.

Typical Wallisian house on Uvea (Wallis) — thatched roof, corrugated walls. (Photo by Jimmy Cornell)

Chapter 34: French Polynesia

1. Geography

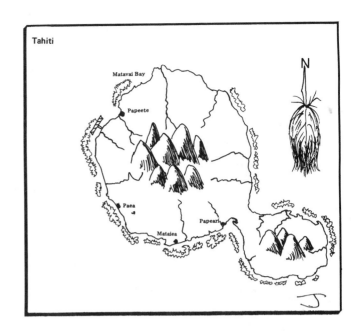

Tahiti

French Polynesia is a collection of five island groups which take up the entire eastern portion of Polynesia. The total land area is about 1500 square miles (4000 km²) spread over 130 islands. The main group is the Society, which has about 14 islands, mostly volcanic. Tahiti, with the capital city of Papeete, is in the Society group, located at the west end of French Polynesia. It is the largest island at 400 square miles (1040 km²). To the south of the Societies are the Austral islands. There are seven in that group, mostly volcanic. To the east is Tuamotu, a chain of about 80 low, flat atolls. In the southeast corner is Mangareva, a cluster of volcanic islands known formerly as Gambier. Finally, in the north, are the Marquesas, about 14 mostly volcanic islands. The geographic characteristics vary from group to group and island to island. Most of the volcanic islands are rugged, steep, lush, and fertile. The atolls are typical reef islands. The island of Bora Bora is so steep that the airport runway is built on a reef island offshore.

2. People and Culture

The history of French Polynesia varies with each group. Tahiti was a favorite of explorers like Cook, Wallis, and Bougainville. It was the scene of the famous *Bounty* mutiny in 1789. Contact continued to increase with Tahiti becoming the home of many beachcombers and traders. A thriving business developed shipping pork raised in the islands to the British settlements in Australia. Whalers called frequently, and Papeete grew up as a whaling town. Diseases introduced by the newcomers greatly reduced the population.

British Protestant missionaries arrived in 1797, and began converting the islanders. They did not make many converts at first. However they were careful to support the Pomare family, who were involved in a struggle to acquire titles in the islands' complicated social system. After both successes and failures, the Pomare family, helped in many ways by the missionaries, succeeded in defeating its enemies. It became the royal family of Tahiti, and Pomare II abolished the native religion and forced all his subjects to convert to Christianity. The local religion had been steadily losing favor anyway. It required a large number of human sacrifices, and had been unable to protect islanders from the ravages of European diseases and economic control.

Strange turns of events ended in the islands coming under the control of France rather than Britain.

Going to church in French Polynesia. (Photo by D. Charnay courtesy Tahiti Tourist Development Board)

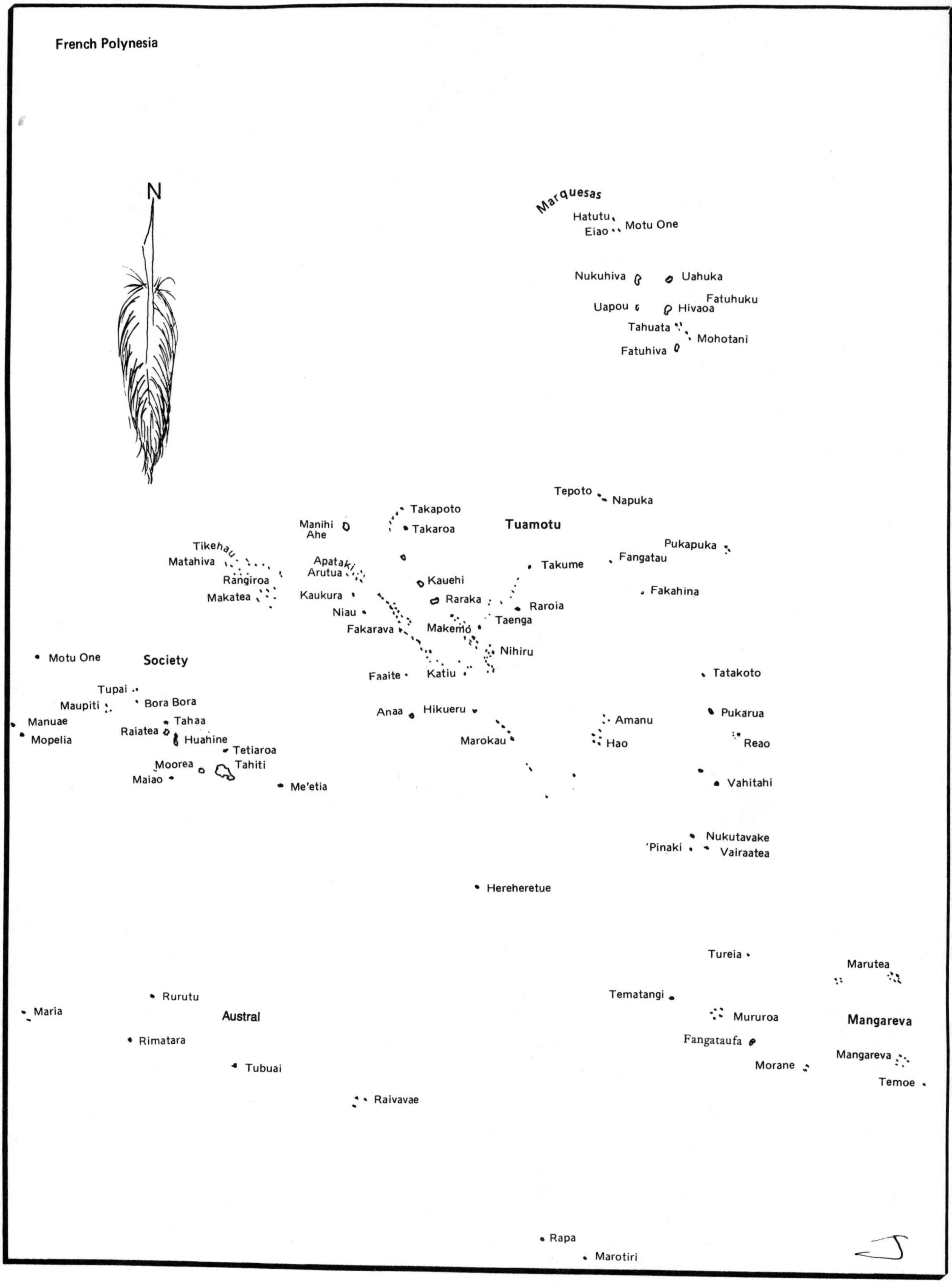

N

Marquesas

Hatutu Motu One
Eiao

Nukuhiva Uahuka
Fatuhuku
Uapou Hivaoa
Tahuata Mohotani
Fatuhiva

Tepoto Napuka

Takapoto Tuamotu
Manihi Takaroa
Ahe Pukapuka

Tikehau Takume Fangatau
Matahiva Apataki Fakahina
Rangiroa Arutua Kauehi
Makatea Kaukura Raraka Raroia
Niau Taenga
Fakarava Makemo
Nihiru
Motu One Society Tatakoto
Faaite Katiu
Tupai Amanu Pukarua
Maupiti Bora Bora Anaa Hikueru Hao Reao
Manuae Tahaa Marokau
Mopelia Raiatea Huahine Vahitahi
Tetiaroa
Moorea Tahiti
Maiao Me'etia Nukutavake
'Pinaki Vairaatea

Hereheretue

Tureia Marutea
Tematangi
Rurutu Mururoa Mangareva
Maria Austral
Rimatara Fangataufa Mangareva
Tubuai Morane Temoe
Raivavae

Rapa
Marotiri

Downtown Papeete, Tahiti. (Photo courtesy **Pacific Daily News)**

After the Protestants had long been established, French Catholic missionaries arrived on Tahiti, but were not well treated. Thus, French naval ships began putting pressure on island leaders. Britain hesitated at making the islands a protectorate, and the French moved in. They were able to persuade some of the chiefs to sign a treaty, and the islands of the Societies became a French protectorate. The French also annexed the Marquesas, the Australs, and Tuamotu. Some islands held out, but eventually all came under French control. Britain and France almost went to war over this. When the French took over, the Tahitians resisted. For several weeks, the French were besieged in Papeete by the Tahitian army hiding in the valleys. Eventually the Tahitians were defeated and the French took complete control. They sent Catholic missionaries to the Marquesas, which today are predominantly Catholic. In the 1950s, there was an independence movement, but its goals were rejected by voters.

The people of French Polynesia number 167,000. Of these 77% are Polynesian, 14% European (mostly French), and 9% Chinese. About 120,000 live on Tahiti. Papeete, the capital, is a modern city. Away from Tahiti, there are fewer cash job opportunities, and the people live more from subsistence. Those who want jobs usually move to Tahiti.

3. Economy and Resources

The main export crops are coconut oil (from copra), vanilla, fruit, fish, pearls, and other items. These do not match imports. Yet the economy is in fairly good shape, due mainly to tourism and the French military nuclear testing bases. Both of these pump needed money into the economy and support many other businesses. About 160,000 tourists a year visit Tahiti. Also, the employees of the French bases spend much money in the islands. The bases create many jobs and construction projects. France also helps directly by financing part of the government operations.

4. Political Status

French Polynesia is an Overseas Territory of France. The people are French citizens. They vote in French elections and elect their own representatives to the French Parliament. Traditionally the main power of local government was the high commissioner appointed by France. The elected assembly and local government council did not have much power. In 1977, France granted the assembly the power to fire the high commissioner if it did not like his policies. In 1984, a new internal autonomy system was begun. The high commissioner lost much of his power, which was transferred to the president of the government council. The government council is chosen by the elected assembly. The locally elected government, with Polynesian President Gaston Flosse, now has almost complete control over internal affairs. France remains sovereign, however, and controls defense and foreign affairs, including the 200-mile zone.

5. Major Problems

The main problems in French Polynesia are its relationship with France, the drift of the people into Tahiti, and the French nuclear testing.

There is a small, vocal movement for independence. The French residents oppose this, as they prefer continued association with France. Many Polynesians also fear independence. They do not want to lose their comparatively high standard of living that is dependent on France. Full independence does not seem likely, as France wants to hold on to its territories.

Urban drift creates the usual problems of overpopulation in Papeete: unemployment, crime, and a breakdown of traditional values and customs. It is also taking people away from the easy going lifestyles of their home islands, and draining those islands of an important part of their population.

The nuclear testing is very controversial. Even though the French tests are now underground, other countries are worried about nuclear radiation fallout, poisoning the ocean, and other possible effects. Almost all Pacific island groups have protested the French tests. France uses two atolls in the Tuamotus for their tests, much as the United States did in the Marshalls in the 1950s. The French Polynesians are also worried about long range effects of testing on their own islands. Many have complained, and there are many who want the French to stop. But the French bases have contributed much to the economy. If they pulled out, the economy would be in trouble.

France has received much bad publicity from its program, especially with the sinking of the Greenpeace ship *Rainbow Warrior* in New Zealand in 1985. The ship had been on its way to French Polynesian waters to protest a nuclear test. French agents blew up the ship, killing one of its crew. France remains determined to continue the tests, claiming it needs the testing to maintain an independent nuclear deter-

rent force. There are about 5000 French military personnel in French Polynesia.

Since 1982, French Polynesia was struck by no less than six typhoons, causing much damage to many islands.

Early in 1984 there was a violent strike by hotel workers in Tahiti. Three hotels were closed, and many tourists were trapped. Most Tahitians were shocked at the violence. Eventually the strike was settled and the strikers went back to work. The strike was expensive and unusual for the islands. The scene was repeated in October 1987, when Tahiti's dock workers went on strike. The port of Papeete was shut down and violence erupted, causing France to send in units of the Foreign Legion to help restore order.

Moorea: ''Moua Roa.'' Spectacular scenery is the rule in French Polynesia. (Photo courtesy Tahiti Tourist Development Board)

Fishing on Tahiti. In the background is the island of Moorea. (Photo courtesy Tahiti Tourist Development Board)

CHAPTER REVIEW

Vocabulary: Tahiti, Papeete, Societies, Marquesas, Tuamotu, Austral, Mangareva

Questions:

1. Why did these islands come under French control instead of British?

2. What are the mainstays of the economy today?

3. What is the controversy over the French nuclear testing?

4. What are the arguments for and against independence?

For Further Reading:

Carter, John (ed.), *PACIFIC ISLANDS YEAR BOOK*, 15th edition, Sydney: Pacific Publications, 1984.

Emory, Kenneth Piler, *MATERIAL CULTURE OF THE TUAMOTU ARCHIPELAGO*, Honolulu: Department of Anthropology, Bishop Museum, 1975.

Newbury, Colin, *TAHITI NUI*, Honolulu: University of Hawaii Press, 1980.

Stanley, David; and Dalton, Bill, *SOUTH PACIFIC HANDBOOK*, Chico, California, 1982.

Thomas, Robert, *THE MARQUESAS ISLANDS*, Laie, Hawaii: Institute for Polynesian Studies, 1978.

Chapter 35: Rapa Nui (Easter)

1. Geography

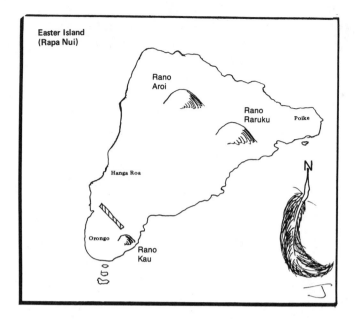

Rapa Nui, also known as Easter Island, represents the southeast point of the Polynesian triangle. The closest inhabited neighbor is tiny Pitcairn, 1500 miles (2400 km) to the west. It is thus farther away from other inhabited places than anywhere in the world. It sits out in one of the emptiest parts of the Pacific.

Rapa Nui is one volcanic island of about 65 square miles (170 km²). There are three extinct volcanoes on the island. Most of the island is a flat or gently rolling plateau. The ground is fertile but very rocky. At one time the island had trees, but the inhabitants evidently used up most of them. There were no coconuts. Cliffs surround most of the coastline. The island has many caves. Rainfall is 100 inches (250 cm) per year but very irregular.

2. People and Culture

There is much controversy surrounding the history and culture of pre-contact Rapa Nui. When the Europeans discovered them, the Polynesian-speaking inhabitants had just finished a series of civil wars. Then came slave raiders who carried off many people, and smallpox practically wiped out the entire population. It reached a low of about 100 people. In 1864, Catholic missionaries came to the island, and in 1888, Chile annexed Easter. Slowly, the population began to recover and increase.

The main controversy over Easter Island deals with the giant stone statues and the origin of the people who made them. The pre-contact population had carved hundreds of unique stone statues, many up to 30 feet (9 m) high. The engineering technology needed to move these statues was great. Most of the statues had been knocked off their platforms during the civil wars. One theory is that one tribe had enslaved another and forced them to build the statues. All the work on the statues caused a shortage of food as not enough people farmed and fished. Soon the enslaved tribe rebelled and wiped out its captors. The people then moved underground to caves. Cannibalism was rampant. After this period the islanders developed the bird cult, with yearly rituals centered in Orongo Village. The first athlete who could swim over to a small offshore island and

return with a newly laid egg of a tern won for his sponsor the title of birdman of the year. The birdman was then able to terrorize all the other contestants until the next contest.

In addition to the stone statues, Easter Islanders had their own form of writing. All the people who could read the writing were killed in the slave raids. Today no one can read it. This was the only Pacific culture to develop writing. There are many other interesting remnants from the ancient times. Petroglyphs (rock drawings) are all over the island. There are also stone foundations for houses, stone chicken coops, and many burial sights among the ruins of the statue platforms.

What were the statues for? How were they moved? Who built them? These questions have been debated by scientists for years. Some believe Rapa Nui was settled by civilized tribes from Peru. The language of the islanders, however, is Polynesian, closely related to Tahitian. Most believe the statues represented the ancestors of the statue builder. Archeolgical evidence indicates all the statues were constructed between 1100-1700 AD. The statue building stopped suddenly when the intertribal wars began. Many partially completed statues were left still at the volcano quarry or halfway down the mountain where they remain today. The statues are called *Moai*, the platforms are called *Ahu*.

Today there are 2400 people on Easter. They all live in the one town of Honga Roa. They live in Chilean-style houses, and use horses and some cars to go out to their farms and ranches. Chile declared the entire island a national park and historical monument in 1935. Hanga Roa and its immediate vicinity are the only areas allowed for settlement.

Recently there has been much modernizing and

other development on the island. There are new public works projects, a new port, and a satellite phone link to Santiago, Chile.

3. Economy and Resources

The people live mainly from their own crops. In pre-contact days these were only bananas, sweet potatoes, yams, sugar cane, taro, and tapioca. Many food plants have been introduced since. Wool from locally raised sheep was exported, but that has dropped off. The only other money earners are tourism and government jobs. For tourists, there are a few modern hotels. Many of the tourists are scientists and students interested in Rapa Nui's archeology, history, and culture. The Chilean government supports all the administrative services and pays for the government jobs. Currently the United States is interested in extending the runway to use Easter as an emergency landing strip for the space shuttle. This would mean a permanent NASA station on the island, and provide some money from rent agreements.

4. Political Status

The island is a dependency of Chile. It is considered a province of the 5 Region Valparaiso, Chile. The Governor is appointed by the Chilean government in Santiago, and traditionally had been a Chilean military governor. In 1984 Chile appointed the first Rapa Nui Governor, Sergio Rapu, an archeologist and curator of the local museum. Previously islanders had very little voice in government affairs. The people do, however, have full Chilean citizenship.

The government of Chile maintains some small military bases on the island.

5. Major Problems

Isolation and economy are Rapa Nui's main problems. Chile, which itself is not a very developed country, loses money in taking care of Easter Island. There does not seem to be much that can be developed, except perhaps tourism. Agriculture could be improved, at least for local consumption to reduce imports. The waters around Rapa Nui are rich in fish and lobster. License fees for the 200-mile zone might help Chile defray some of the cost of the island.

Chile has received much criticism for its authoritarian control over Easter and the lack of local input in the island's government. In 1983, some islanders sent a petition to the United Nations, claiming Rapa Nui islanders had no say in government affairs and no elected council. They accused Chile of colonial exploitation. In late 1984, a council was formed of the 35 family heads, but it was not recognized by Chile. One problem that bothers the islanders is that they don't legally own much of the island. There is one Chilean company that owns a huge chunk of the island for the sheep ranch, and the whole island is considered a park. However the appointment of a Rapa Nui Islander as governor might help answer some of the islanders' concerns. But they will probably still continue to look for ways to increase their say in the control of their island.

The giant stone statues of Rapa Nui. (Photo by Jimmy Cornell)

CHAPTER REVIEW

Vocabulary: Honga Roa, Rapa Nui, *Ahu, Moai,* petroglyphs

Questions:

1. What is unique about the physical characteristics of Easter?

2. What are the mysteries of the island's pre-history?

3. What is the island's relationship with Chile?

For Further Reading:

Carter, John (ed.), *PACIFIC ISLANDS YEAR BOOK,* 15th edition. Sydney: Pacific Publications, 1984.

Englert, Fr. Sebastian, *ISLAND AT THE CENTER OF THE WORLD,* New York: Charles Scribner's Sons, 1970.

Mann, Peggy, *EASTER ISLAND — LAND OF MYSTERIES,* New York: Holt, Rinehart, & Winston, 1976.

Stanley, David; and Dalton, Bill, *SOUTH PACIFIC HANDBOOK,* Chico, California: Moon Publications, 1982.

Chapter 36: Hawaii

1. Geography

Hawaii is the only major island group of Polynesia located entirely in the northeast Pacific. The chain actually extends all the way to Midway Atoll, but traditionally Hawaii is considered to include eight main islands. All are volcanic, and seven are inhabited. Each island has its own unique geography. In general, all are rugged, but also have large valleys and coastal lowlands. There is plenty of rainfall, except where the rain is blocked by mountains. The wet sides are very lush, the dry sides are desert-like.

Hawaii is also the name of the largest island, nicknamed the "Big Island." It has active volcanoes, including Kilauea, considered the most active in the world. The peaks of the two largest mountains, active Mauna Loa and extinct Mauna Kea, are nearly 14,000 feet (430 m) above sea level and occasionally have snow in the winter. Maui, the second largest island, has a huge volcanic crater, now dormant. Kahoolawe is dry and uninhabited. The U.S. Navy uses it as a bombing target. Molokai has a very relaxed atmosphere and is the home of a famous leper colony. Lanai is practically one huge pineapple plantation. Oahu is the main island with the capital of Honolulu. It is the most developed and most populated. Kauai is the wettest and considered by many to be the most beautiful. Niihau is privately owned by one family. All the people living there work for that family and many are full-blooded Hawaiian. The total area of the islands is about 6500 square miles (16,638 km²).

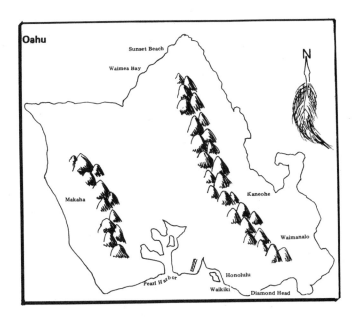

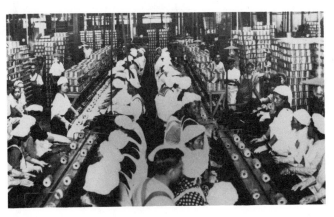

Pineapple canneries on Oahu, Maui, and Kauai once provided employment for many, but are gradually being phased out due to the high cost of labor. (Hawaii State Archives photo)

2. People and Culture

The original Hawaiians probably migrated from somewhere in French Polynesia. Shortly after Captain Cook's death in 1779, the islands were conquered and united by Kamehameha I. As explained in Chapter 9, this independent kingdom was later overthrown by the Hawaii sugar planters, and the islands eventually were annexed by the United States.

The population of original Hawaiians was almost wiped out by introduced diseases. Many Chinese, Japanese, and Filipinos were brought in to work in the fields, and today their descendants outnumber Hawaiians. Caucasians and Japanese are the main ethnic groups. There is a large mixed-race population, many of whom are part Hawaiian. Pure Chinese, Filipinos, other Asians, Portuguese and Pacific islanders, like Samoans, make up the rest of the population. The number of remaining pure Hawaiians is very small by comparison.

Oahu is the most modern and developed island in the Pacific. Of Hawaii's total population of about 1,000,000, nearly 800,000 live on Oahu. Over 600,000 of those live in Honolulu. Honolulu is a modern city with big buildings and an active economy. On the other islands life can be quite different: much slower, more relaxed, more rural. Although almost no one in Hawaii survives by subsistence anymore, there is still much farming and fishing. Most Hawaiians, even on the outer islands, live in modern homes with electricity, running water, and the usual amenities of American life.

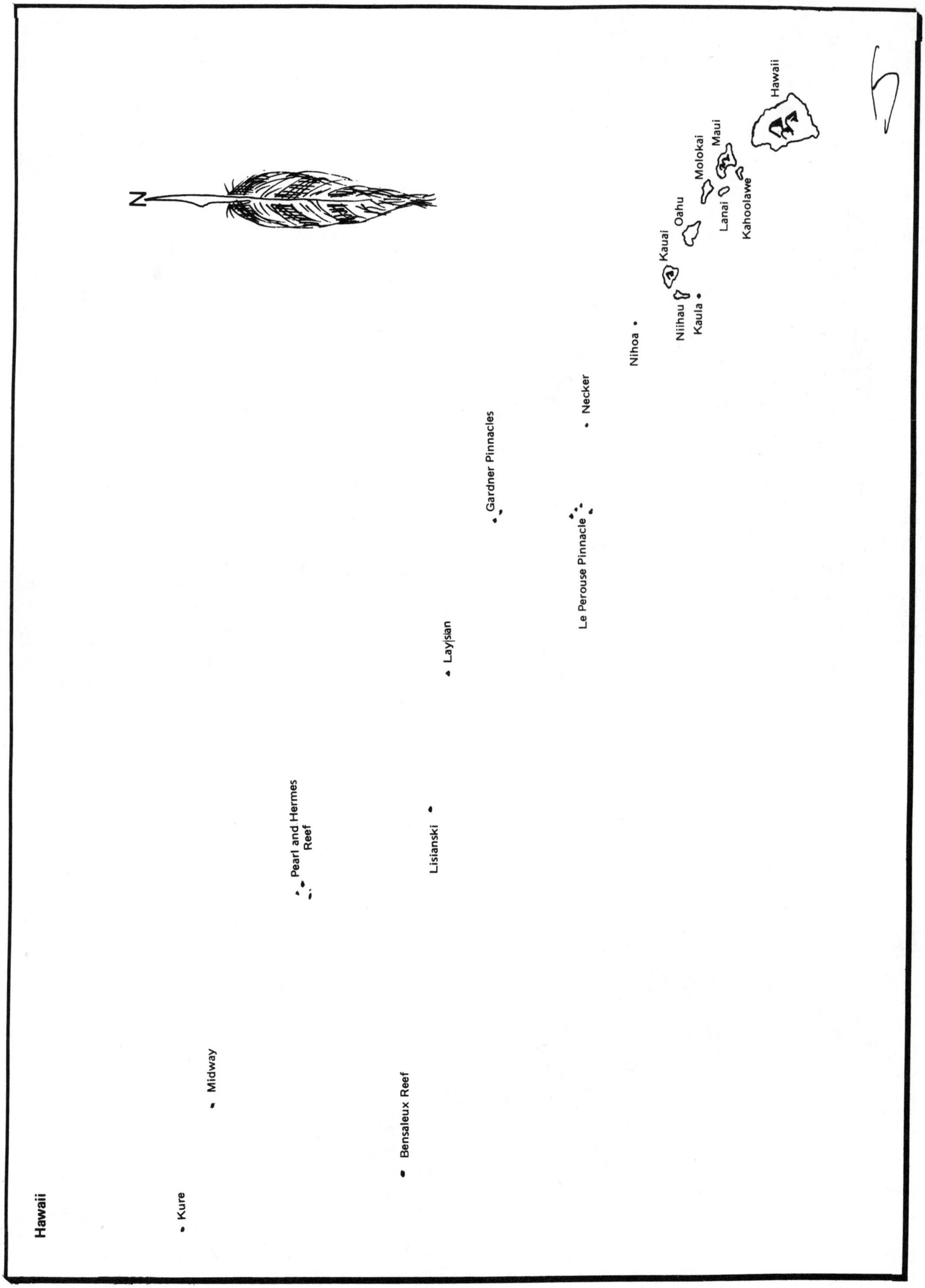

Hawaii

Kure •

Midway •

Bensaleux Reef •

Pearl and Hermes
Reef • •

Lisianski •

Layjsian •

Gardner Pinnacles •

Le Perouse Pinnacle • •

Necker •

Nihoa •

N

Niihau
Kaula •

Kauai

Oahu

Molokai
Lanai Maui
Kahoolawe

Hawaii

Famous Diamond Head looms in the background of this view of Honolulu, the largest city in the Pacific. (Hawaii Visitors Bureau photo)

3. Economy and Resources

The economy of Hawaii is based on tourism, the U.S. military, and agriculture. The three main crops of Hawaii are sugar, pineapple and marijuana. Marijuana, of course, is illegal. Unfortunately, it brings in millions of dollars to the state each year. The U.S. military has several bases on Oahu, and more than 100,000 military and their dependents are stationed in Hawaii. This also brings in much money to the state. Tourism is the single largest industry. Millions of Japanese and U.S. mainlanders visit Oahu each year. Many of them make it to the neighbor islands as well. There are modern hotels on all the major islands. Even Lanai has a small hotel, and a major luxury hotel complex is under construction.

Hawaii imports heavily. This causes Hawaii to have one of the highest costs of living in the United States. Though the balance appears bad, it is made up for by military spending and tourism. Over 5,000,000 tourists visited Hawaii in 1986.

4. Political Status

Hawaii is a state of the United States. It elects voting representatives to the U.S. Congress. The people are U.S. citizens and can vote in all national elections. Hawaii elects its own governor and legislature locally. As a U.S. citizen, any Hawaiian may move to the U.S. mainland. This also means, since Hawaii is a state, any mainlander may move to Hawaii.

5. Major Problems

The state's major problems are overpopulation and the high cost of living. Overpopulation helps cause many other problems for Hawaii. Oahu is much too crowded. It has neither the space nor the resources to support the almost 800,000 who live there now. Every year, thousands more statesiders move to Hawaii to live and work. This creates housing shortages, job shortages, and puts a strain on the utilities and welfare systems. Any U.S. citizen has a right to live in any U.S. state. Many mainland Americans see Hawaii as a tropical paradise that is warm all year round. Their influx creates problems because islands are different. They have very fixed limits as to the number of people they can support. If Los Angeles were an island, it could never support the millions who live there. It doesn't have enough water. But since it is part of a mainland, it can build pipes and aqueducts to bring water hundreds of miles to the city. Islands can't do these things as easily. The problem is not resolved. For now, Hawaii must try to live with the situation.

Racial conflicts sometimes cause other problems. Hawaii has always been a melting pot, with many mixed marriages. But at times, the different groups have not always gotten along. In the early seventies, some Hawaiians and part Hawaiians began to resent the invasion of stateside *haoles*. There were even some well publicized attacks on tourists in the early eighties that were attributed to racial bitterness. Part of this was due to a feeling that Hawaiians used to be independent with their own government, but now the mainlanders and Japanese appeared to control everything. However, the bitterness does seem to be diminishing. In 1986, a Hawaiian, John Waihee, was elected governor. The year 1987 was declared the "Year of the Hawaiian" in Hawaii, and there are many signs that the racial pride of Hawaiians and part Hawaiians is moving in positive directions. This bodes well for the ability of all the groups to live together in harmony.

Aerial view of Waikiki, Honolulu. (Hawaii Visitors Bureau photo)

Turn-of-the-century Honolulu. Most of the domestic servants of the S.N. Castle household in Manoa were Japanese. Couples who worked for affluent haole families were given living quarters plus a small salary. (Hawaii State Archives photo)

CHAPTER REVIEW

Vocabulary: Oahu, Honolulu, Kamehameha, Hawaii, Maui, Molokai, Lanai, Kahoolawe, Kauai, Niihau, *haole*

Questions:

1. Why did Hawaii become a United States possession?

2. Why are there so many Japanese, Chinese, and Filipinos in Hawaii?

3. How does being a state hurt Hawaii's ability to deal with overpopulation?

4. On what is the Hawaiian economy based?

For Further Reading:

Burrows, Edwin G., *HAWAIIAN AMERICANS*, Anchor Books, 1970.

Carter, John (ed.), *PACIFIC ISLANDS YEAR BOOK*, 15th edition, Sydney: Pacific Publications, 1984.

Rayson, Ann, *MODERN HAWAIIAN HISTORY*, Honolulu: Bess Press, Inc., 1984.

Stanley, David; and Dalton, Bill, *SOUTH PACIFIC HANDBOOK*, Chico, California: Moon Publications, 1982.

INDEX

CHARTS

DIAGRAMS AND ILLUSTRATIONS

MAPS

ISLAND MAPS